IMAGES
of Rail

RAILROAD DEPOTS OF NORTHEAST OHIO

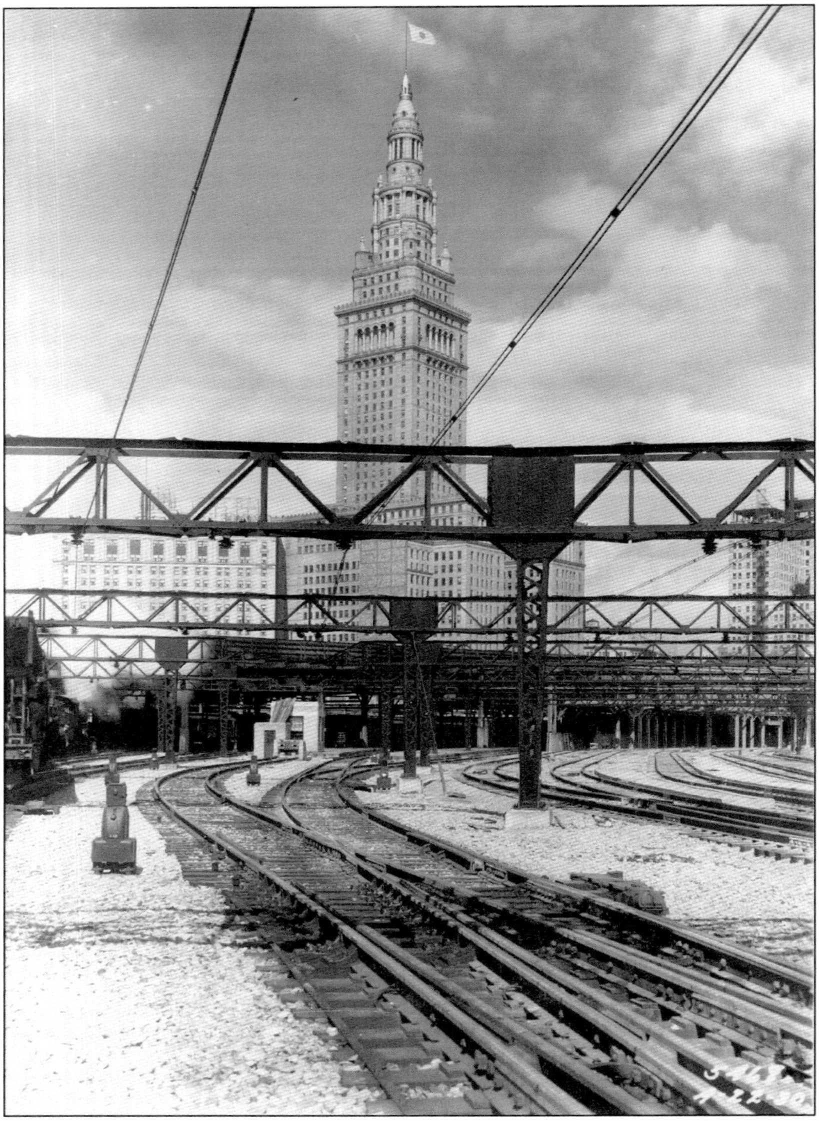

Cleveland Union Terminal was the greatest railroad station project in this corner of Ohio, and Terminal Tower still remains a distinctive part of the Cleveland skyline. More than just a railroad terminal, the Terminal Tower complex was built between 1926 and 1931 and eventually served the Baltimore and Ohio, Big Four, Erie, New York Central, Nickel Plate, and Cleveland's rapid transit system. (Cleveland State University Library Special Collections.)

On the cover: Elyria was a major station on the Lake Shore and Michigan Southern (LS&MS) Railway in the early 1900s. In this *c.* 1907 view, passengers and their baggage await boarding. The depot was a typical 1870s design of the LS&MS repeated at many locations between Buffalo and Chicago. A track elevation project around 1925 led to the eventual replacement of this depot with a New York Central–designed passenger depot that still stands. (Mark J. Camp collection.)

IMAGES
of Rail

RAILROAD DEPOTS OF NORTHEAST OHIO

Mark J. Camp

ARCADIA
PUBLISHING

ISBN 978-0-7385-5115-9

Published by Arcadia Publishing
Charleston, South Carolina

Printed in the United States of America

Library of Congress Catalog Card Number: 2006939774

For all general information contact Arcadia Publishing at:
Telephone 843-853-2070
Fax 843-853-0044
E-mail sales@arcadiapublishing.com
For customer service and orders:
Toll-Free 1-888-313-2665

Visit us on the Internet at www.arcadiapublishing.com

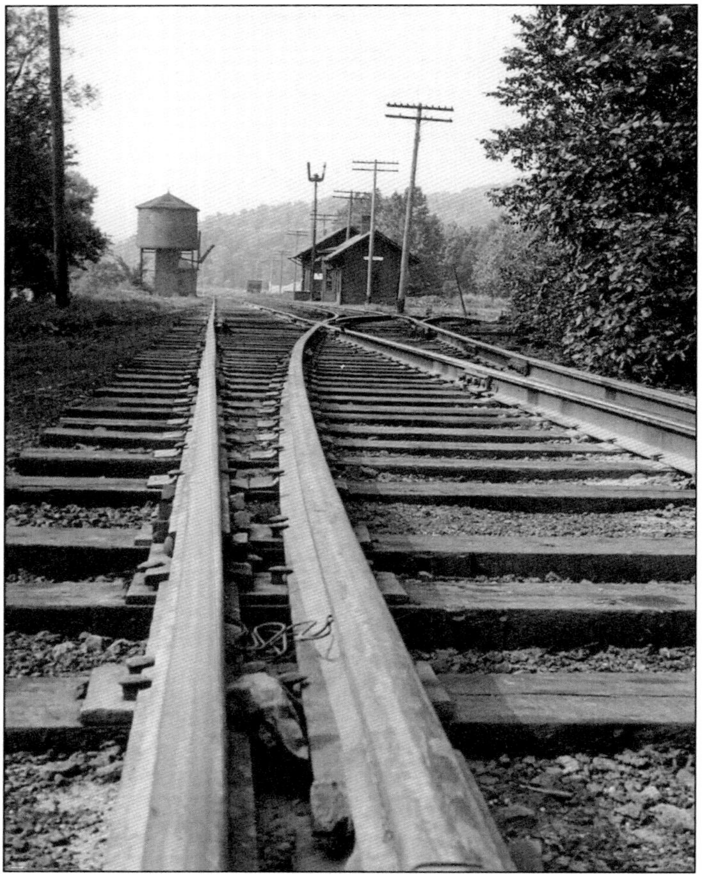

The small-town depot was just as important to its respective community as the big-city depot. Although the city depot offered all kinds of amenities to the train traveler, the small-town depot was the center of activity in many a northeast Ohio town. The rails paint an interesting path as they stretch to the Valley Railway depot and water tank at Peninsula in the Cuyahoga Valley. (Peninsula Library and Historical Society collection.)

Contents

ACKNOWLEDGMENTS

Without the assistance through the years of the following organizations this book would be much less complete: the Akron Canton and Youngstown Historical Society, Akron-Summit County Public Library Special Collections Department, Allen County Historical Society, Amherst Historical Society, Andover Public Library, Ashtabula County District Library, Ashtabula County Genealogical Society, Cleveland Public Library, Cleveland State University Library Special Collections, Conneaut Public Library, Conneaut Historical Railroad Museum, Elyria Public Library, Erie Lackawanna Historical Society, Geneva Public Library, Lake County Historical Society, Morley Library Genealogy and Local History Room, the New York Central Historical Society, Nickel Plate Historical and Technical Society, Oberlin College Library, Peninsula Library and Historical Society, the Toledo-Lucas County Public Library Local History Department, University of Toledo Carlson Library, Western Reserve Historical Society of Cleveland, and all the libraries and associations of northeast Ohio that maintain historical collections. Among the individuals that I owe a debt of gratitude for contributions to this book are Howard Ameling, Charles Bates, Randy Bergdorf, Robert Chilcote, Richard J. Cook, John B. Corns, John Eles, Carl Thomas Engel, Charles Garvin, Herbert H. Harwood, Clyde Helms, Kirk Hise, John Keller, Robert Lorenz, Willis A. McCaleb, Dave McKay, Max Miller, Phil Moberg, David P. Oroszi, Paul W. Prescott, John A. Rehor, Robert Runyan, W. C. Thurman, and Bruce Young. Some contributed photographs and historical data, others published articles and books that aided in the research, and others provided inspiration, leadership, and friendship over the years. Some are gone now, but their memory lives on in their pictorial recordings of railroad history. I also greatly appreciate the assistance of Kevin Capurso of the University of Toledo during the research and the scanning of photographs.

Historical information for this book came from *Reports of the Ohio Railroad Commission, Annual Reports of the Public Utilities Commission of Ohio, Poors Manuals, Railroad Gazette, Railway Age*, and other trade journals; *The Encyclopedia of Cleveland History, Centennial History of the Pennsylvania Railroad Company 1846-1946*; various newspapers of northeast Ohio; numerous centennial, bicentennial, and sesquicentennial compilations and histories of northeast Ohio communities; and firsthand interviews conducted over the last 40 years.

INTRODUCTION

Northeast Ohio was destined to become a major transportation corridor in the 1850s; it was directly in the path of railroads stretching westward from eastern markets to Chicago. Some of Ohio's earliest railroads were projected to connect Lake Erie with the Ohio River and points south. Painesville, Ashtabula, and Conneaut each had competing plans. Cleveland, already a major lake port and canal port, sought to connect to larger cities across the Midwest. By 1900 the Lake Shore and Michigan Southern Railway (LS&MS) and New York Chicago and St. Louis Railroad paralleled the Lake Erie coast on their way to Buffalo and Chicago; further south the Baltimore and Ohio Railroad (B&O) connected Pittsburgh with Chicago, as did the Pennsylvania Railroad, and the Erie Railroad ran between New Jersey and Chicago. Like spokes of a wheel, the Cleveland, Cincinnati, Chicago and St. Louis, LS&MS, New York Chicago and St. Louis, B&O, Pennsylvania, Wheeling and Lake Erie, and Erie Railroads spread away from downtown Cleveland, the railroad hub of northeast Ohio.

The railroads established stations at regular intervals along their lines to serve the traveling public and shippers; to provide necessary water and fuel for locomotives; to provide repairs for motive power; and to provide transfer facilities with other lines. Stations that served particular towns, or around which a community grew, became the sites of depots—shelters for passengers and freight and the railroad staff responsible for overseeing this business. Northeast Ohio communities became the sites of some 125 depots, busy debarking points for the traveling public, businessmen, professionals, and servicemen from the late 1800s to the 1950s. The typical railroad depot was a frame or brick structure with a waiting room on one end and a freight room on the other end with an office in between. This was known as a combination depot and was commonly erected in communities where business was anticipated to be moderate but not to the point of overtaxing the facility. Each railroad had a set of plans for the building of depots by their construction crews. Unique architectural features often distinguished depots of a particular line, but some features and props were common to most depots. These included a vestibule or bay window in the central office area that extended trackside, allowing the agent or operator a clear view up and down the tracks. Extended eaves provided protection to passengers standing along the loading platform on the trackside of the building. In larger combination depots the waiting room was divided providing separate waiting areas for women and children and men. Ticket counters connected the office area to the waiting room(s). Wooden benches and a potbelly stove were part of the decor of waiting rooms for many years. The office area contained the telegraph, which, before the telephone, was the connection of many a small community to news of the world. A timetable rack, station clock, typewriter, rubber stamps, and railroad calendar were standard equipment in the early years. Often a lever in the bay window would allow the operator to adjust the order board, a semaphore-like signal on the trackside of the building, to indicate to the train crew whether they had passengers or a message of importance to be retrieved at the depot. Mail bags and baggage and freight wagons also had to be strategically placed on the platform for stopping passenger trains so the transfer was quick and efficient. The freight room was usually unfinished, unheated, windowless, equipped with wide or double doors, and open to the rafters. The floor and platform were sometimes at a higher level to allow easier transfer of items to boxcars spotted on a depot siding, often behind the building. Depots had the name of the station clearly displayed on the ends of the buildings, either stenciled directly on the walls or on a separate town board. Some lines also displayed the name on the trackside of the depot or attached to a post along the loading platform. Larger communities and those that were deemed more important by the railroads, like county seats or junction points, often had separate passenger and freight depots. These were designed by railroad staff or by architectural firms employed by the railroads. Growths in passenger and freight business sometimes led to the replacement of combination depots with separate larger structures. Union depots were built where more than one line served a community and the railroads agreed to share a facility.

Most of these structures have become obsolete and unneeded today. Railroad passenger service began to decline as automobiles became the standard mode of transportation. Depots were retired and in many cases demolished. Some were moved to serve other purposes. Water tanks and coaling stations disappeared when steam locomotives were replaced by diesels in the 1940s–1950s. Interlocking towers were gradually replaced by new ways of traffic control involving radios and computers. One centralized traffic control facility could do the work once accomplished by many tower men. The formation of Amtrak in 1971 led to the closing of many remaining passenger depots. Luckily historical preservation began gaining strength around this time as well, and a number of surviving depots have been restored and returned to a portion of their former glory and importance they played in the history of communities small and large in northeast Ohio. Following is a selection of illustrations of these structures, mainly passenger and combination depots, across 11 northeast Ohio counties. The boundaries of this compilation are the Pennsylvania-Ohio border and central Erie and Huron Counties, Lake Erie to the north and the southern borders of Huron, Medina, Summit, Portage, and Trumbull Counties. Future studies will extend the study into other parts of the Buckeye State. As with any historical compilation it is far from complete, but fortunately many images have survived on early postcards mailed across the United States. Although most of the photographers remain anonymous, they have made a great contribution to our history. The author is still seeking added information and photographs of railroad structures in this area. Readers are urged to contact the author through the Railroad Station Historical Society Web site (www.rrshs.org) or at the University of Toledo (www.utoledo.edu/eeescience/Camp/).

One

Baltimore and Ohio Lines

August 1873 marked the opening of the Lake Shore and Tuscarawas Valley Railway (LS&TV), linking Lorain and Elyria with Uhrichsville on the Tuscarawas River. This was primarily a coal-hauling line, but three daily passenger trains were on the schedule. Tracks from Elyria north to the lake were originally laid by the Elyria and Black River Railroad and acquired by the LS&TV in 1872. Financial difficulties led to its reorganization as the Cleveland, Tuscarawas Valley and Wheeling Railway in 1875 and then the Cleveland Lorain and Wheeling Railroad (CL&W) in 1882. In 1893, the CL&W consolidated with the Cleveland and Southwestern Railway, which ran between Cleveland and Medina. The CL&W eventually connected Cleveland and Lorain with Bridgeport on the Ohio River. The CL&W came under the control of the B&O Railroad in 1909. The first train chugged along the Valley Railway from Cleveland to Canton in late January 1880. In 1895, after financial problems, it became the Cleveland, Terminal and Valley Railroad (CT&V). Being controlled by the B&O Railroad since 1890, the CT&V was purchased by the B&O in 1915, when the B&O ran four passenger trains each day. Beginning in June 1934, the B&O switched its passenger trains to the new Cleveland Union Terminal, converting the old Canal Road passenger depot to freight offices. The last B&O passenger service in Cleveland was in December 1962.

In 1882, the Pittsburgh, Youngstown and Chicago Railroad was built through Youngstown and Warren to Akron. The Akron and Chicago Junction Railroad, opened for freight service in 1891, linked Akron with Chicago Junction, later Willard. These two lines became part of the main line of the B&O between Pittsburgh and Chicago. The Pittsburg and Western Railroad (P&W) grew with the takeover of several smaller Pennsylvania and Ohio lines and by 1887 stretched from Youngstown through Girard, Niles, Warren, and Newton Falls. In 1886, the Painesville and Youngstown Railway incorporated to build a line south from Painesville. Later that year it was renamed the Pittsburg, Painesville and Fairport Railway and eventually connected Fairport Harbor with Niles. It became part of the P&W, which in turn became part of the B&O.

The B&O engineering offices had a set of standard designs that were used to construct depots up and down their lines. Frame combination depots were the order for smaller communities; county seats and important junction points received brick structures. In the early 1900s, a new set of designs was used to replace many of the smaller frame combination depots.

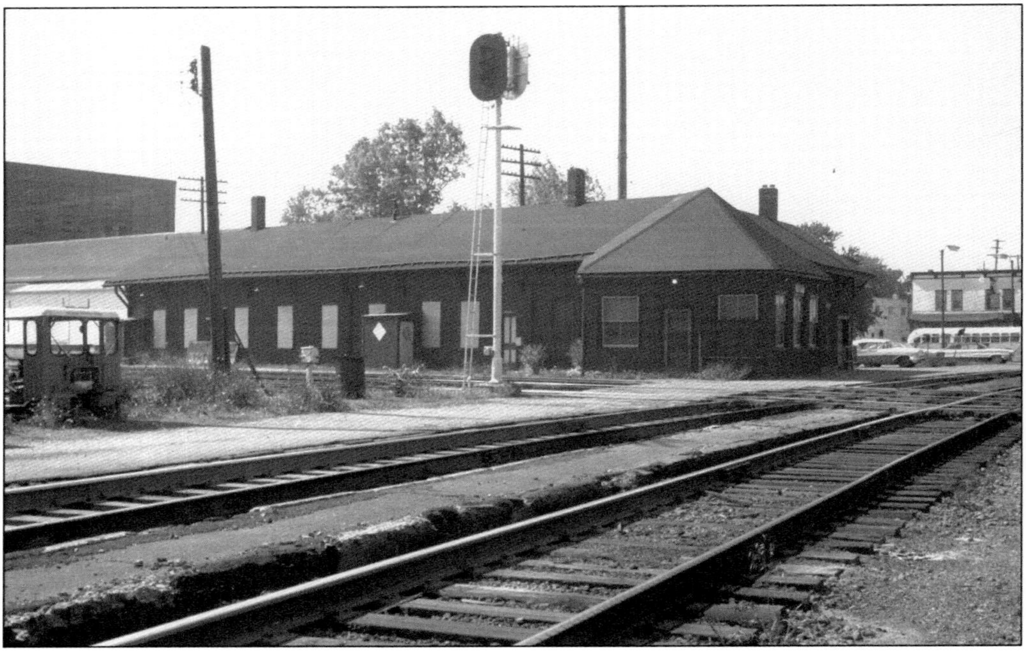

August 1872 marked the arrival of the first passenger train of the LS&TV in Lorain. In 1882, when the Nickel Plate was opened across northern Ohio, this depot was erected at the junction with what was now known as the CL&W. This photograph from August 1967 shows the joint B&O-Nickel Plate passenger depot at the diamond in downtown Lorain. The view is down the B&O tracks. Only the B&O freight house remains.

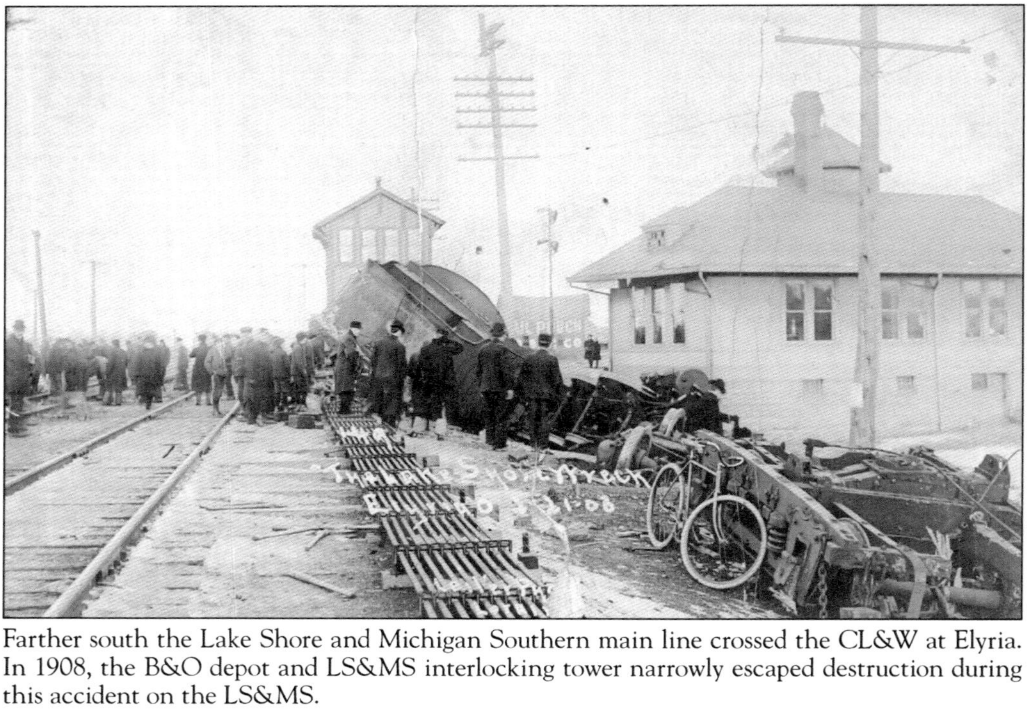

Farther south the Lake Shore and Michigan Southern main line crossed the CL&W at Elyria. In 1908, the B&O depot and LS&MS interlocking tower narrowly escaped destruction during this accident on the LS&MS.

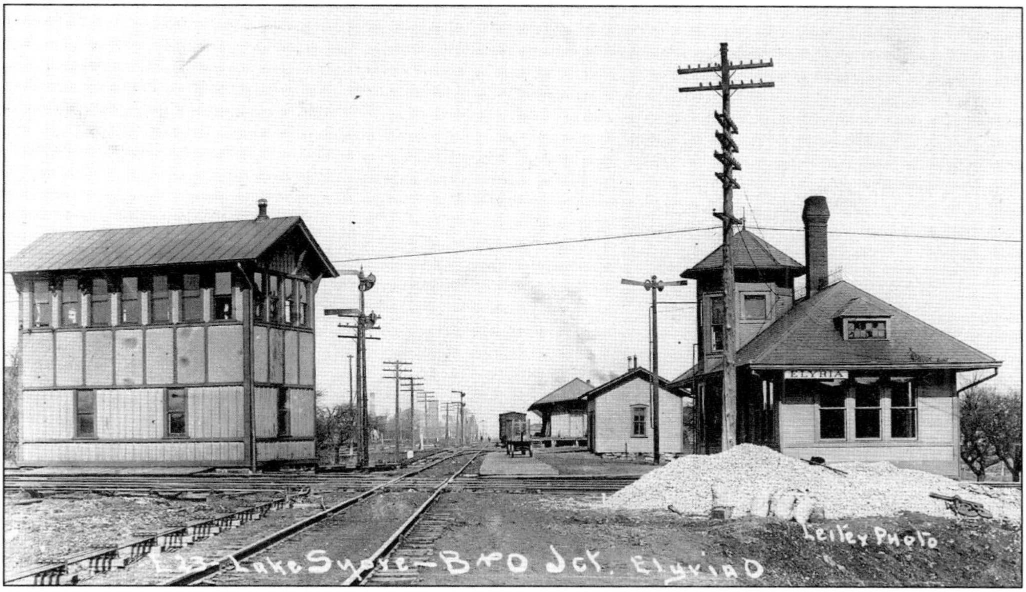

Elyria's CL&W, later B&O, depot sat at the crossing of the LS&MS on the south side of Huron Street. This turreted building served passengers; the smaller building in the distance was a freight house. Across the tracks is an interlocking tower of LS&MS design. Note the series of pipes along the tracks that carried the links to switches and signals controlling the crossing. The tower man set the interlocking by pushing long levers in the second floor of the tower. The B&O later enlarged the freight house on the north side of Huron Street. All significant B&O structures in Elyria are gone. (Mark J. Camp collection.)

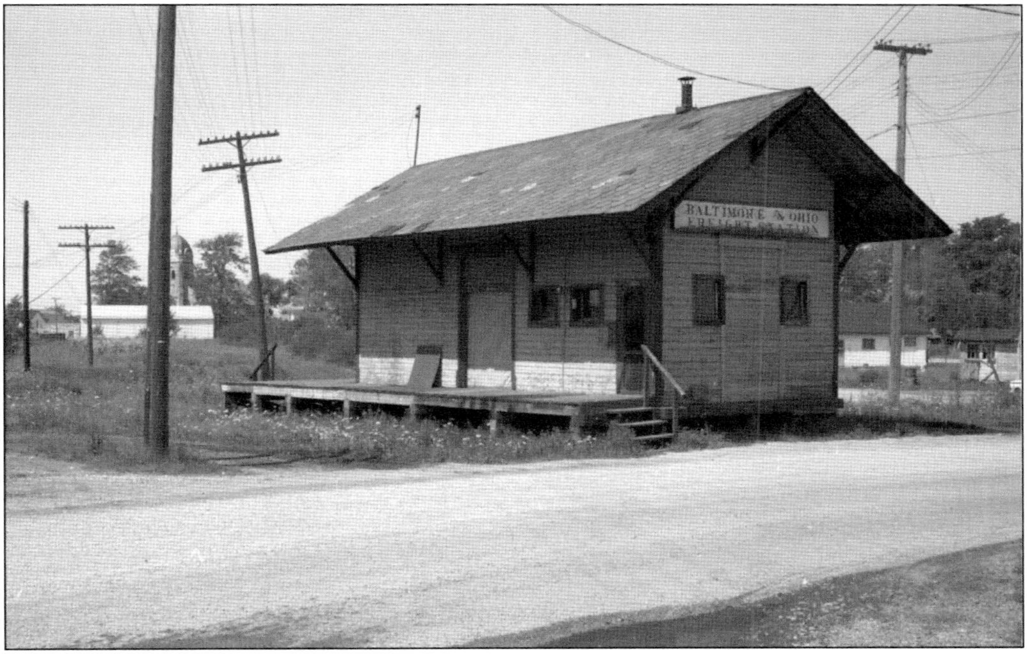

The CL&W (B&O) built this freight house on the wye at Grafton for transfer business with the Big Four. The building, photographed in 1967, remains in 2006.

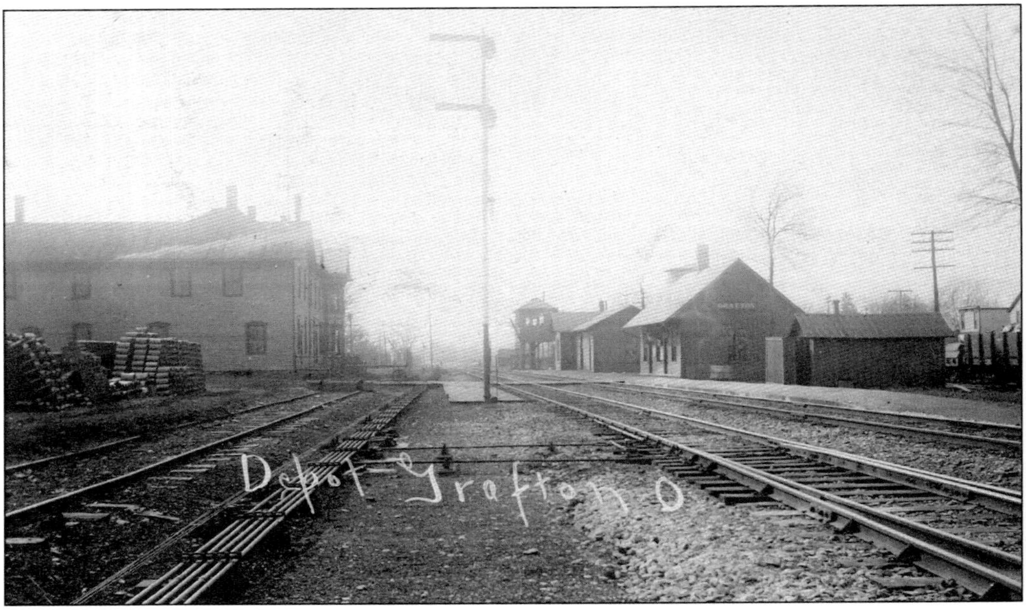

The CL&W crosses the Big Four, later New York Central Railroad (NYC), at Grafton. This *c.* 1907 view looks down the Big Four showing the older Big Four passenger depot, the replacement depot, and the Big Four interlocking tower on the right and a railroad hotel on the left. A tile plant was a major shipper at Grafton. Only the tower, now restored, remains from this scene. (Mark J. Camp collection.)

The CL&W depot at Erhart serves as a typical model of a small-town passenger depot. Insulators mark where the telegraph wires entered the agent's office. A train bulletin board with chalked arrivals and departures of the daily passenger trains and signs of Western Union and United Express companies decorate the walls. A simple order board indicates the local is scheduled to stop. To the left is a freight shed, and to the right is a coal shed and outhouse. The depot has been gone since the mid-1950s. (Mark J. Camp collection.)

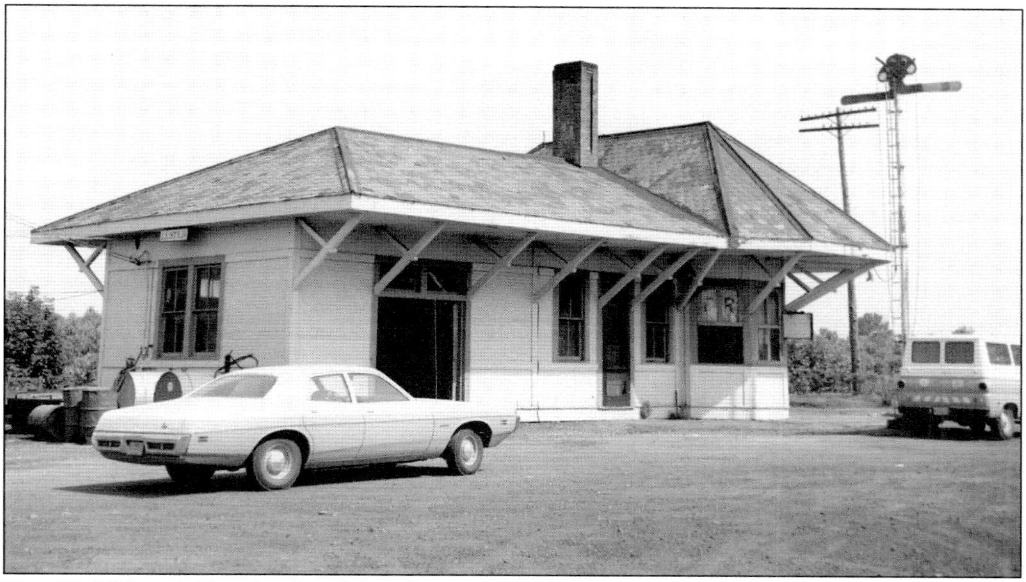

The CL&W and Cleveland and Southwestern Railway crossed at Lester, originally just a rural railroad station, but today a small community. The Lester depot, probably dating from around 1893, was designed to provide the agent with unobstructed views up and down both the line to Cleveland and Medina and the one to Lorain and Sterling. The depot was located within the wye. This view dates from July 1971. It is still in railroad use.

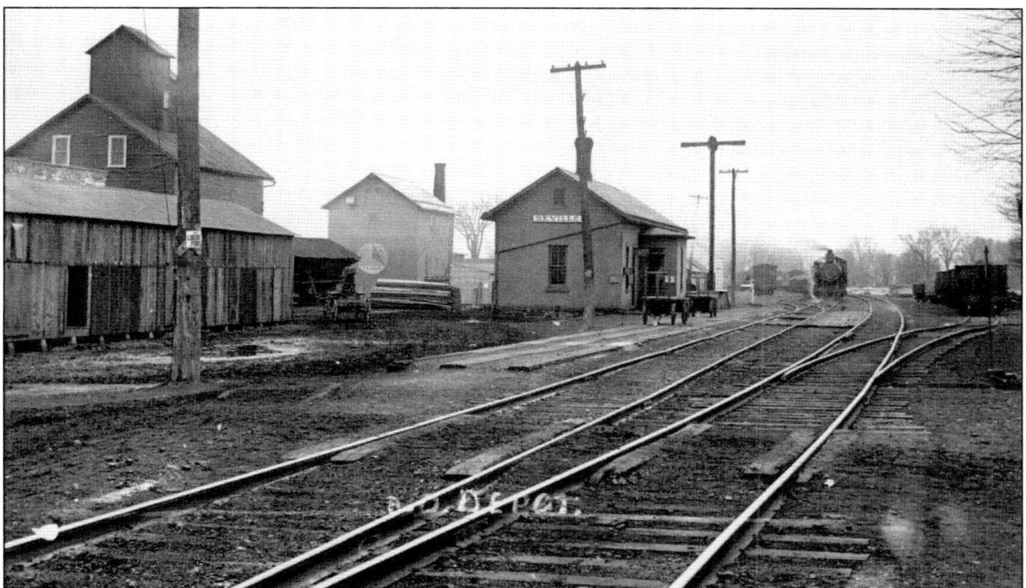

The B&O depot at Seville was one of the few brick depots along the line. It dates from the late 1800s. It was torn down sometime after the late 1970s. (Mark J. Camp collection.)

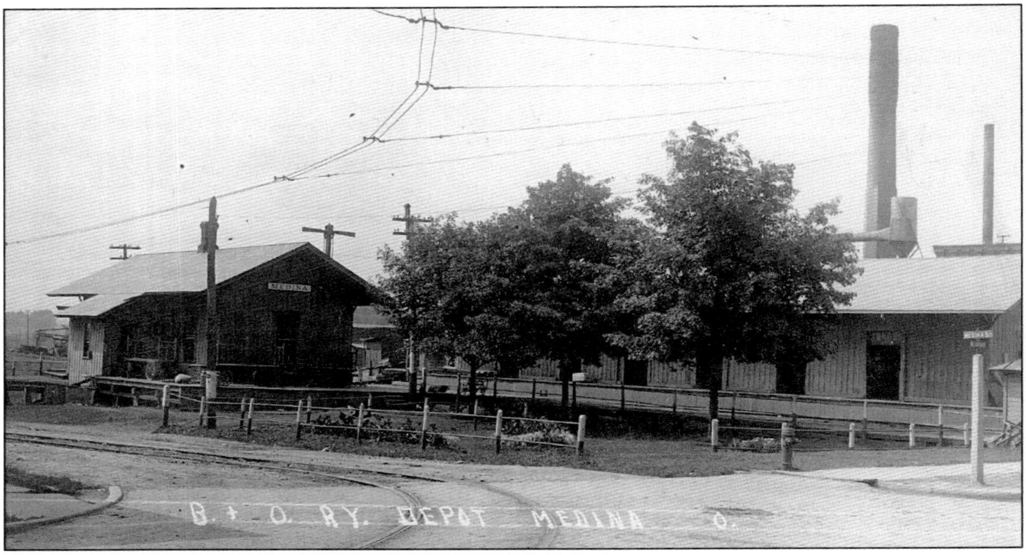

The former B&O depot at Medina resembles the Erhart depot. The Cleveland, Southwestern and Columbus interurban tracks curve behind the depot in this 1908 view. The Medina County seat was a busy place, requiring the construction of a long freight house across the tracks. Behind it are stacks of the A. I. Root Company, an innovator in the beekeeping field and still a major manufacturer of candles. A cutoff built between Lester and Lafayette removed Medina from through traffic by the early 1900s. The 1894 freight house remains on site, but the passenger depot was relocated to a local stonecutting firm. (Mark J. Camp collection.)

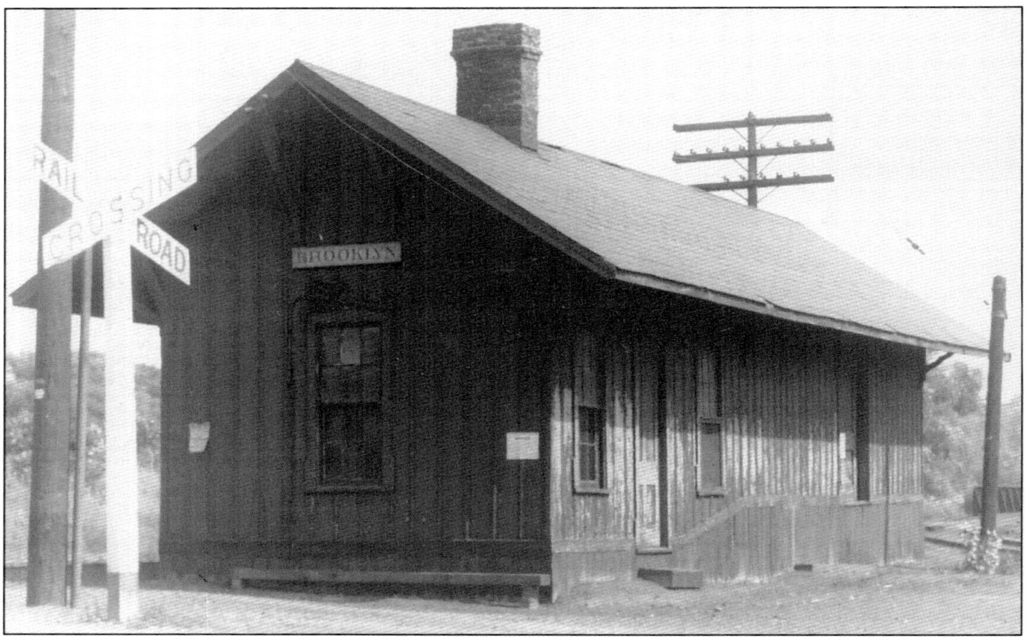

On the former Cleveland and Southwestern line is this combination depot at Brooklyn, probably built in the early 1890s. At one time a raised freight loading platform extended from the building. This view probably dates from the late 1950s or early 1960s. The structure has since disappeared. (Photograph collection of Cleveland Public Library.)

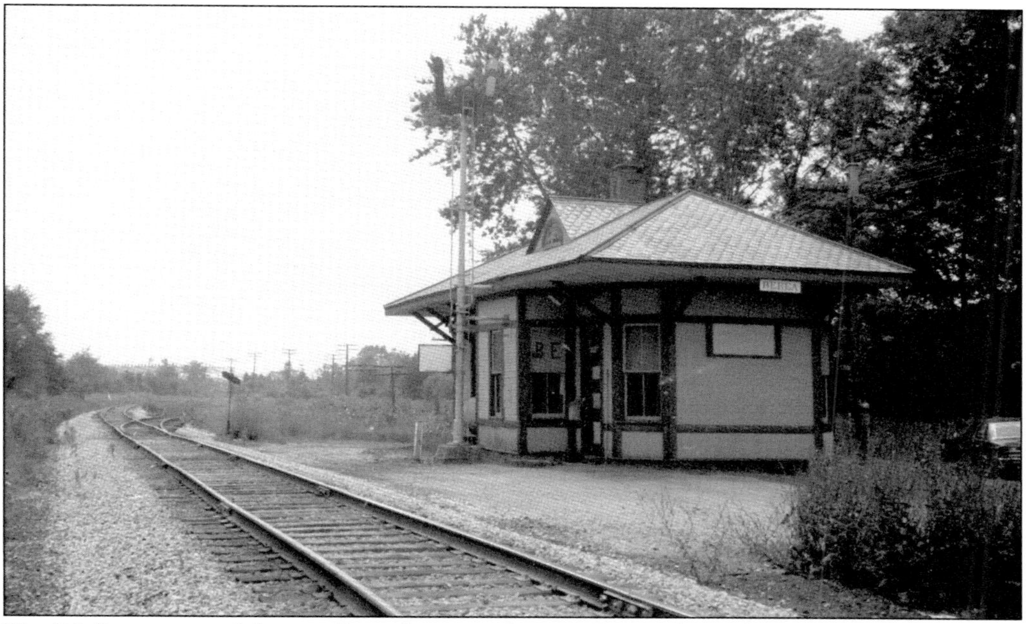

The B&O maintained this small combination depot at Berea, shown here in July 1968. After its closing it was moved to the former Trolley Land USA, a once-operating electric railway display near Olmsted Falls. Farther south, Strongsville had a similarly designed depot that was made more striking by a conical tower over the operator's bay. The Strongsville depot was removed in the late 1950s.

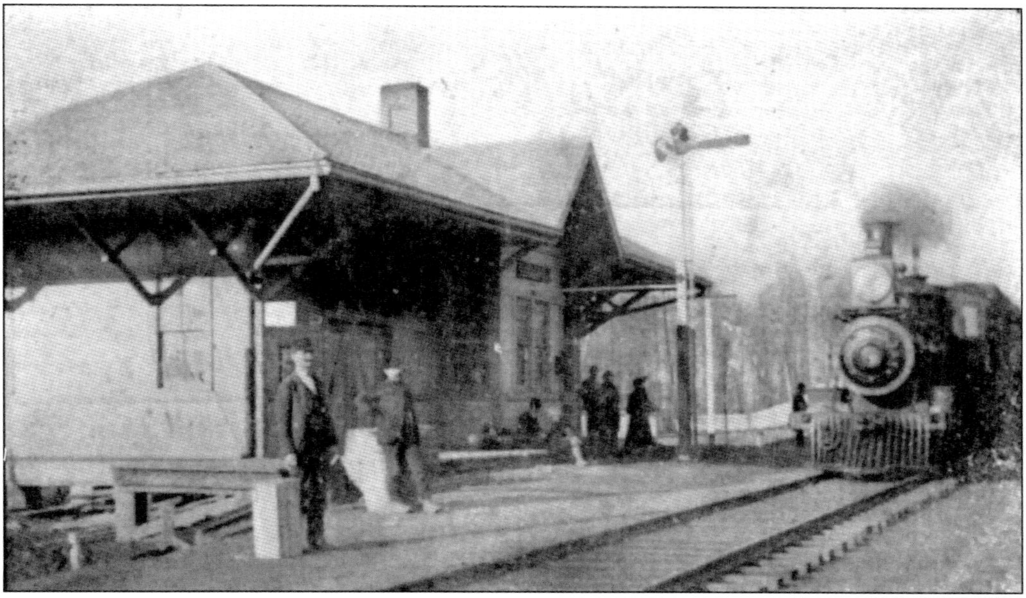

The CL&W built this structure around 1895 east of Liverpool and called it East Liverpool. The town never grew in the direction of the depot, so a hack always waited to transport visitors into town. Liverpool became Valley City. The depot finally became part of "downtown" Valley City when it was moved as a 1976 bicentennial project to become a local historical museum and meeting room. (Mark J. Camp collection.)

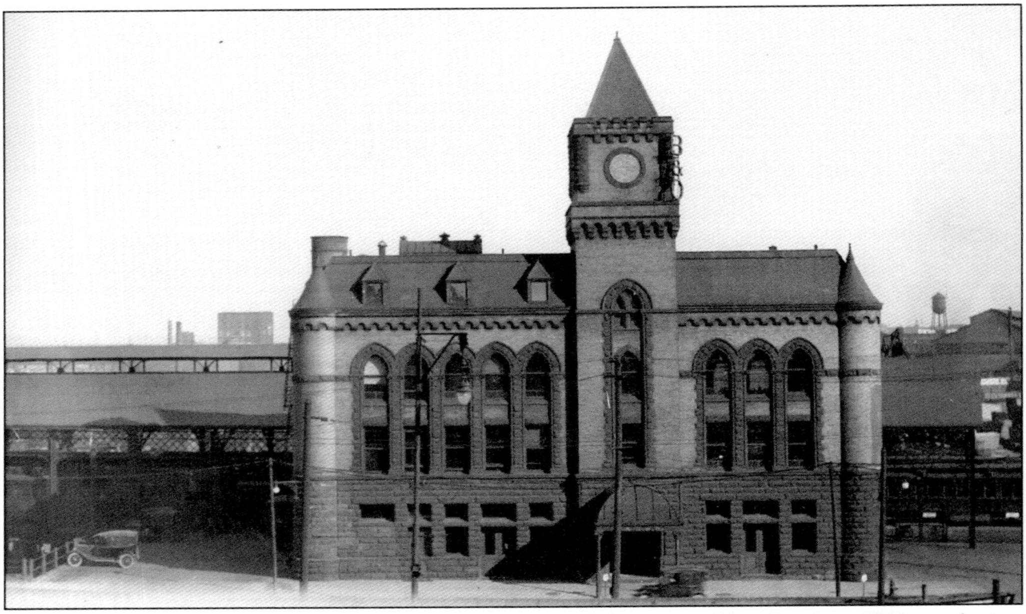

The CT&V opened this imposing structure on Canal Street in Cleveland in 1898, replacing an earlier 1880 Valley Railway building at the foot of Water Street. A large freight house was located on Columbus Avenue. The depot served the B&O until all B&O passenger service was shifted to Cleveland Union Terminal in June 1934. The large train shed was shortly removed, and the building entered nonrailroad use. A fire destroyed the clock tower and original roof. The lower view dates from September 1971. The building remains in poor condition although there have been attempts at restoration and reuse. A new B&O freight house built in 1954 was demolished in 2001. (Above, photograph collection of Cleveland Public Library.)

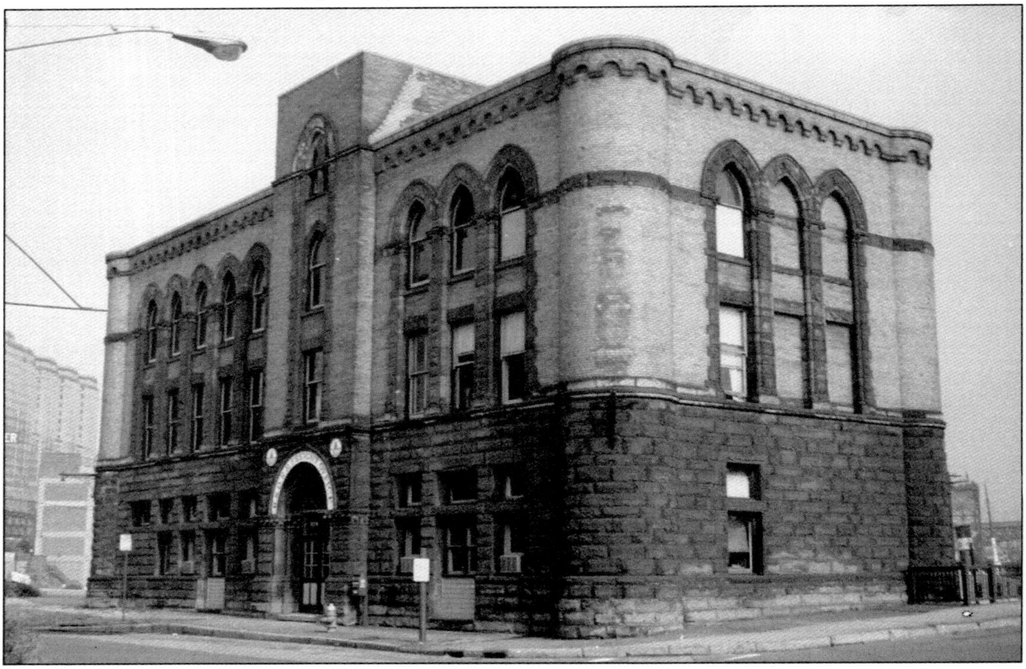

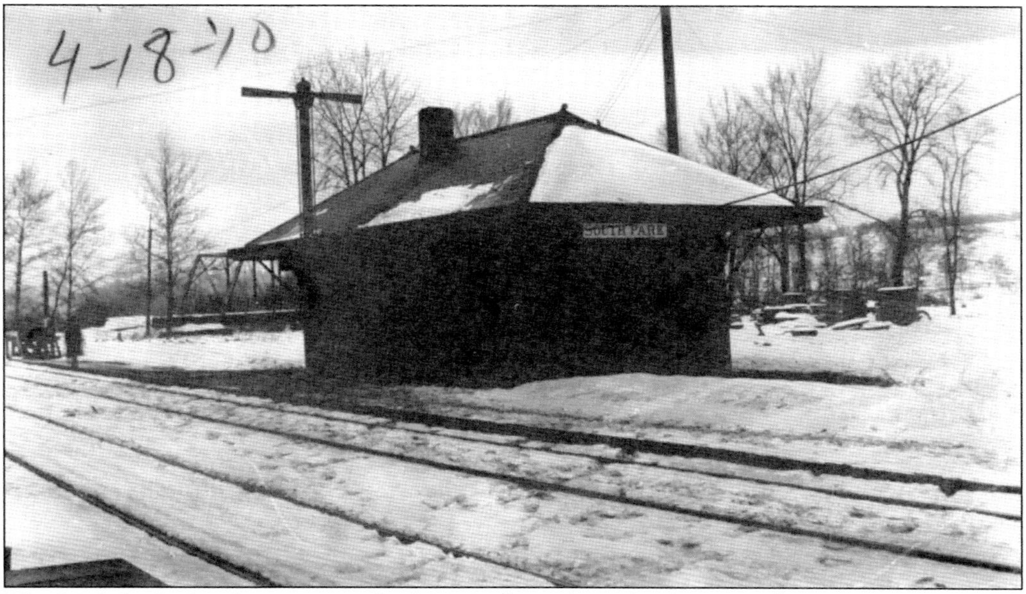

The B&O built this depot to standard B&O plans along the former Valley Line at South Park around 1909. It was gone by the late 1960s. (Mark J. Camp collection.)

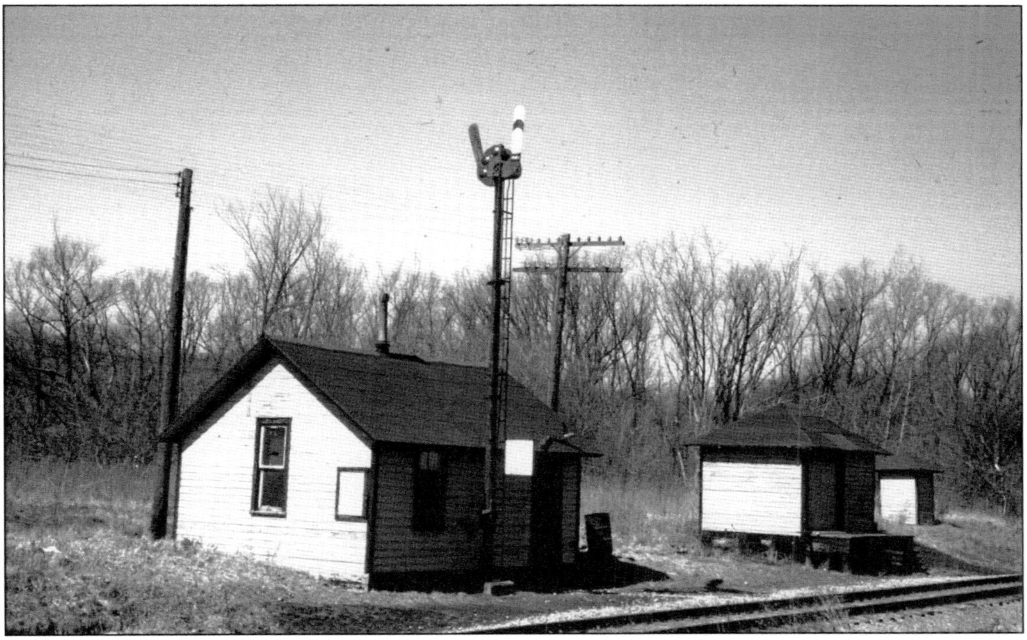

Jaite, formerly Vaughn Station, became a company town to house and provide services to the employees of the Jaite Company Paper Mill built around 1905. This depot/telegraph office and adjacent freight house are of CT&V design. Surprisingly, these small structures survived and have been faithfully restored by the National Park Service, just across the street from its offices at Cuyahoga Valley National Park.

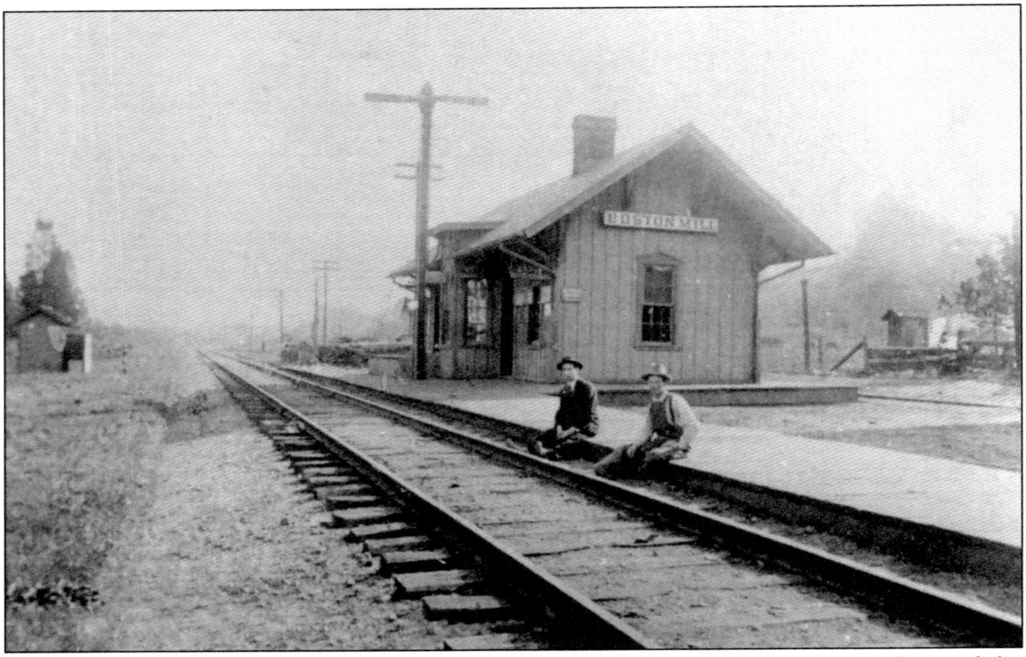

The Valley Line built nearly identical depots at Boston Mill and Peninsula. Residents of the Cuyahoga Valley flocked to this new mode of transportation, finding it much speedier than the old Ohio and Erie Canal. Both had busy freight agents around 1900 because of stone shipments from nearby building stone quarries. The 1913 flood devastated the Valley Line, but these two depots survived to serve the railroad until their retirement. Peninsula eventually disappeared, and Boston Mill was moved to Peninsula in 1967. It became a boutique for a number of years. The restored Boston Mill depot opened in August 2004 and now serves the Cuyahoga Valley Scenic Railroad and the National Park Service. (Peninsula Library and Historical Society collection.)

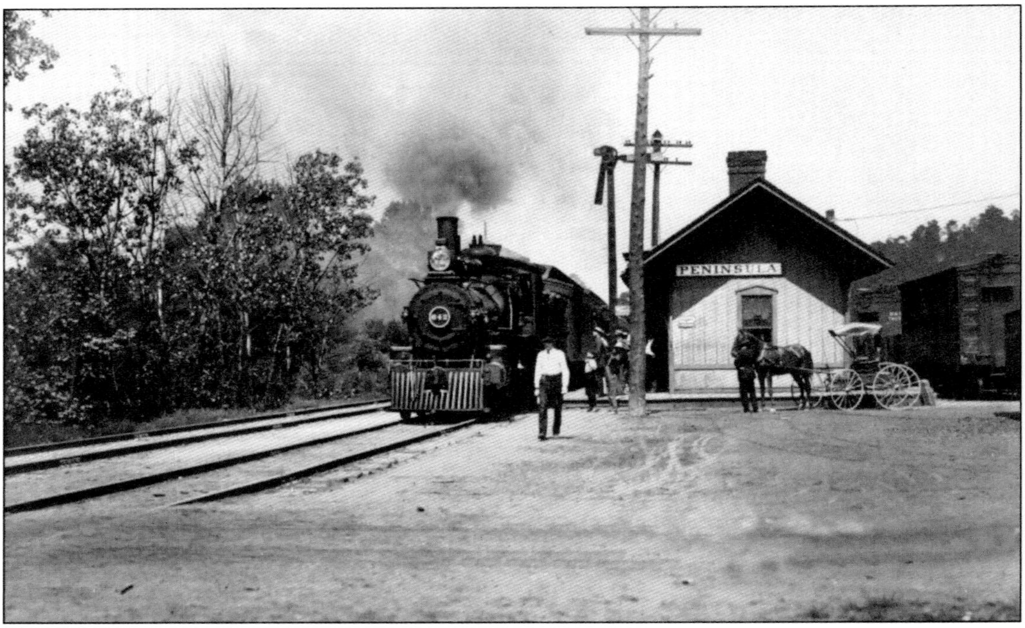

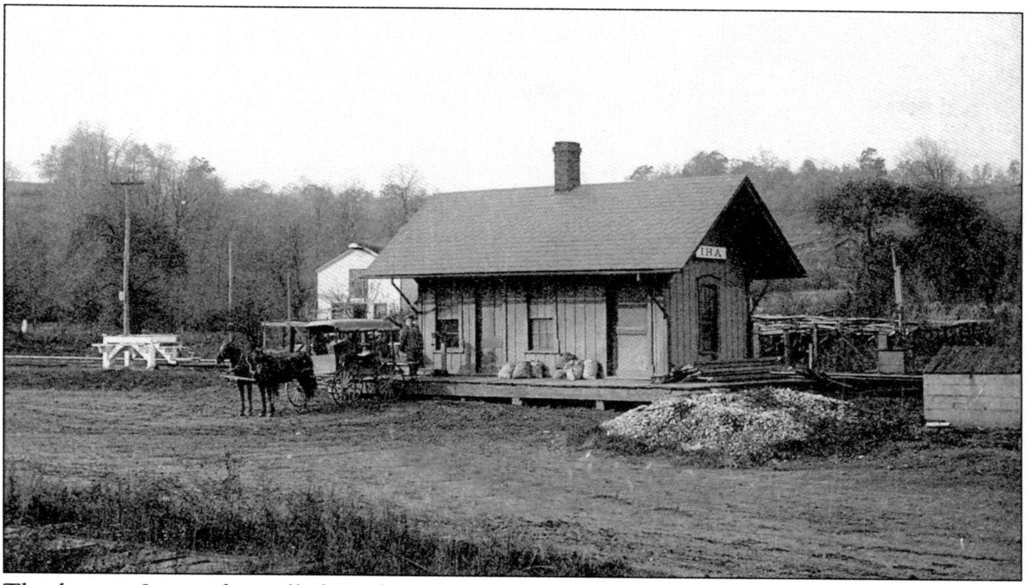

The depot at Ira was first called Hawkins, but confusion with another stop called Haskins led to its renaming. The original Valley Line depots at Boston Mill, Botzum, Brecksville, Everett, Ira, and Peninsula were all built from the same plans, and except for changes in length and window-door arrangement, were nearly identical. Unfortunately only the restored Boston Mill depot and Everett depot, which was disassembled and its lumber used to build a garage, are known to still exist. (Peninsula Library and Historical Society collection.)

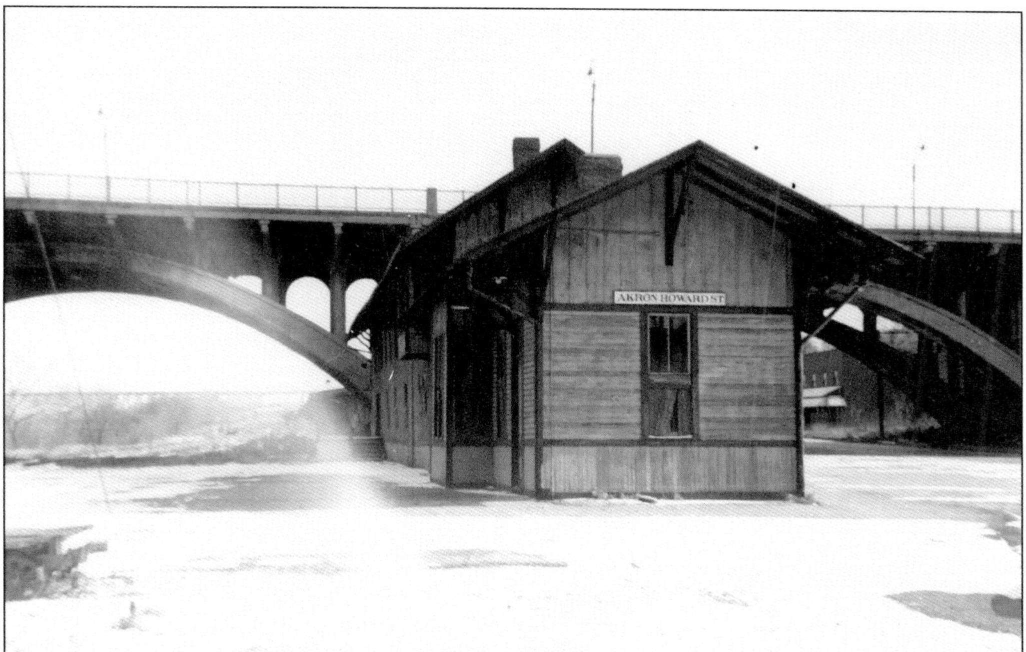

The B&O had a stop at Howard Street in Akron. The depot did not survive long after this photograph was taken in January 1965. (Max Miller collection.)

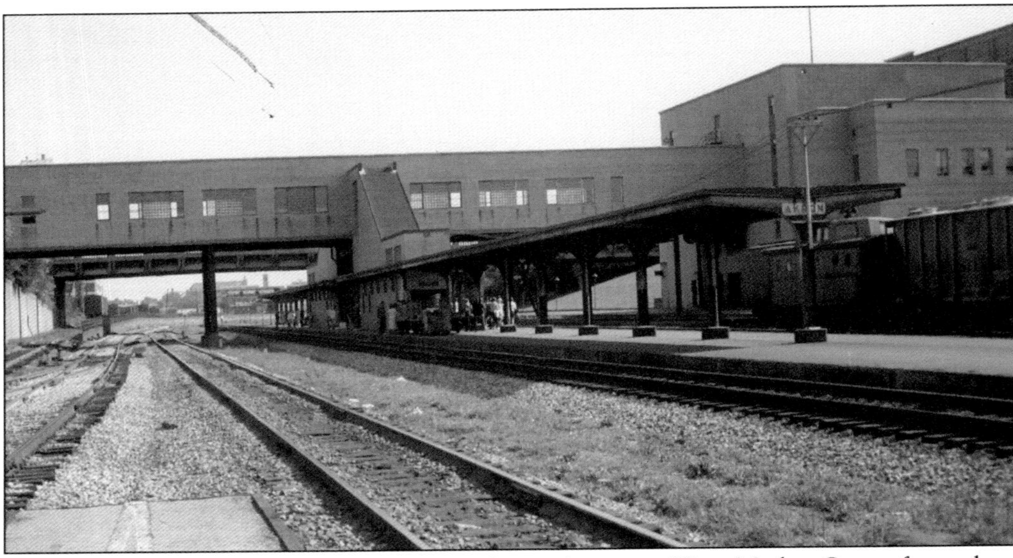

The Valley Railway had a large two-story frame depot on West Market Street from about 1852 until the 1890s. The B&O and Cleveland, Akron and Canton (PRR) jointly built Union Depot (see page 27) which opened in October 1891. This $100,000 brick and stone edifice was located on East Market Street. For a time, the Erie also ran trains into this depot. By the 1920s citizens were campaigning for a new depot—one more indicative of "modern" Akron. The depot remained in service until completion of new Union Depot (above) in 1950. (Charles Garvin photograph, 1966.)

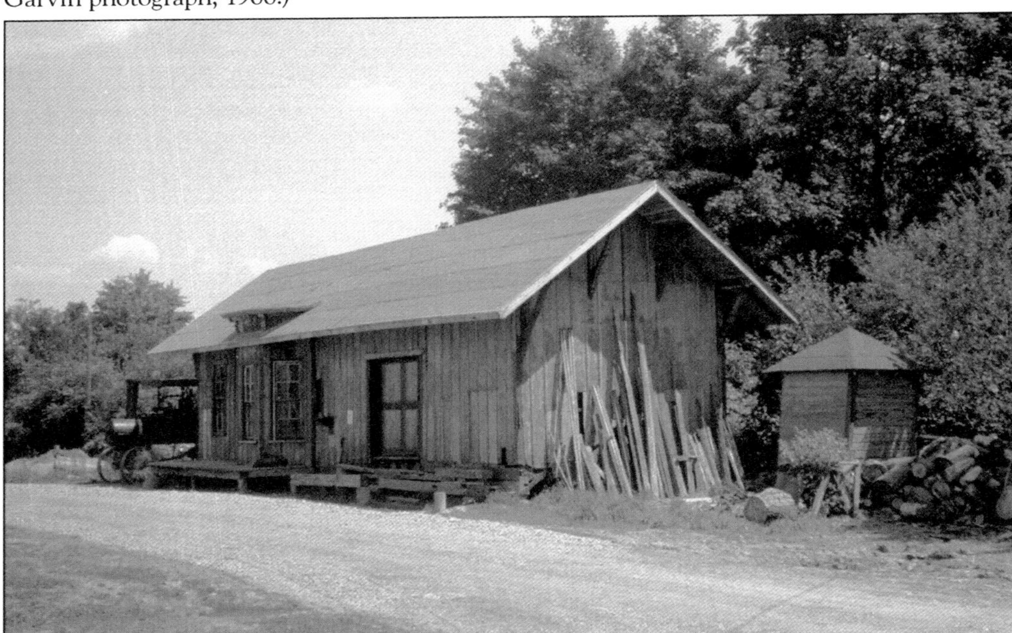

Note the similarity of the *c.* 1878 Valley Railway depot from Aultman with those between Akron and Cleveland. After the depot closed, it was moved in November 1967 to become part of Century Village, a historical village in Burton in Geauga County. Since being photographed in 1970 the depot has been completely restored.

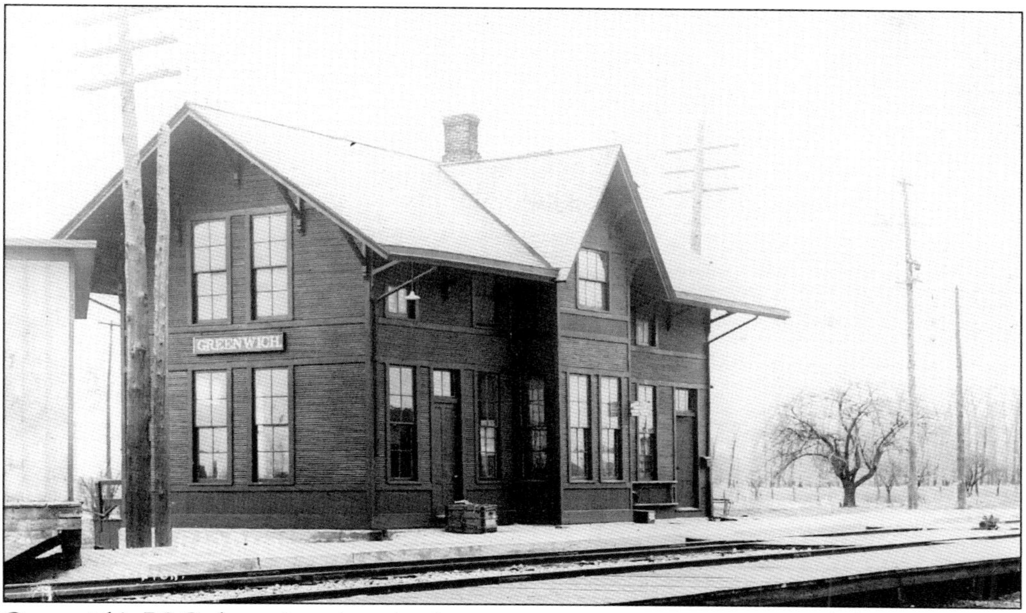

Greenwich's B&O depot is unique in that it was a two-story structure with living space for the agent on the second floor. Greenwich was a new town established as the railroad was built through and an important junction with the Big Four in 1891. The depot has been gone since the mid-1900s, but a small former telegraph office remained in 2000. (Mark J. Camp collection.)

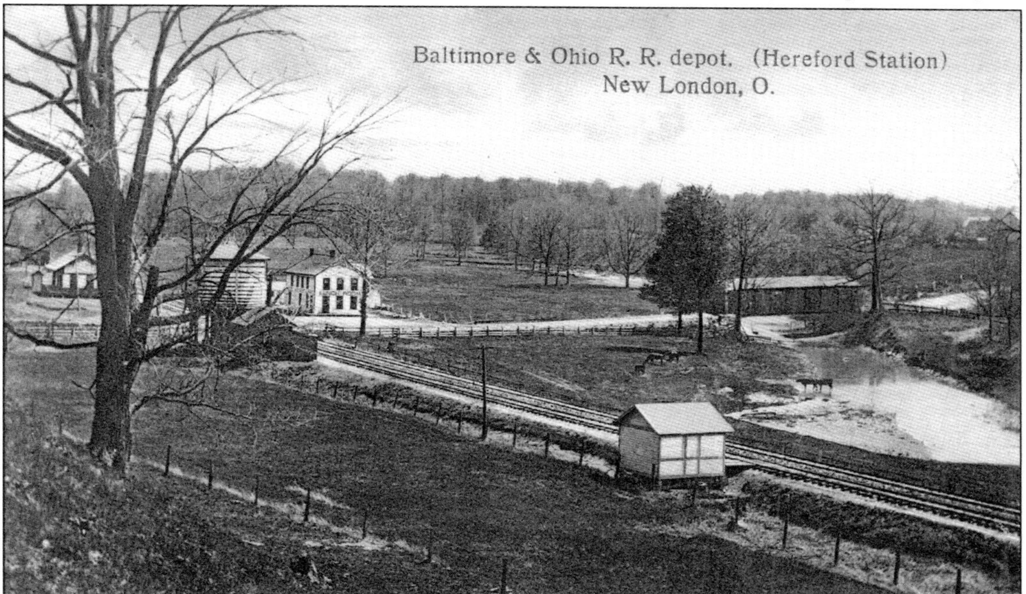

Shown is a bucolic scene at Hereford station around 1908. In the foreground is a handcar shed and behind a covered bridge over Buck Creek. A pump house and water tank obtain a reliable source of water from the nearby creek. A two-story lunch room was a beehive of activity before the day of dining cars. At the far left is Hereford's small standard-design combination depot, dating from 1891. Except for the creek and track line, little remains today to recreate this scene. (Mark J. Camp collection.)

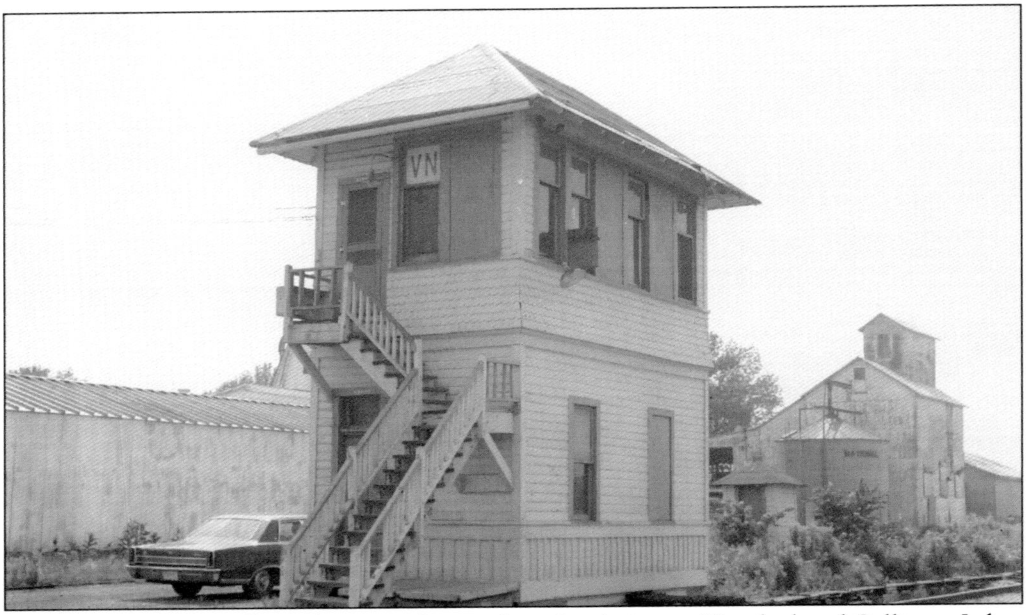

Nova once had a small combination depot of similar design to Hereford and Sullivan. It has been gone for sometime, but surprisingly Nova tower, seen in 1977, still stood in 2001. This building design was repeated many times along the B&O lines.

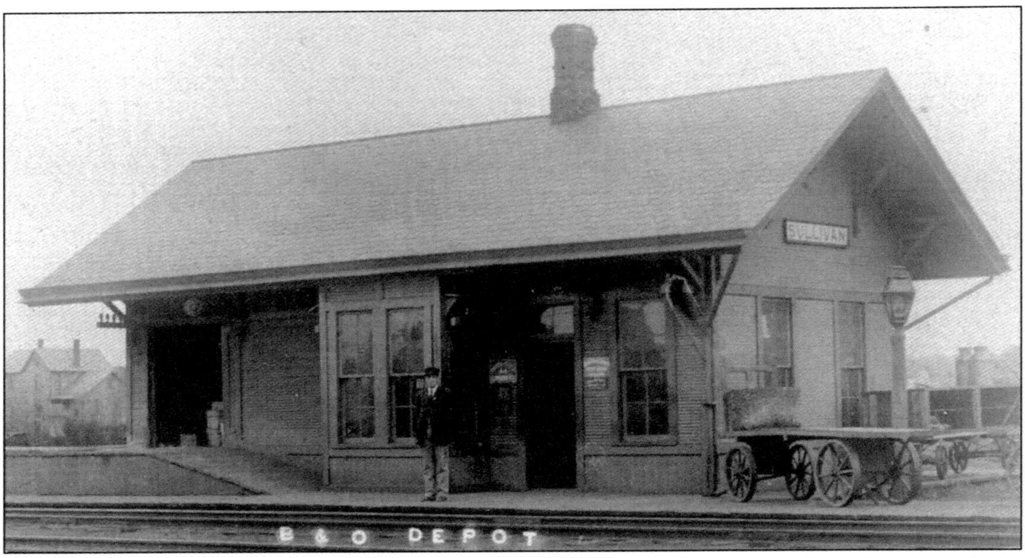

Sullivan serves as a typical example of the standard-design small-town combination depot built along the Akron and Chicago Junction Railroad (later the B&O) in 1891–1892. The plans called for boxy single-floor depots with simple arched roofs, horizontal slat siding, unadorned window and door frames, vertical wainscot, rectangular bays, and raised freight platforms. In the early 1900s, the railroad realigned its track through Sullivan to lessen the grade east to Lodi. The Sullivan depot, shown here around 1909, was later moved north of the tracks and now, in a modified state, serves as a residence. (Mark J. Camp collection.)

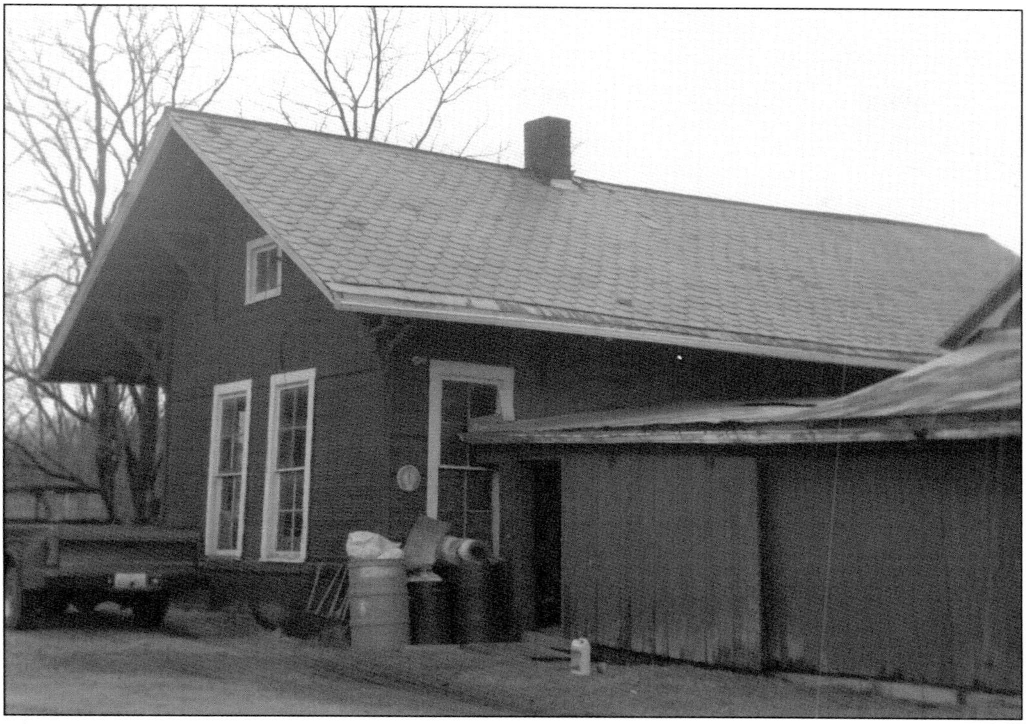

The top view shows the original 1891 depot at Homer in use as an outbuilding at a local residence in 1998. A new alignment of the former Akron and Chicago Junction Railroad (B&O) was put in use in the early 1900s. Instead of moving the old depot, the B&O built one of their standard plan combination depots on the new grade, now located about a half mile north of town. Note the freight end of the depot has high windows to allow more light and allow stacking of freight against the walls, out of sight from the outside. Discarded stone from an earlier bridge lies to the right. Somewhat fancy his and hers outhouses are behind the depot. The newer depot no longer exists. (Mark J. Camp collection.)

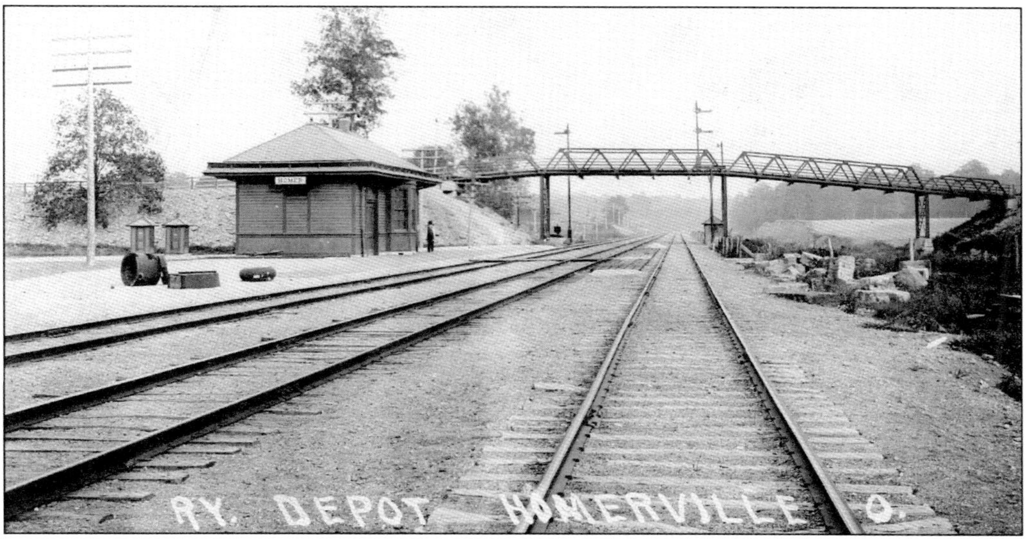

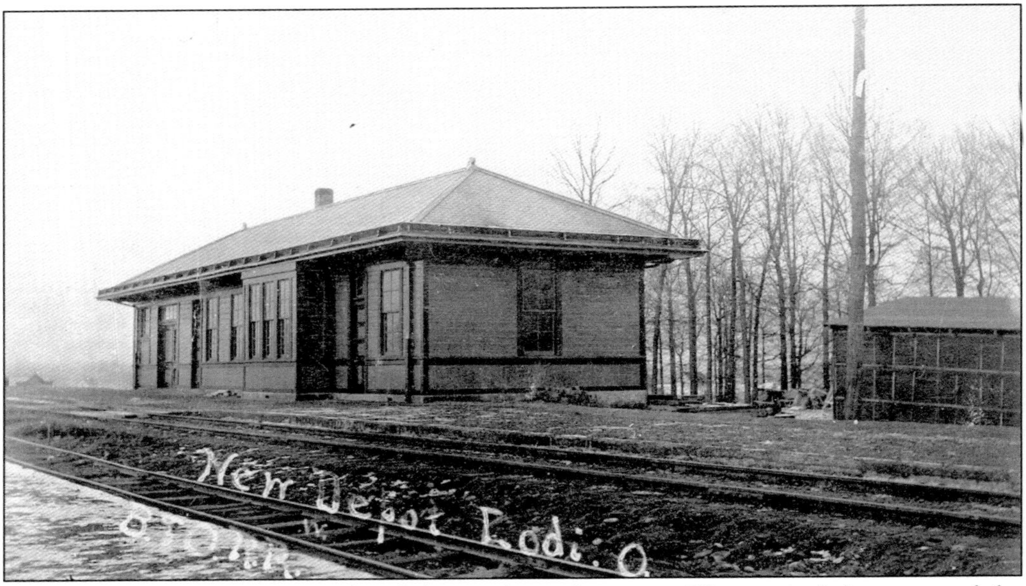

Lodi's B&O depot was also replaced during the realignment. The original depot was of the same design as Homer's earlier depot, and the second depot was built to the same plan as the newer depot at Homer. This *c.* 1907 view shows the brand-new depot, which differs from Homer in having two waiting rooms. The B&O passes over the Wheeling and Lake Erie here on an impressive stone arch viaduct. After the passenger depot was closed by the B&O it was moved nearby and converted into a residence. A B&O freight house remains in railroad use. (Mark J. Camp collection.)

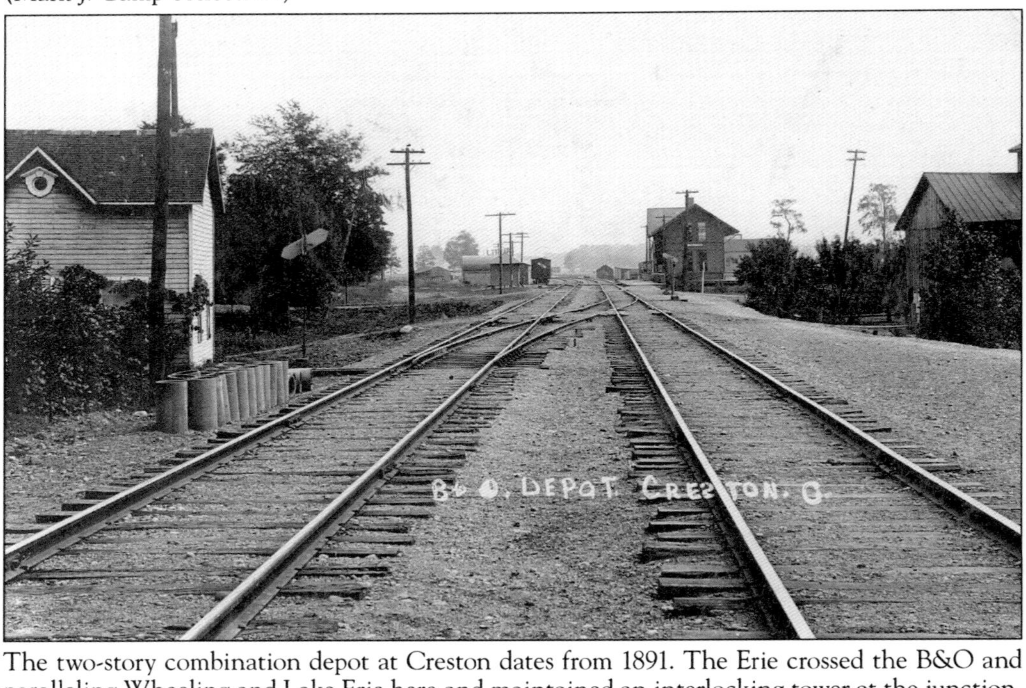

The two-story combination depot at Creston dates from 1891. The Erie crossed the B&O and paralleling Wheeling and Lake Erie here and maintained an interlocking tower at the junction. The depot is a copy of the one at Greenwich. (Mark J. Camp collection.)

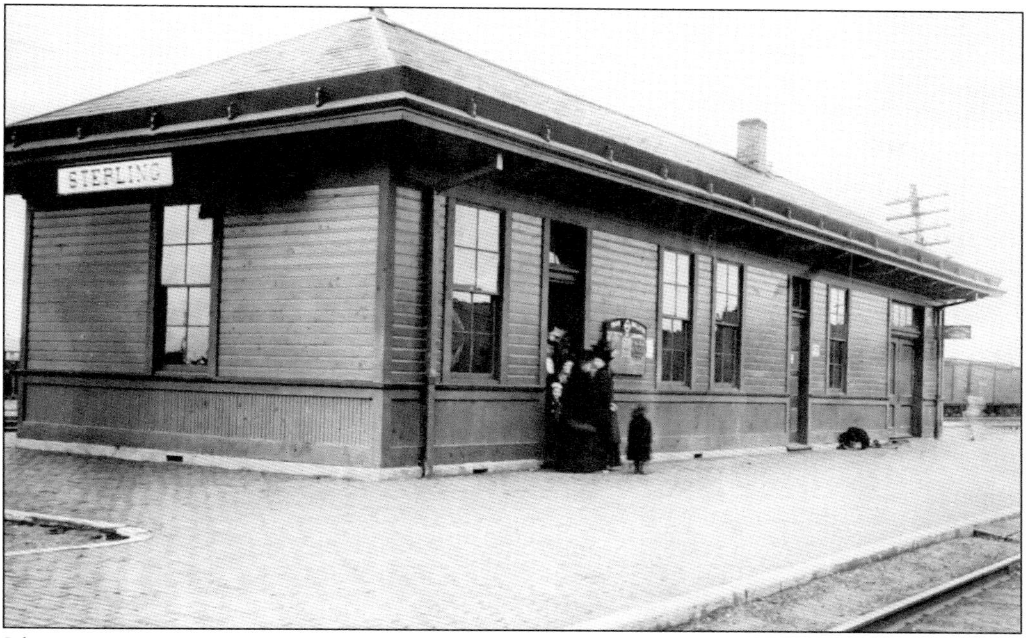

The B&O erected a standard-design passenger depot at the crossing of the Erie in Sterling around 1910. This replaced an earlier V-shaped union depot of Atlantic and Great Western (A&GW) design. This is the Erie side of the depot; the B&O ran on the other side of the depot. Only an Erie tower remained here in the late 1960s. (Mark J. Camp collection.)

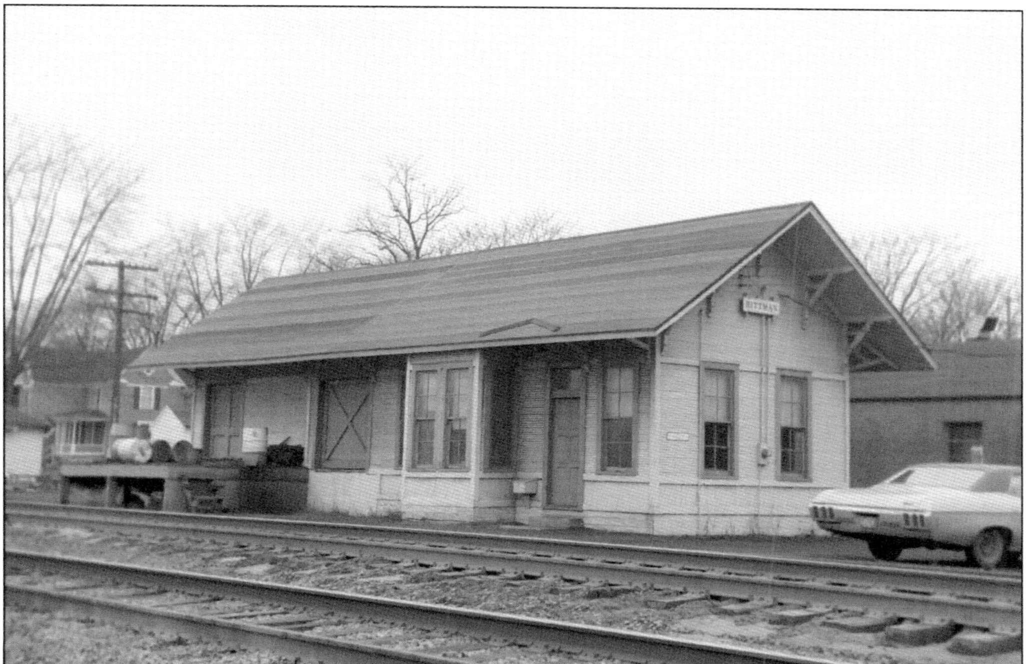

Rittman's B&O combination depot is another standard-plan Akron and Chicago Junction structure. In 1974, it seemed to be mainly a maintenance facility.

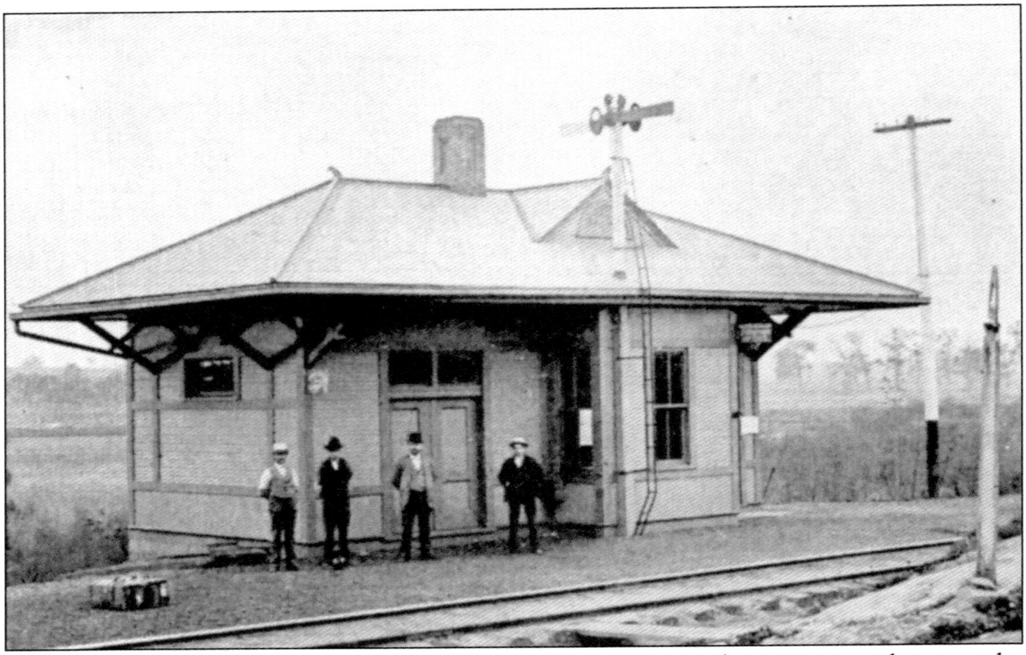

Easton was originally served by the LS&TV. The above depot dates to its predecessor, the CL&W, and probably was built around 1882. Note its similarity to the depot at Valley City, farther north on the line. In 1891, Easton gained a depot on the Akron and Chicago Junction Railroad (B&O). This depot is seen in a 1966 view below when it was part of a small company. Although modified, its railroad heritage is evident. (Above, Mark J. Camp collection; below, Charles Garvin photograph.)

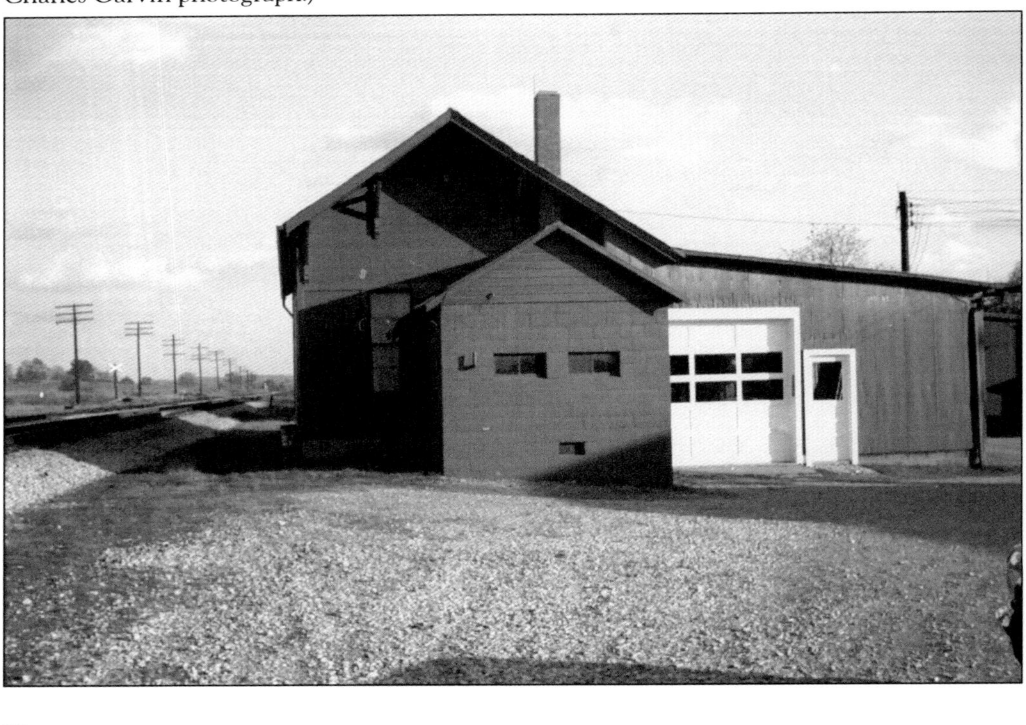

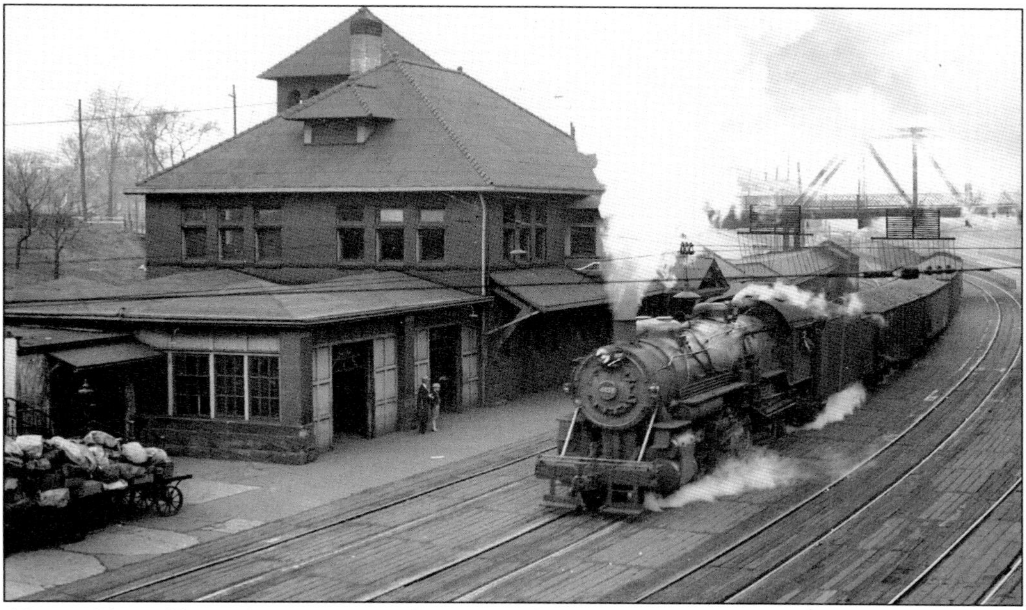

Above, Akron Union Station is in its last years of passenger service in this 1948 photograph. A B&O coal train passes the 1891 depot on its way to Cleveland. This depot was demolished in 1951 and replaced by new Union Depot about five blocks away, shown below. The stone structure was dedicated on April 28, 1950, by the Akron Union Passenger Depot Company, a subsidiary of the B&O and PRR lines. An enclosed concourse extends from the main building across eight sets of tracks. Passengers were accommodated for 21 years, but in 1971, Akron was not included among the original Amtrak routes and the depot was eventually closed. The depot is now part of the University of Akron; students can catch a snack rather than a train in the above track concourse. (Above, W. C. Thurman photograph; below, 1966 Charles Garvin photograph.)

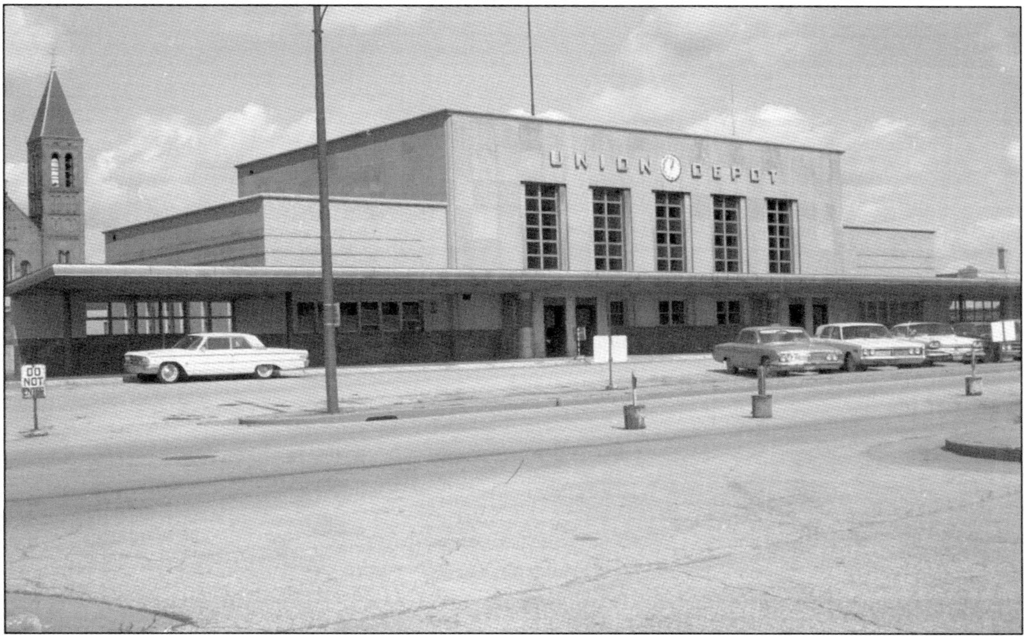

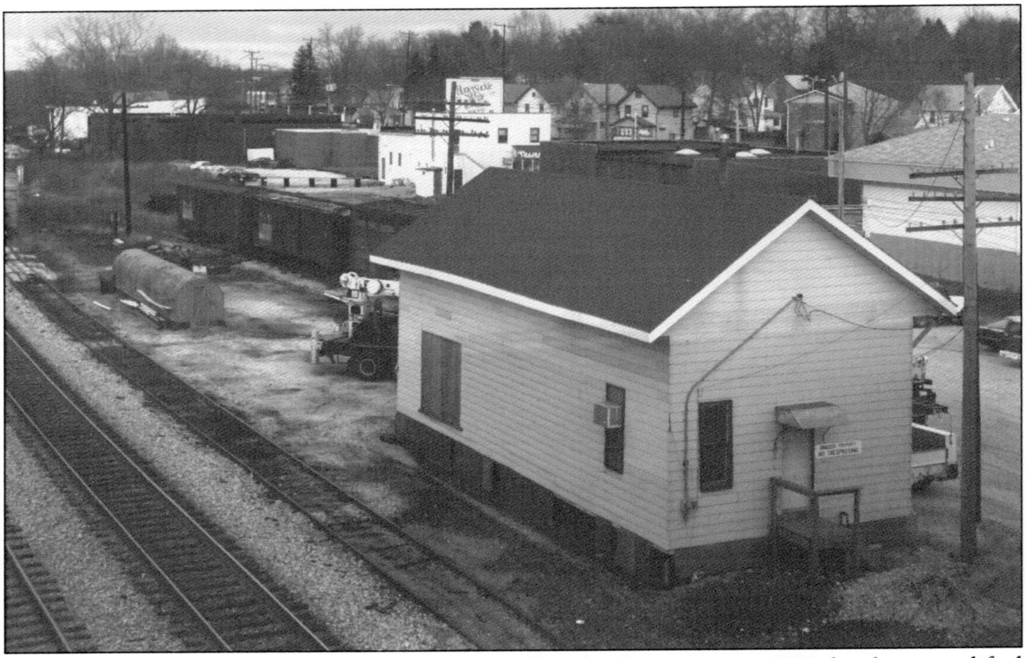

A small suburban depot was built in Cuyahoga Falls. The depot, seen in 1990, has been modified through the years but continues to serve CSX as a maintenance facility. The once nearby Pennsylvania Railroad depot is gone.

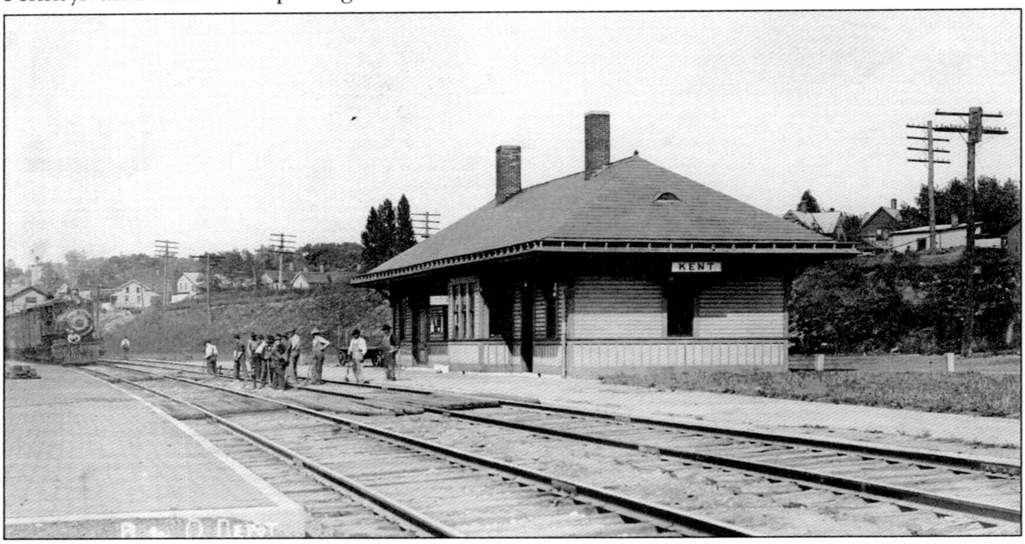

The Cuyahoga River valley through downtown Kent became the right-of-way of both the B&O and Erie predecessors. This *c.* 1907 view shows the passenger depot with gandy dancers at work on the station tracks. The depot is of standard B&O design, dating from around 1905. The Erie's elevated grade lies behind the depot. The end of the Erie freight house is behind the locomotive. The last passenger train to depart this depot was the *Capitol Limited* in April 1971. Both the B&O passenger and freight depots have survived to 2006, although the freight house has been condemned and will probably not last long. The passenger depot still serves CSX as a maintenance facility. (Mark J. Camp collection.)

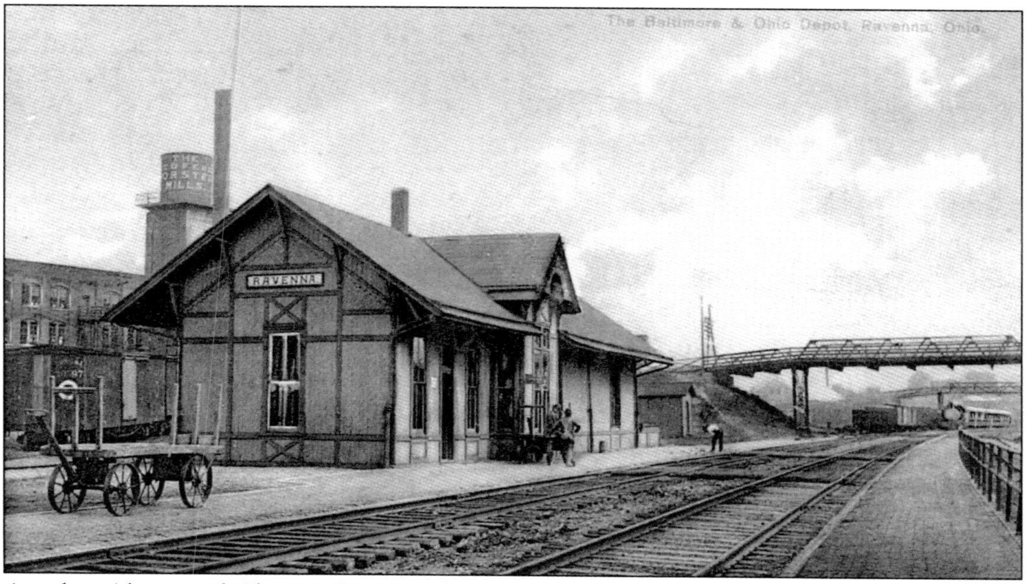

Another Akron and Chicago Junction design depot was built around 1891 in Ravenna. The highway overpasses in the background are also of standard B&O design (an identical bridge can be seen in the view of the Homer depot on page 23). The Ravenna depot was replaced by a metal prefabricated building by the mid-1960s. The only significant B&O structure remaining in Ravenna is RN tower near the former overhead crossing of the Erie. (Mark J. Camp collection.)

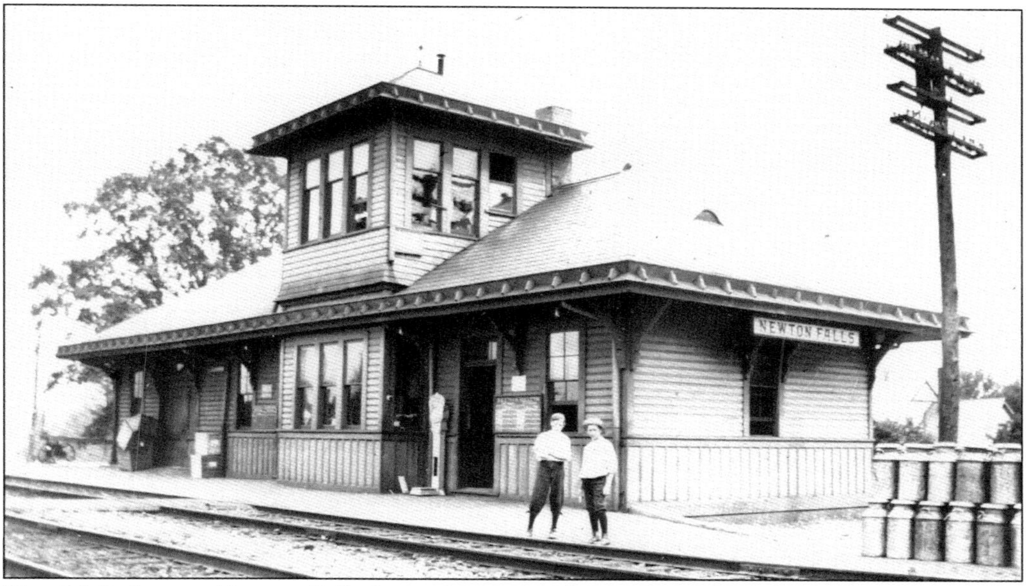

This B&O depot at Newton Falls dating from around 1905 shows the successful combination of a tower and depot. The depot and tower are standardized designs built across the B&O system in the early 1900s. The elevation of the B&O through Newton Falls eliminated an at-grade crossing of the Lake Erie, Alliance and Wheeling Railroad. FN tower controlled the crossing of two B&O lines. Milk was an important commodity at this station. The depot remains as a CSX maintenance facility. (Mark J. Camp collection.)

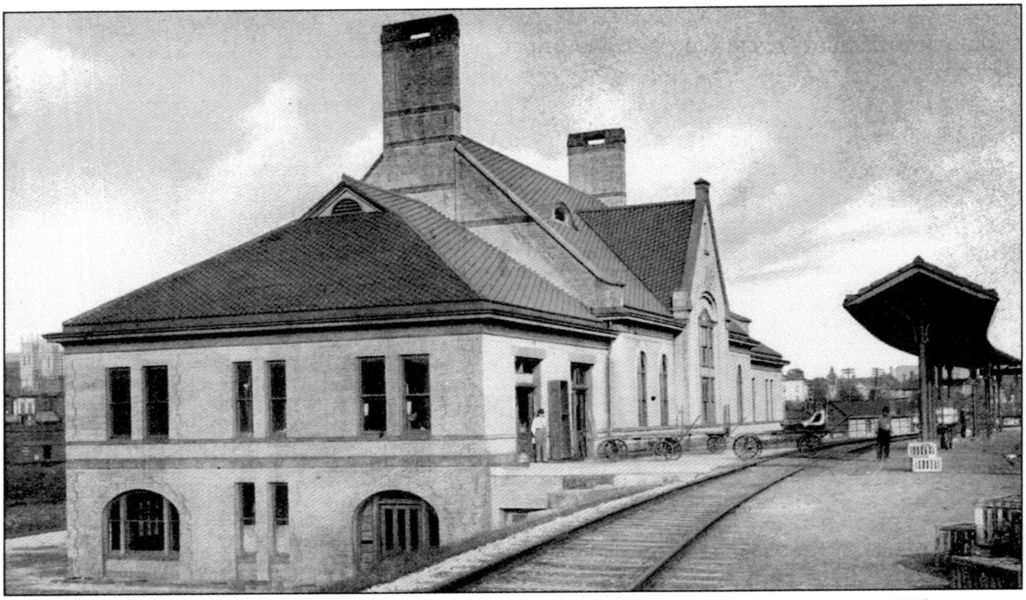

The B&O built this new passenger depot on Mahoning Avenue in Youngstown in 1905 at a cost of about $70,000. The 1913 flood caused havoc across Ohio; Youngstown was no exception. The Mahoning River submerged the first floor of the depot. The raised platform and right-of-way proved a good move by the B&O. A new freight house was added to the Youngstown facilities in 1926. Amtrak brought an end to passenger service in 1971. The depot housed freight offices for several years, and then the building was abandoned in 1981. When demolition was eminent in the mid-1980s, the city purchased the building. It was renovated in 1990 and opened as a restaurant in 1991. (Mark J. Camp collection.)

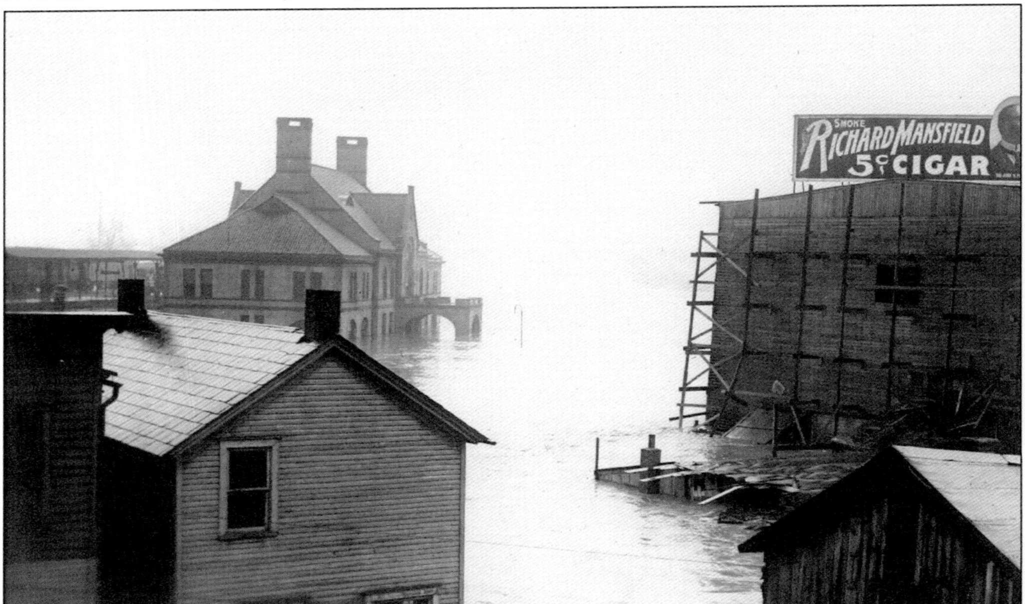

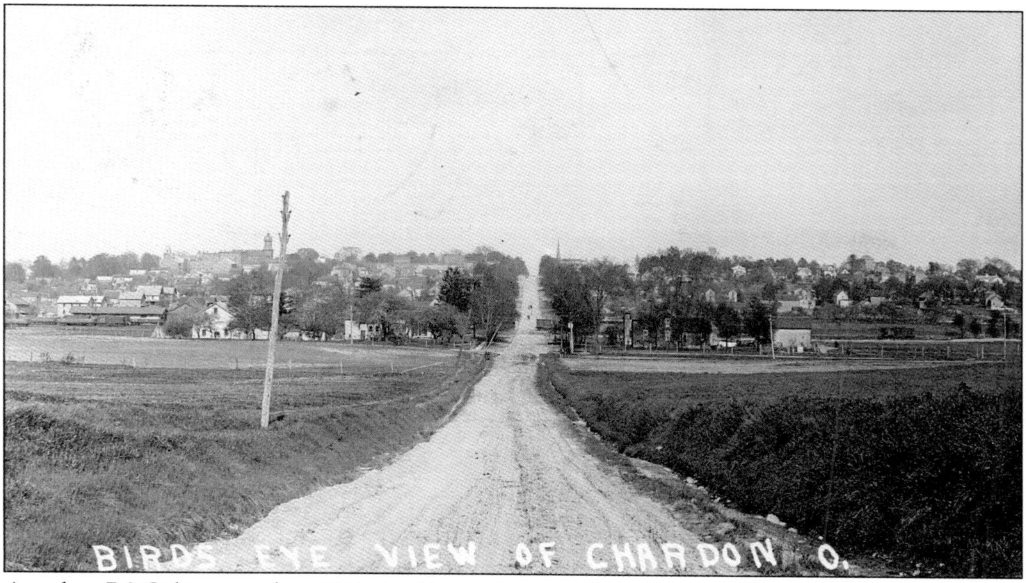

Another B&O line ran from Painesville southeast to Warren and Youngstown. A new B&O depot was built in Painesville in 1905, but by the 1960s only a ramshackle freight house remained. Chardon, as seen above, was initially developed on a high ridge of land left over from the great Ice Age. The Pittsburg, Painesville and Fairport Railroad, later the Pittsburg and Western Railroad (P&W), built through town in the late 1880s. The depot lies to the right in this distant 1915 view. By the late 1960s, Chardon's depot had been greatly shortened and since has been torn down. (Mark J. Camp collection.)

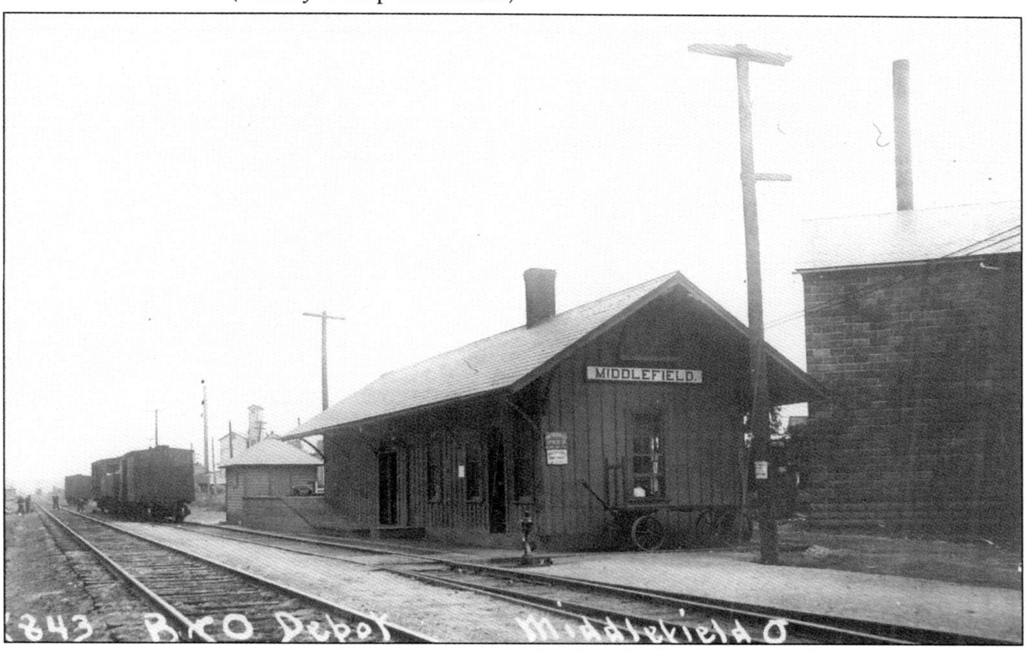

This *c.* 1907 view shows the standard design P&W (B&O) combination depot at Middlefield. The depot was restored in spring 1992 and reopened as a chamber of commerce and small museum. (Mark J. Camp collection.)

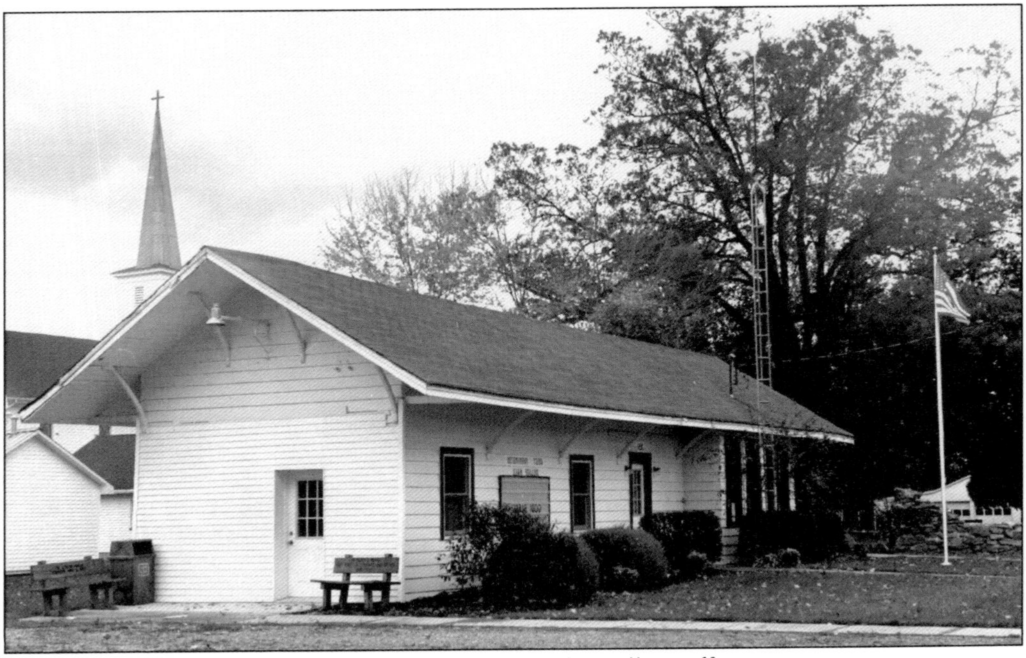

West Farmington's former B&O depot was converted to village offices.

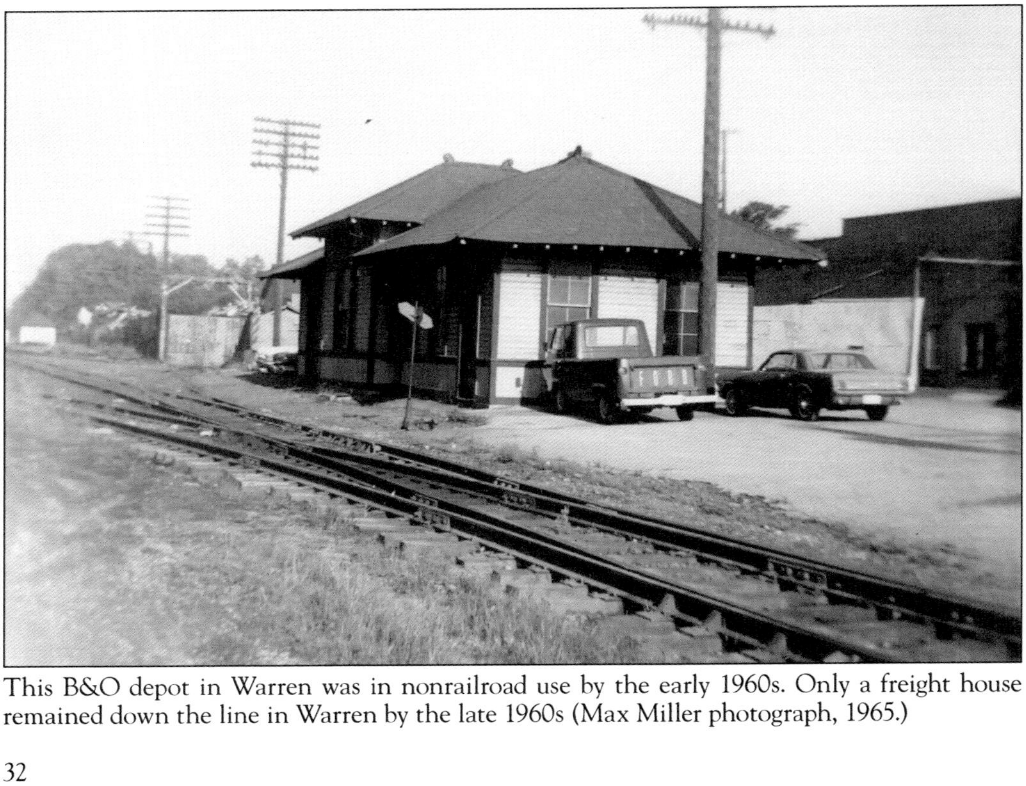

This B&O depot in Warren was in nonrailroad use by the early 1960s. Only a freight house remained down the line in Warren by the late 1960s (Max Miller photograph, 1965.)

Two

Erie Railroad Lines

Work began on the Franklin and Warren Railroad's line from Franklin Mills, now Kent, east to the Pennsylvania-Ohio line in July 1853. Two months later it changed its name to the Atlantic and Great Western Railroad (A&GW). Construction proceeded slowly, with the line eventually connecting points in New York with Dayton, Ohio, in June 1864. In the meantime, the Cleveland and Mahoning Valley Railroad (C&MV), opened between Cleveland and Leavittsburg in June 1856, was running two daily passenger trains to Youngstown by November 1856 and to New Castle, Pennsylvania, in 1858. The C&MV, which tapped rich coal and iron ore fields around Youngstown, was leased by the A&GW in October 1863. Since the A&GW was broad gauge—six feet between the rails—a third rail was laid along the "standard gauge" C&MV to allow trains to reach Cleveland by November 1863. Financial problems led to receivership and control of the A&GW by the Erie Railroad in the late 1860s. The A&GW became the New York, Pennsylvania and Ohio Railroad (NYP&O) in 1880, and the track was narrowed to standard gauge in one day, a remarkable engineering feat, on June 22, 1880. The offices of the NYP&O were in Cleveland. In three years, the line fell under Erie control again. The Erie Railroad offices were moved to downtown Cleveland when the Van Sweringen Brothers gained control in the 1920s. After years of financial difficulties, the Erie merged with the Delaware, Lackawanna and Western in 1960 to become the Erie Lackawanna Railroad (EL), the offices remained in downtown Cleveland. EL passenger service, with the exception of Cleveland-Youngstown commuter service, ended in 1971. A portion of the EL, including the Cleveland-Youngstown line, became part of Conrail in 1976. The last commuter service between Cleveland and Youngstown ran on January 14, 1977. The engineering offices of the Erie Railroad followed sets of standard plans for their mainly frame depots and repeated them regularly along the entire system from Jersey City to Chicago.

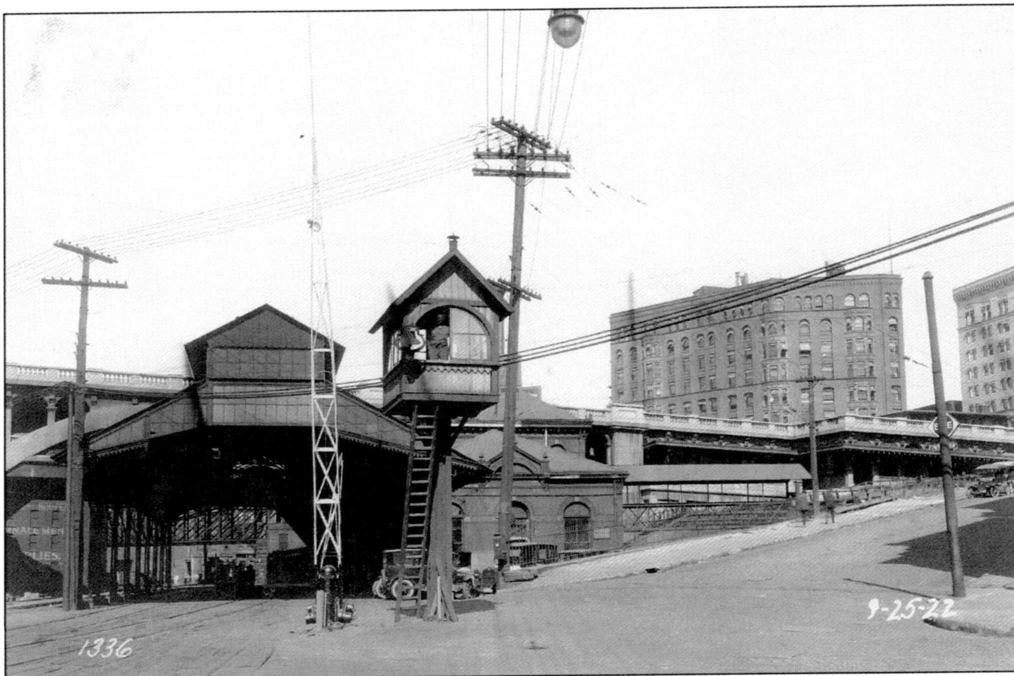

In 1881, the NYP&O built the above depot near the intersection of Columbus and Canal Roads. In the background of this 1922 view is the Superior-Detroit viaduct across the Cuyahoga River. The man in the elevated watch tower controlled the gates. By the 1930s, 20 Erie passenger trains used this depot each day. The Erie used this depot until 1949 when it began to run its trains into Cleveland Union Terminal. The train shed was torn down, and by the 1960s the brick structure became a restaurant/night club. In 1898, the Erie built the structure below at Wilson Avenue and East Fifty-fifth Street to provide a convenient depot for the Erie terminal and shops located nearby. (Above, photograph collection of Cleveland Public Library.)

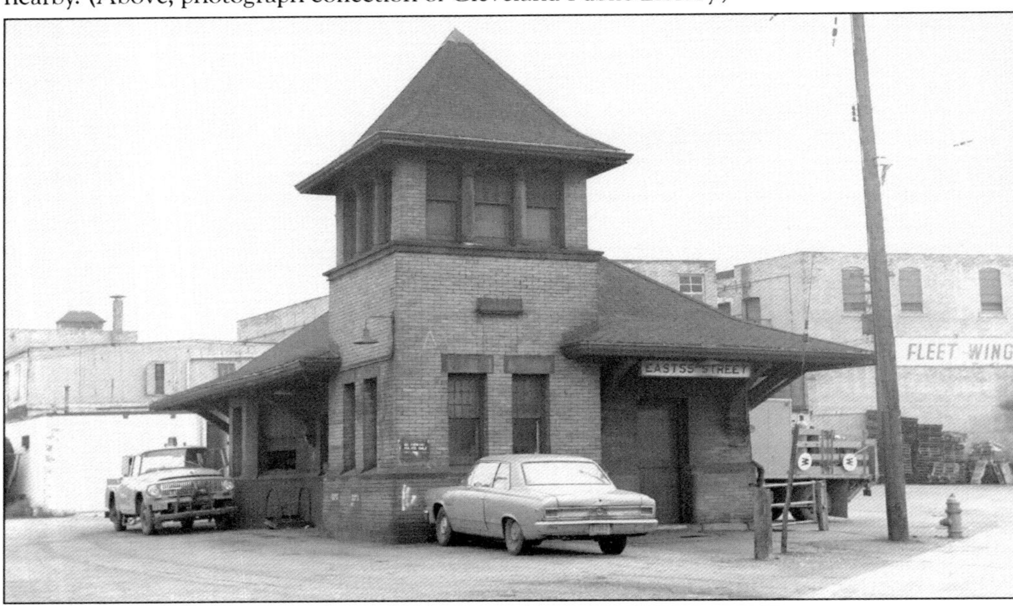

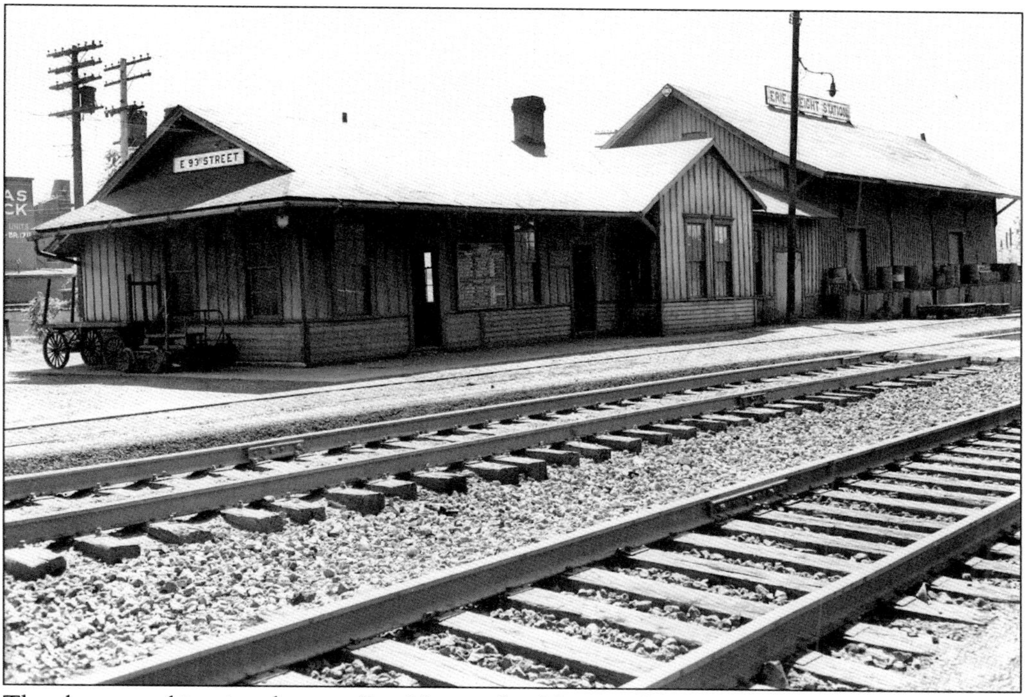

The above combination depot at East Ninety-third Street, photographed in 1949, was originally called Newburgh. Over the years the building had an addition on the passenger end, note the vertical board and change in the wainscot, and the freight end roof was raised to a story and a half. Below is a newer depot built at Lee Road by the Erie in 1948 to serve commuters in this burgeoning suburb of Cleveland. The depot, photographed in 1971, closed when commuter service ended in 1977. (Above, Robert Runyan photograph.)

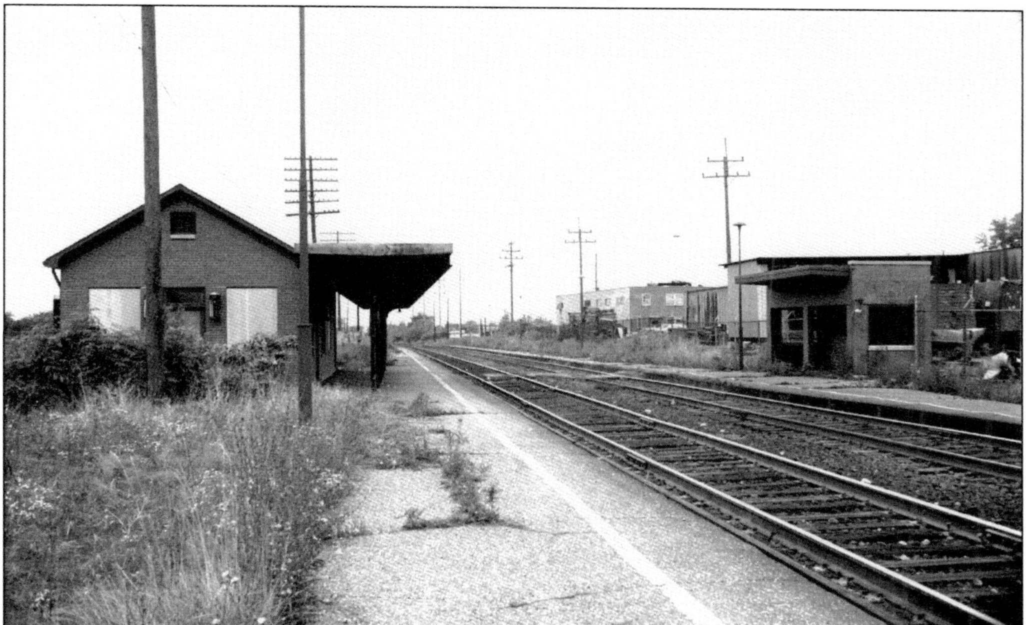

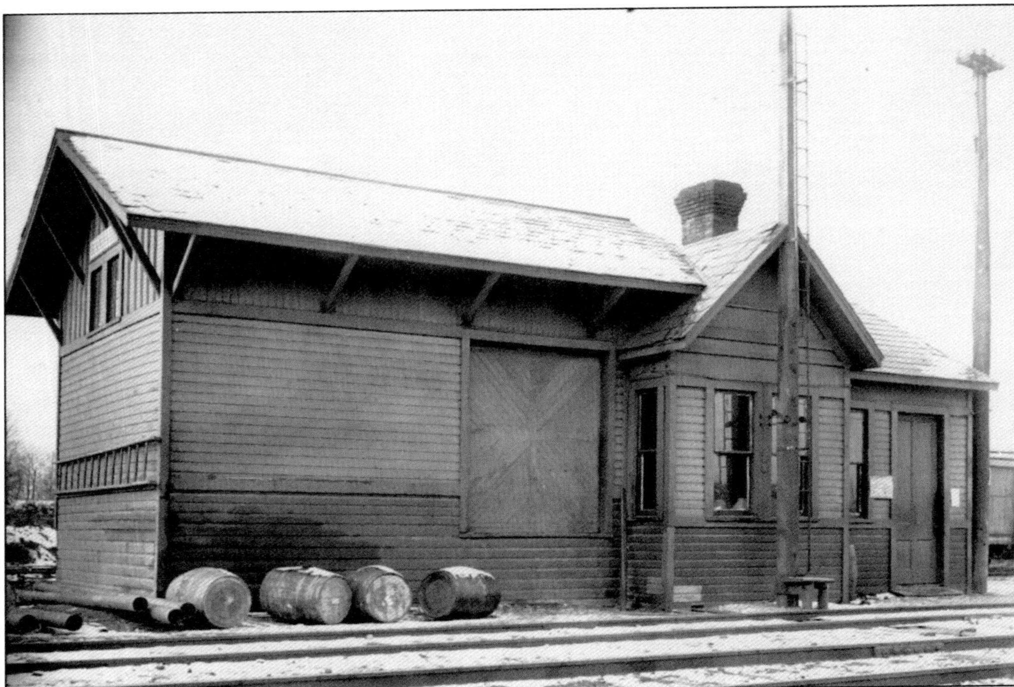

North Randall's Erie depot was built to one of the standard plans of the company. The depot, shown above around 1910, still stands but is boarded and unused. The depot at Solon was of similar design, but the passenger and freight rooms were reversed and the vestibule was rounded instead of squared off with a three-sided lower roof. A branch of the Wheeling and Lake Erie was crossed here. The depot remains in business use, although it has been considerably modified. (Above, Erie Railroad photograph, Mark J. Camp collection.)

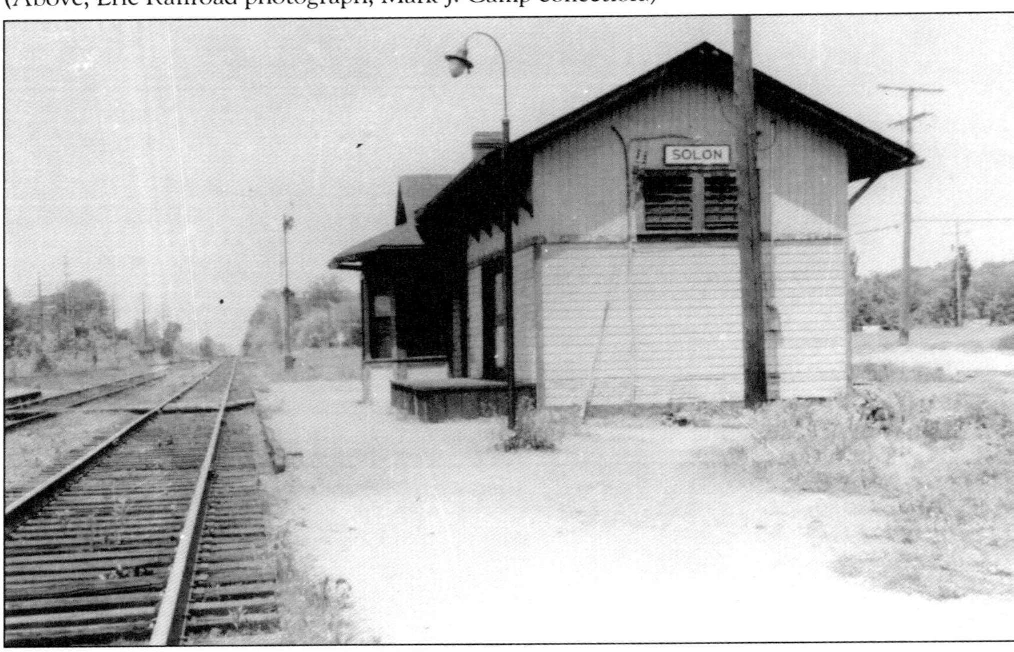

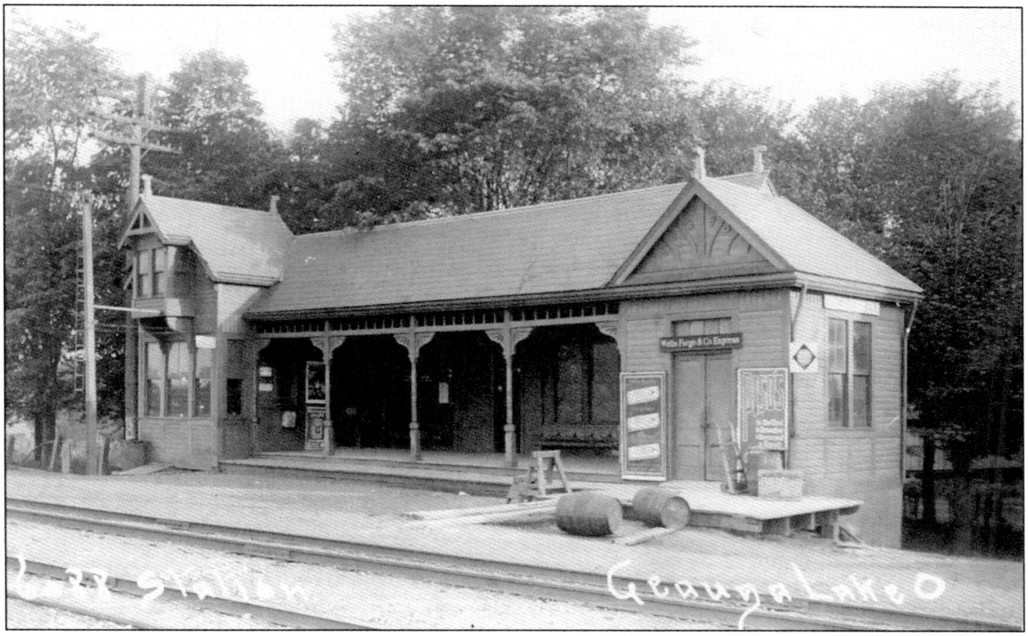

Erie's first depot at Geauga Lake, photographed around 1912, was designed to accommodate the summertime crowds visiting the popular resort, dance hall, and amusement park. Note that passengers waited outside. South of this depot was a wye where NYP&O, later Erie, trains could proceed to the gates of the Geauga Lake Resort and Encampment. The resort drew huge crowds in the 1880s and 1890s. Some Erie depots had commercial advertising plastered to the walls, but this was more common in states east of Ohio. The last depot at Geauga Lake was the stucco structure shown in 1977, below. The newer depot lasted until the fall of 2002. (Mark J. Camp collection.)

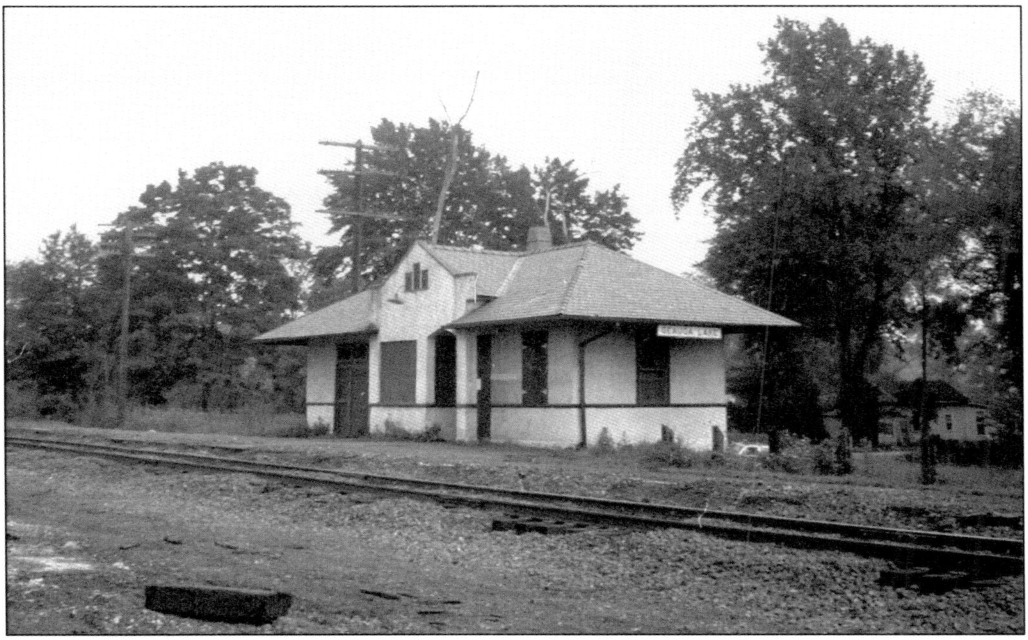

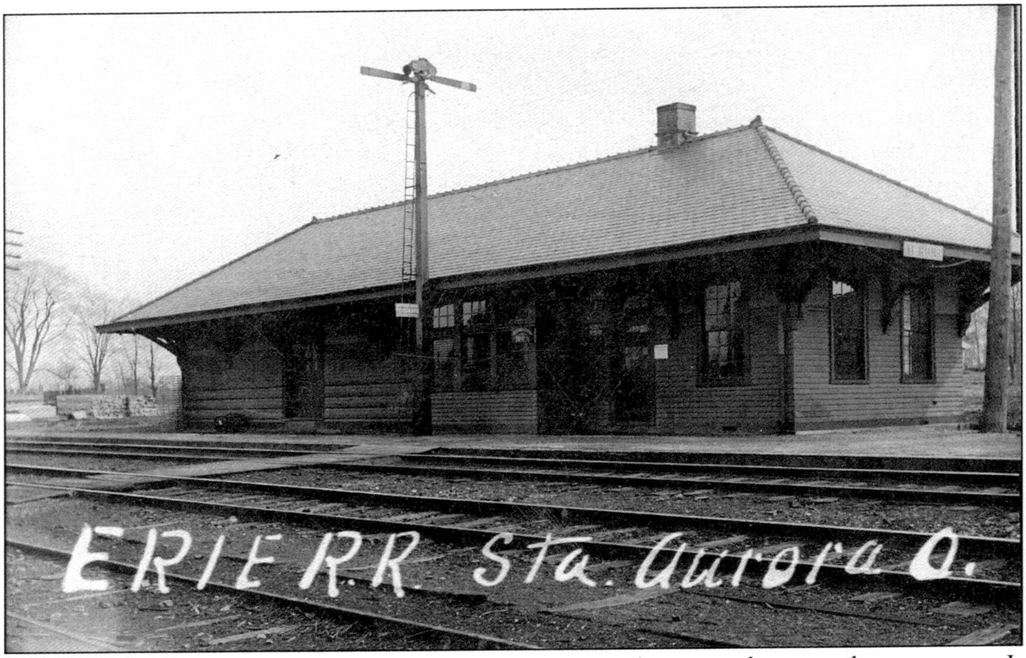

The combination depot at Aurora dates from 1906, a replacement for an earlier structure. It represents another common design used along the Erie. The above photograph dates from 1908. Below is a design at Mantua attributed to the A&GW. The depot is thought to date from around 1872, however, the first regular C&MV trains served Mantua on July 4, 1856. Built to the same plans but shorter in length was the depot at Mahoning. A shorter, plain design served Hiram. Hiram lacked the gingerbread in the eaves and had a corrugated tin roof, obviously quite noisy in a rainstorm. Aurora and Mantua remain, nicely restored, along the trackless roadbed. Hiram and Mahoning are gone. (Mark J. Camp collection.)

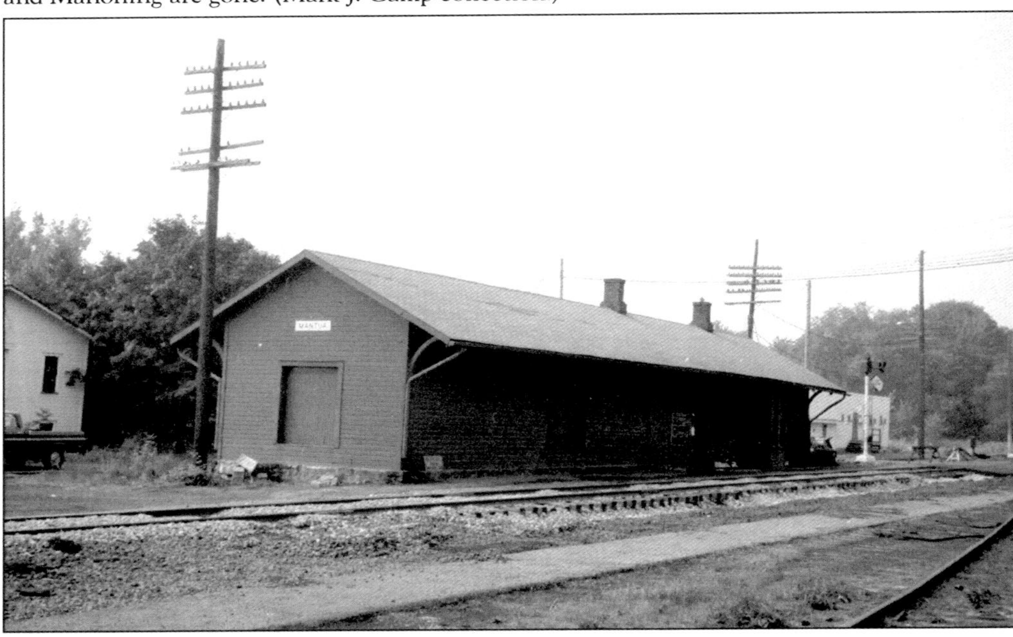

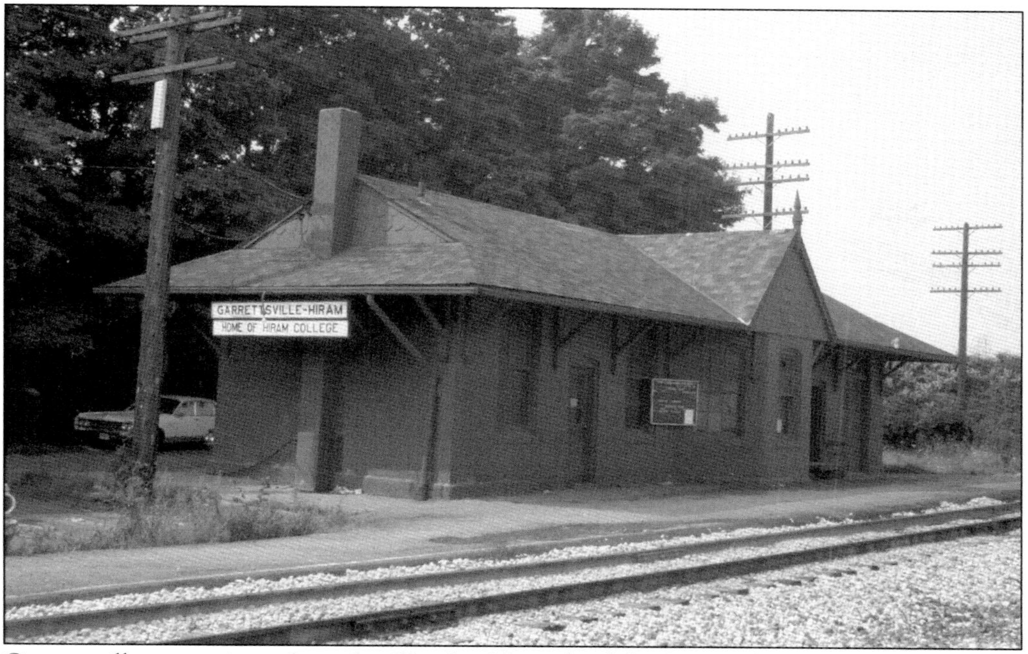

Garrettsville was unique along the Cleveland branch of the Erie Railroad because of its brick construction. It became the stop for Hiram College in later days. Facing the passenger depot was a standardized frame freight house. Only the freight house remains, in use by a local lumberyard.

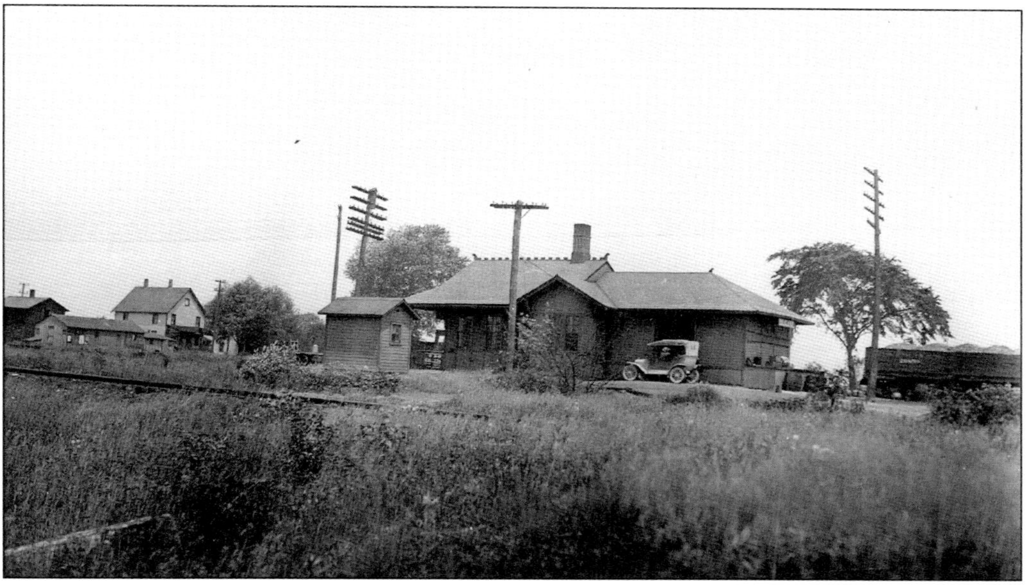

An Erie Railroad–designed depot once sat at the junction of the Erie and Lake Erie, Alliance and Wheeling Railroad at Phalanx. This was one of the more architecturally pleasing designs to come out of the Erie Railroad engineering offices. The depot sat within the wye of the two lines. In June 1914, a photographer under the employ of the NYC snapped this photograph while compiling evaluation photographs of the railroad's property here shared with the Erie. The road to the depot could get quite dusty. (NYC photograph, Allen County [Ohio] Historical Society collection.)

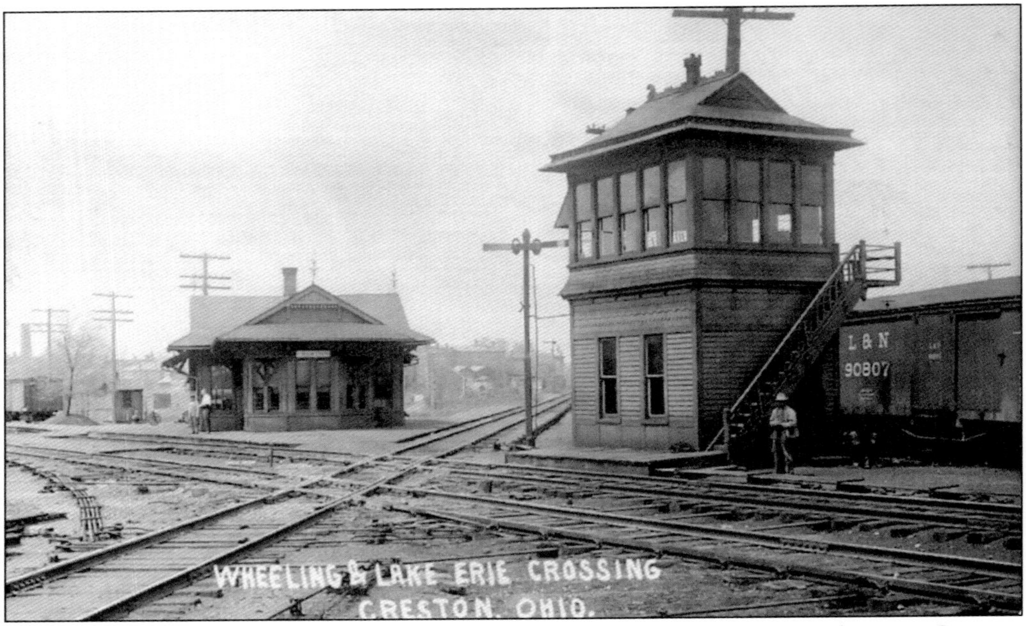

The Erie, B&O, and Wheeling and Lake Erie Railroads shared a passenger depot in Creston. Diagonally across from the depot was an Erie Railroad interlocking tower. Only a vacated freight house remained by the late 1960s. (Mark J. Camp collection.)

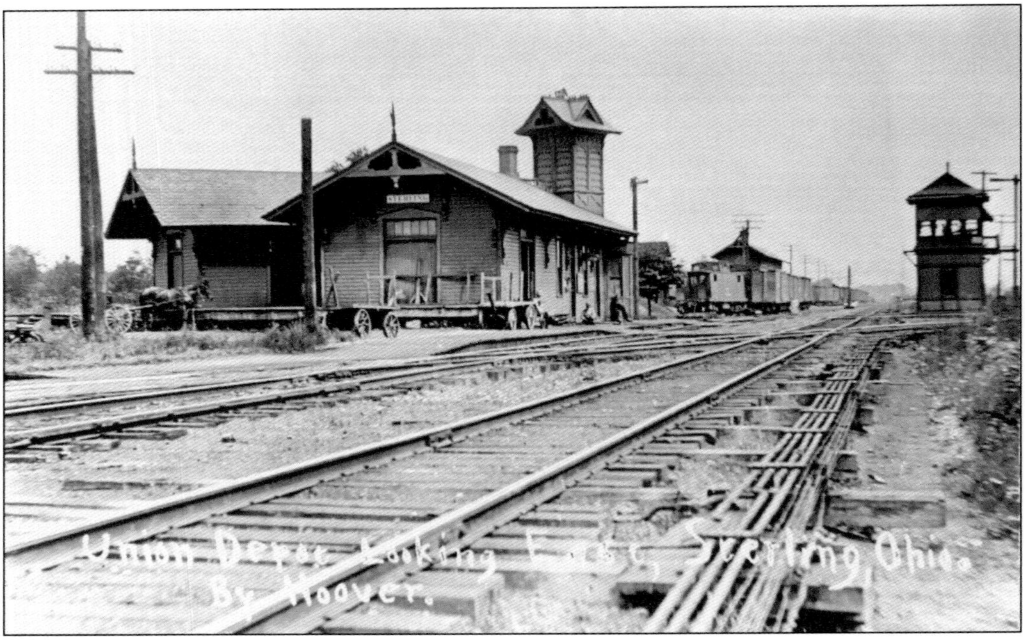

Sterling had a union depot of Erie Railroad design serving the CL&W, B&O, and Erie Railroads. The V-shaped structure, shown here looking east around 1910, was gone by the early 1900s when the depot was replaced with one of standard B&O design. Only an Erie Railroad interlocking tower remained at this once-busy junction by the 1960s. (David P. Oroszi collection.)

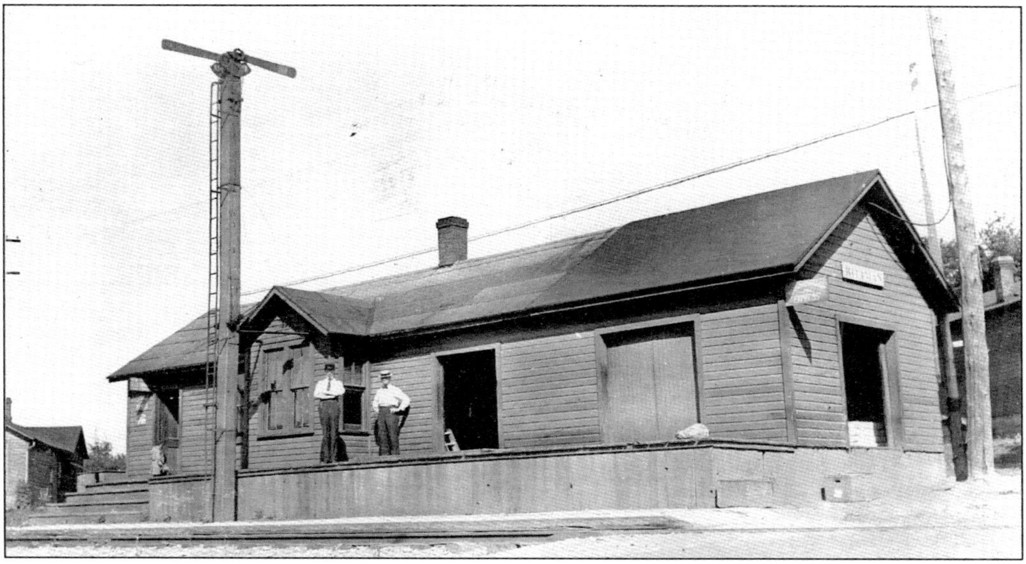

Rittman depot was a busy place in 1908 with nearby salt wells providing regular shipments of bags of processed salt. Note that the freight room dwarfs the passenger end. Apparently the day shift was handled by these two dapper gentlemen. This depot was later replaced with separate freight and passenger depots. The later passenger depot was built to the same plan as Freedom; the freight house was stucco. (Mark J. Camp collection.)

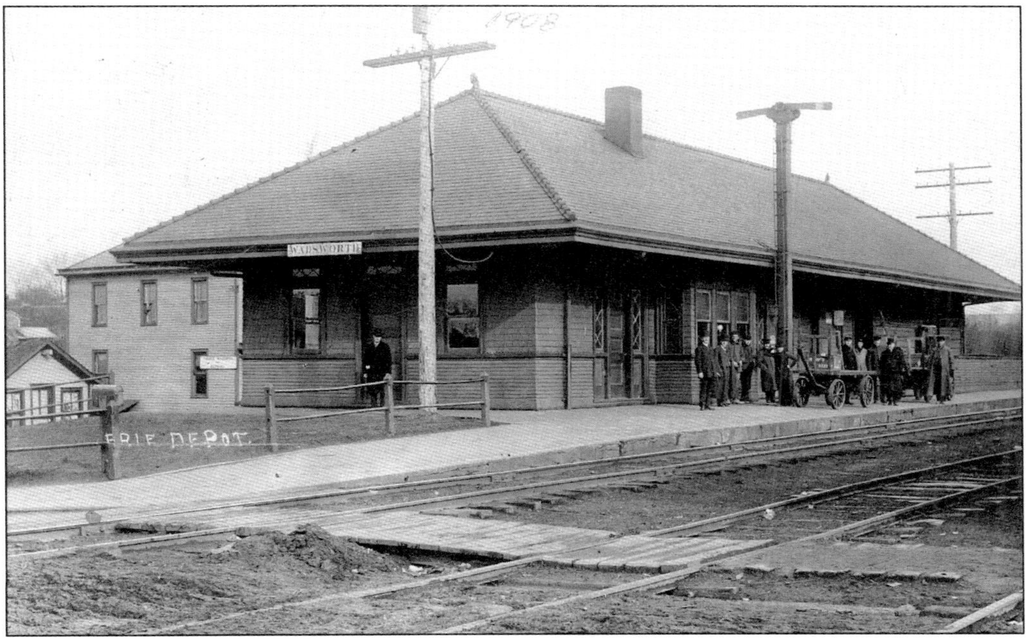

The combination depot at Wadsworth dates from 1900 to 1906 and is similar to the depot at Aurora. The hipped roof was favored by Erie Railroad architects for the larger depots. The structure has been demolished. (Mark J. Camp collection.)

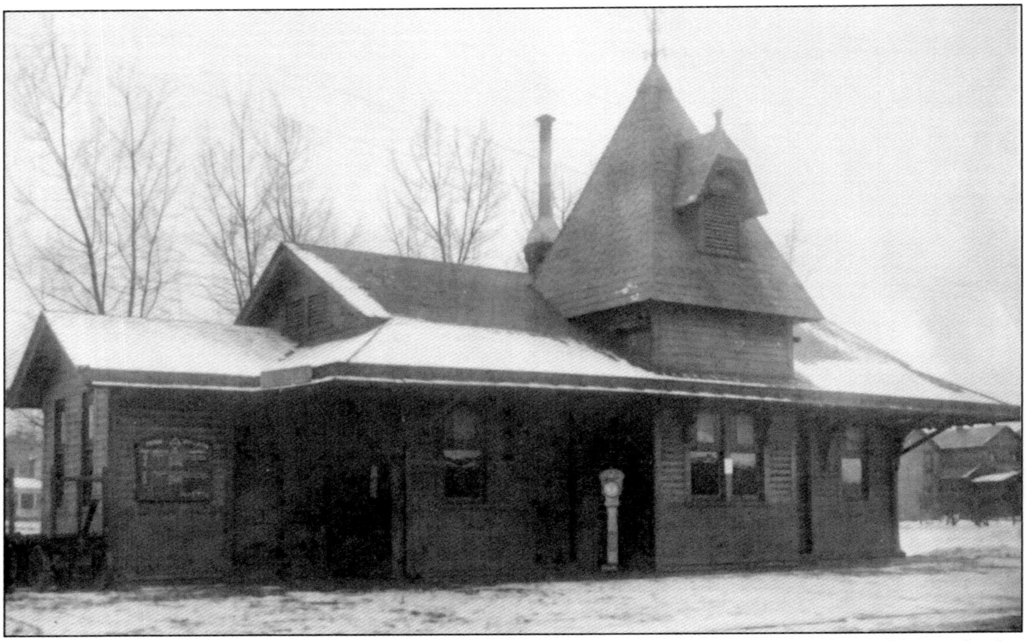

This turreted passenger depot located on Fourth Street in Barberton opened in 1891 with the founding of Barberton. The depot had three waiting rooms and stained glass in the upper sashes of the windows. Nearby was an Erie freight house and the Erie House, a railroad hotel with dining facilities. Next to the depot was a well-manicured garden; in later years the town name was stenciled with stone in the lawn. (Erie Railroad photograph, Mark J. Camp collection.)

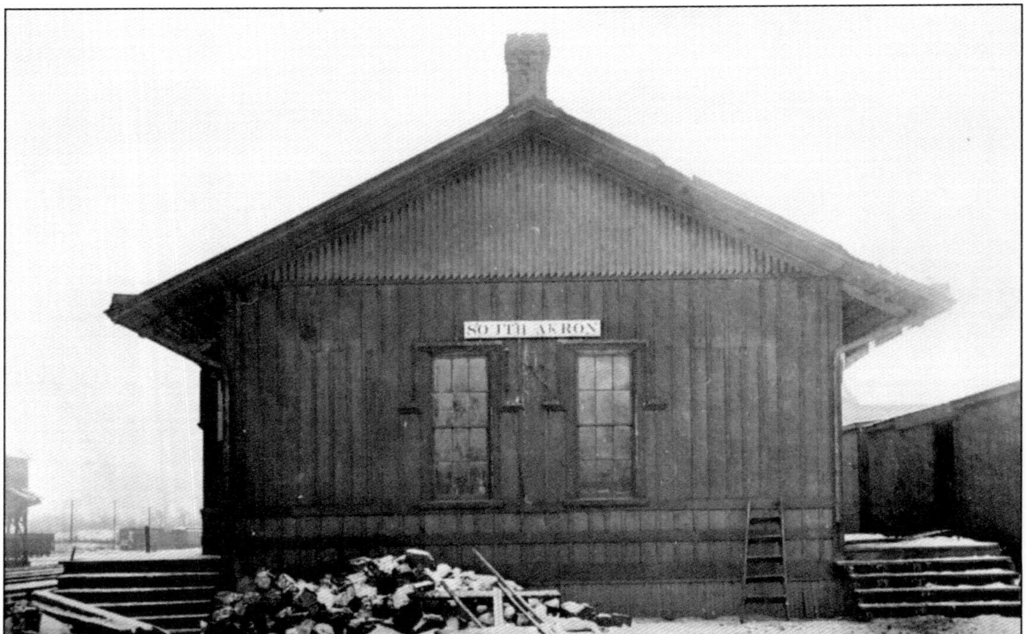

A combination depot was also erected at South Akron. It has been gone since at least the mid-1900s. (Erie Railroad photograph, Mark J. Camp collection.)

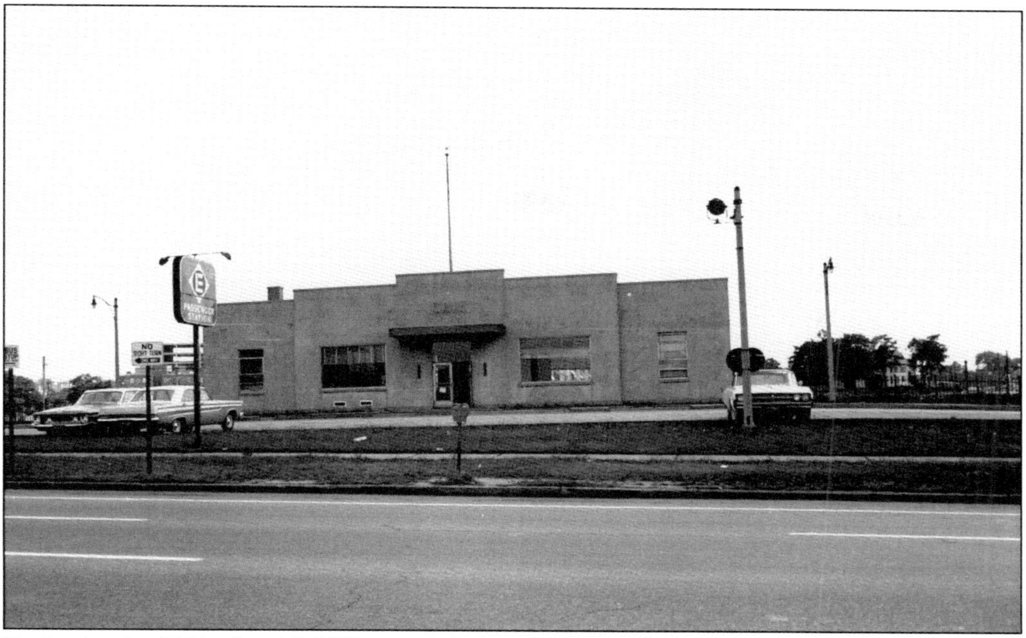

Beginning in 1864, the A&GW operated out of a frame depot in Akron. Union Depot (see page 27) in Akron was built in 1890–1891 at East Market and Canal Streets by the B&O and Cleveland Akron and Columbus Railroads for around $100,000. It eventually served the B&O, Erie, and Pennsylvania Railroads until its replacement in 1947 by a new Erie Railroad passenger depot (shown here) about five blocks away on South Broadway; the B&O and PRR entered new Union Depot in 1950 just north of and across the tracks from the Erie depot. The new Erie structure was faced with Indiana limestone and had an enclosed concourse over three sets of tracks. The 1947 Erie depot has been torn down, and only the brick Erie freight house remains.

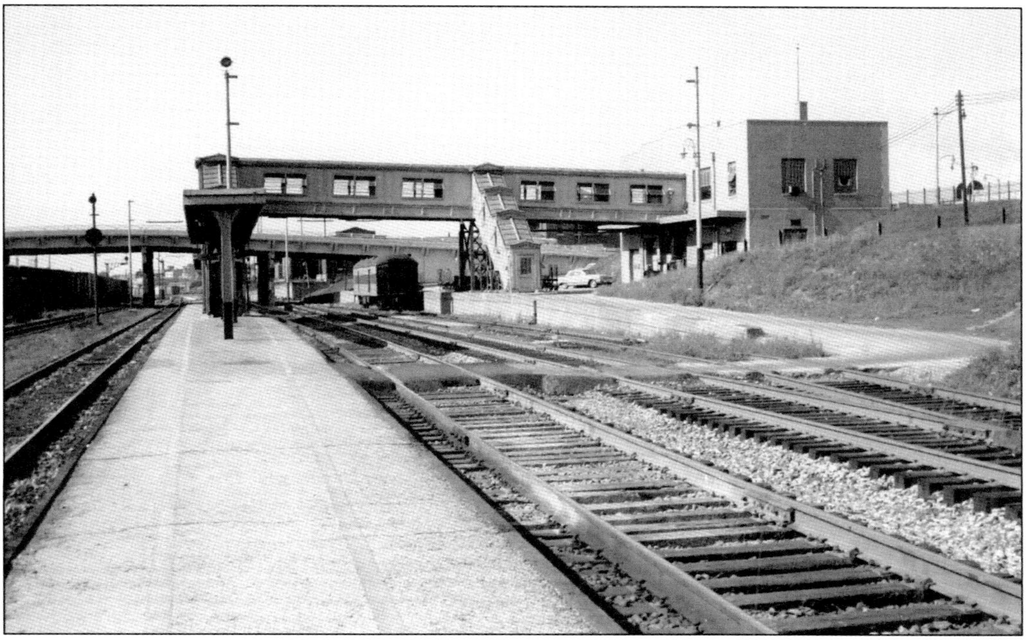

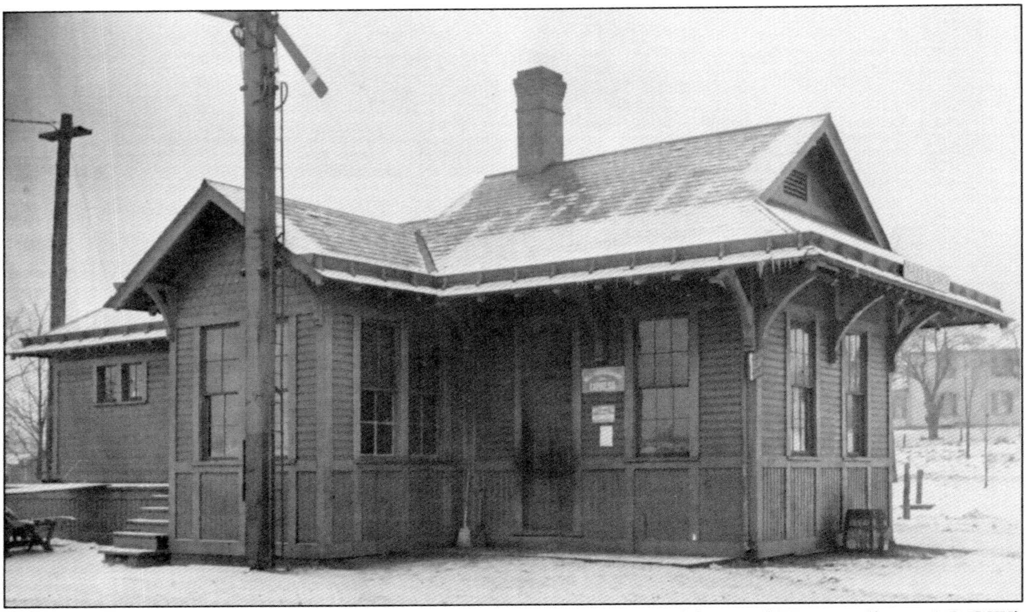

The citizens of Tallmadge celebrated the arrival of the first Franklin and Warren (later A&GW) train on May 26, 1863. The first depot was on Southeast Avenue, but in 1891, it was relocated to East Avenue. This depot burned down in 1903, and the depot pictured above replaced it. Note that it was built to similar plans as Phalanx. It was still there in the late 1960s. (Erie Railroad photograph, Mark J. Camp collection.)

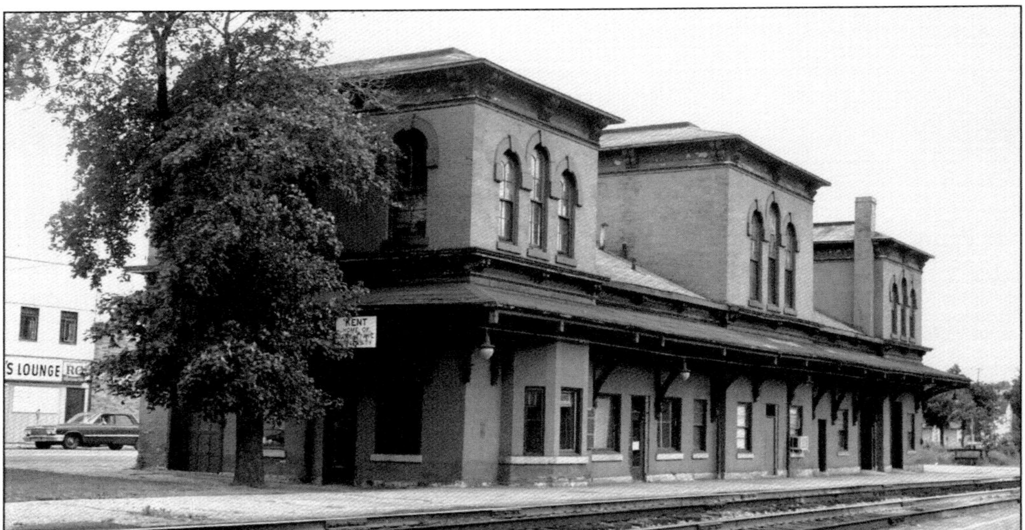

On June 1, 1875, the A&GW opened this imposing passenger depot in Kent, formerly Franklin Mills. The main floor had waiting rooms, a ticket office, a baggage room, and a dining area. The second floor contained a crew dormitory and employee reading room, which operated from 1875 to 1882. Around 1925, the depot restaurant was closed and replaced with a freight room. Passenger service ended in January 1970. The passenger depot sat abandoned until 1977, when restoration began by the Kent Historical Society, and it reopened as a restaurant in 1981. (Mark J. Camp collection.)

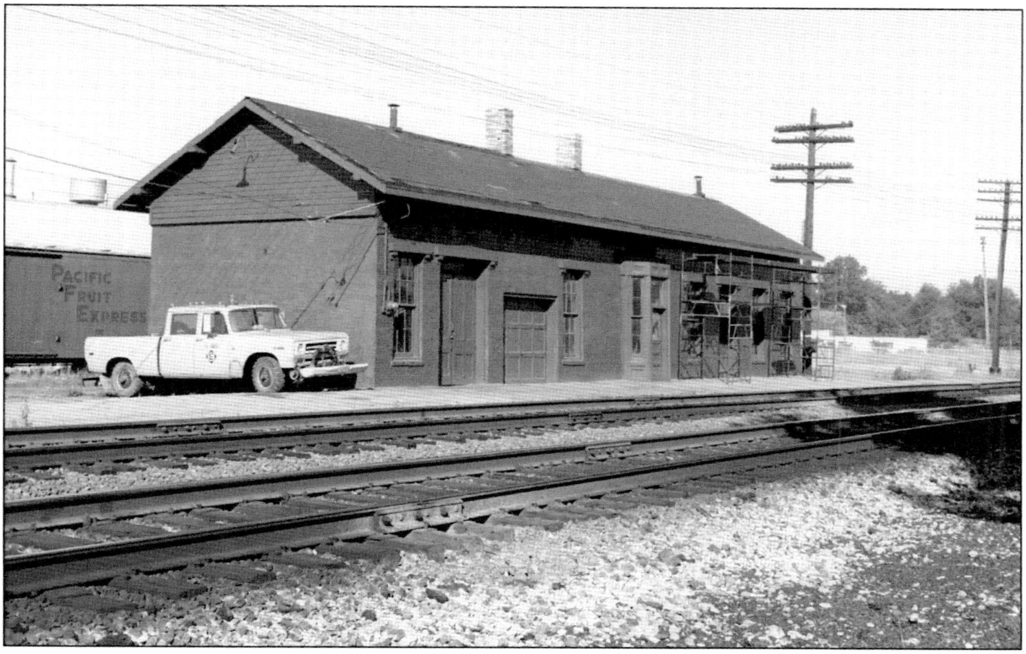

The A&GW first served Ravenna in March 1863. This brick depot served the community for over 100 years. By 1971, the overhanging roof had been cut back, making a rather odd-looking depot. (Herbert H. Harwood photograph.)

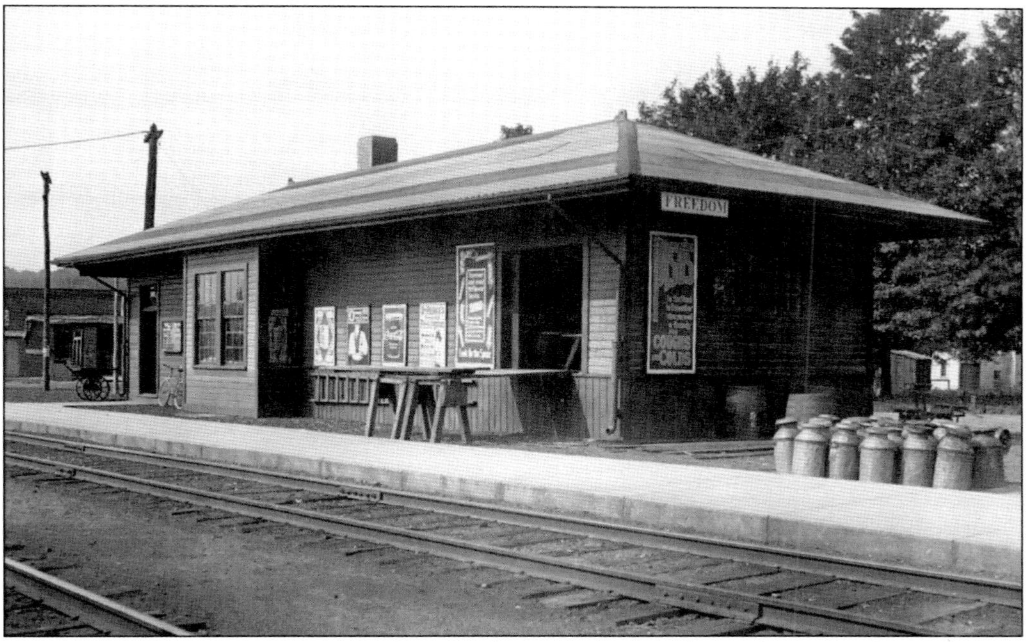

The depot at Freedom, shown around 1910, follows another Erie depot plan. Note the advertising placards, more characteristic of Erie depots in New York and New Jersey. Farmers used this depot to ship their milk to city dairies. (Erie Railroad photograph, Mark J. Camp collection.)

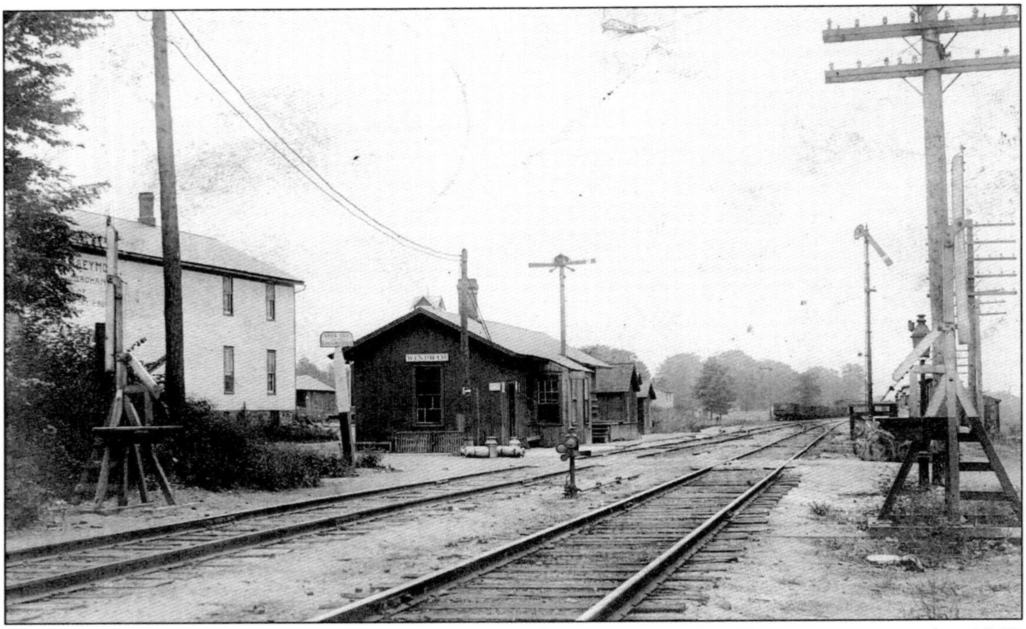

The order board at the rather plain depot at Windham is set to stop the next train in this 1908 view. Although utilitarian, this depot was the key to the outside world for this rural village in the early 1900s. (Mark J. Camp collection.)

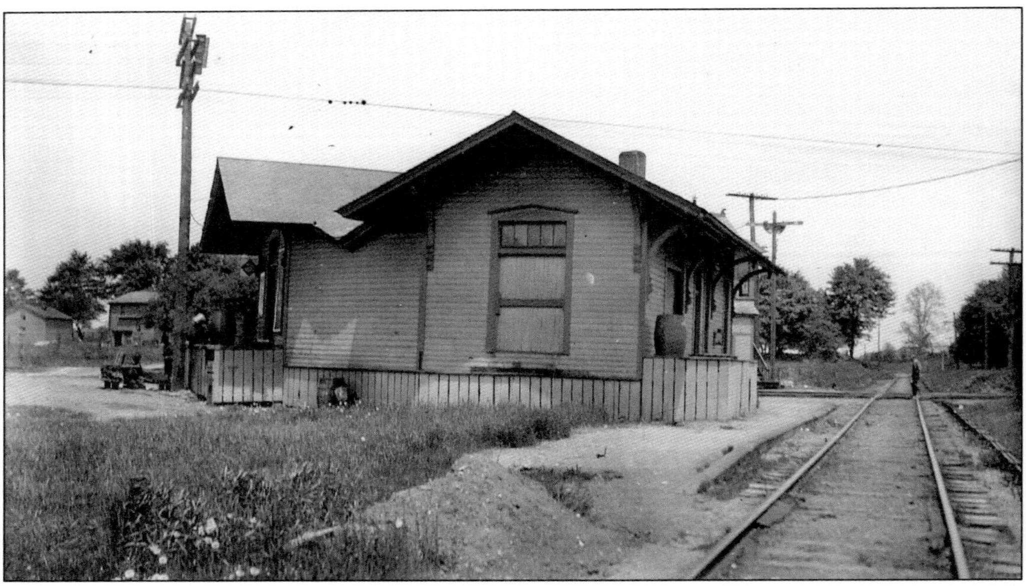

The Erie shared its Braceville depot with the former Lake Erie, Alliance and Wheeling Railroad, an NYC property by the time this May 1919 exposure was made. The depot was V-shaped, stretching along each line. Mostly hidden by the depot is an Erie Railroad interlocking tower. (NYC photograph, Allen County [Ohio] Historical Society collection.)

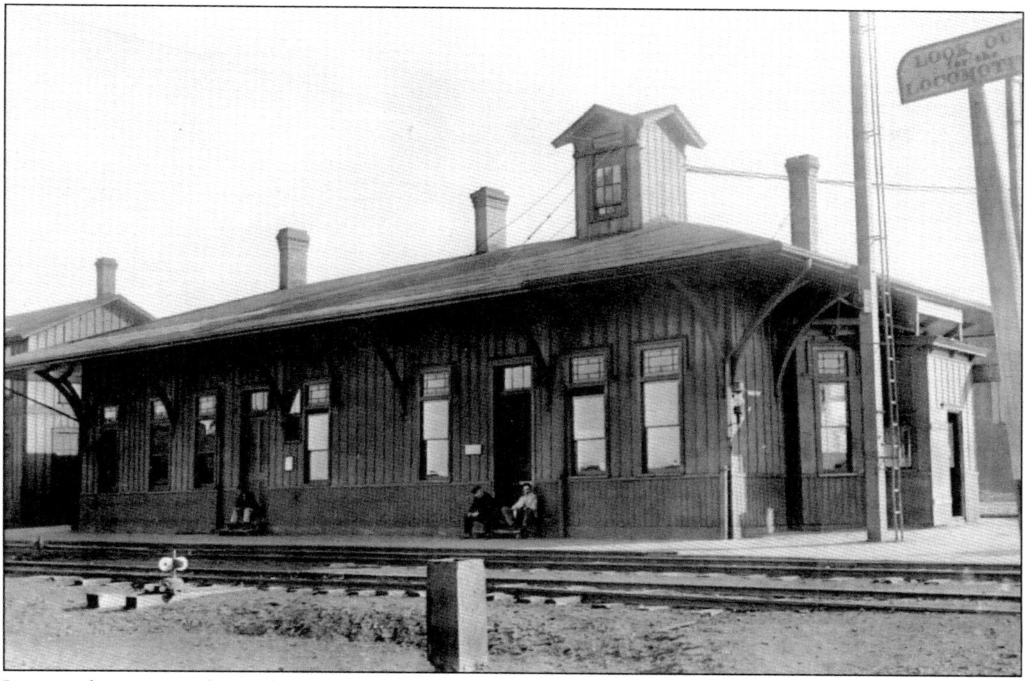

Leavittsburg was where the C&MV line left the main line of the A&GW. This frame junction depot with leaded-glass upper windows was a busy transfer point. The photographer has captured the depot at one of its quieter moments in 1910. By the early 1970s, only an atypical concrete interlocking tower, seen below around 1967, remained. (Above, Erie Railroad photograph, Mark J. Camp collection.)

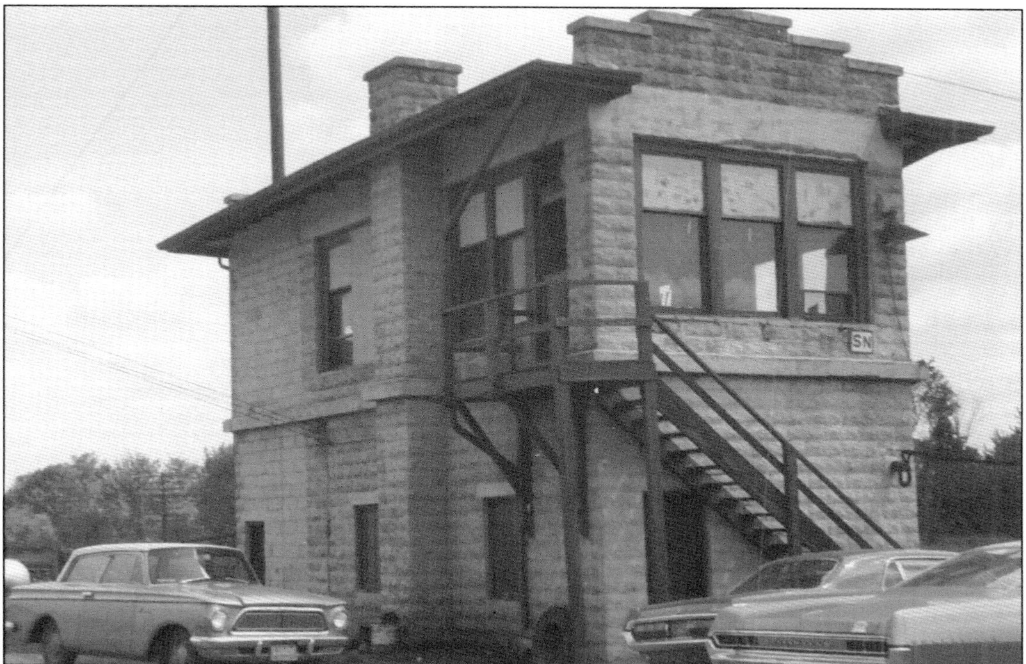

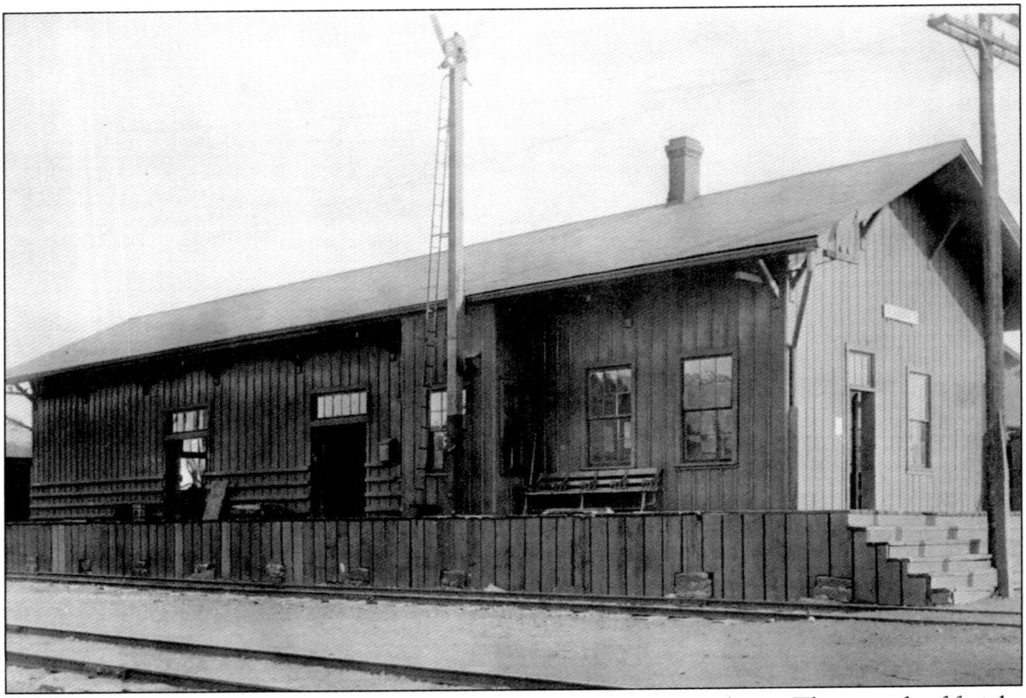

The A&GW or its successor, the NYP&O, built the above Warren depot. The growth of freight business in the Trumbull County seat necessitated the construction of the large brick freight house below in the early 1900s. By the 1960s, the passenger depot had been torn down and the head house of the freight house converted to passenger use. No significant Erie Railroad structures remain in Warren. (Above, Erie Railroad photograph, Mark J. Camp collection.)

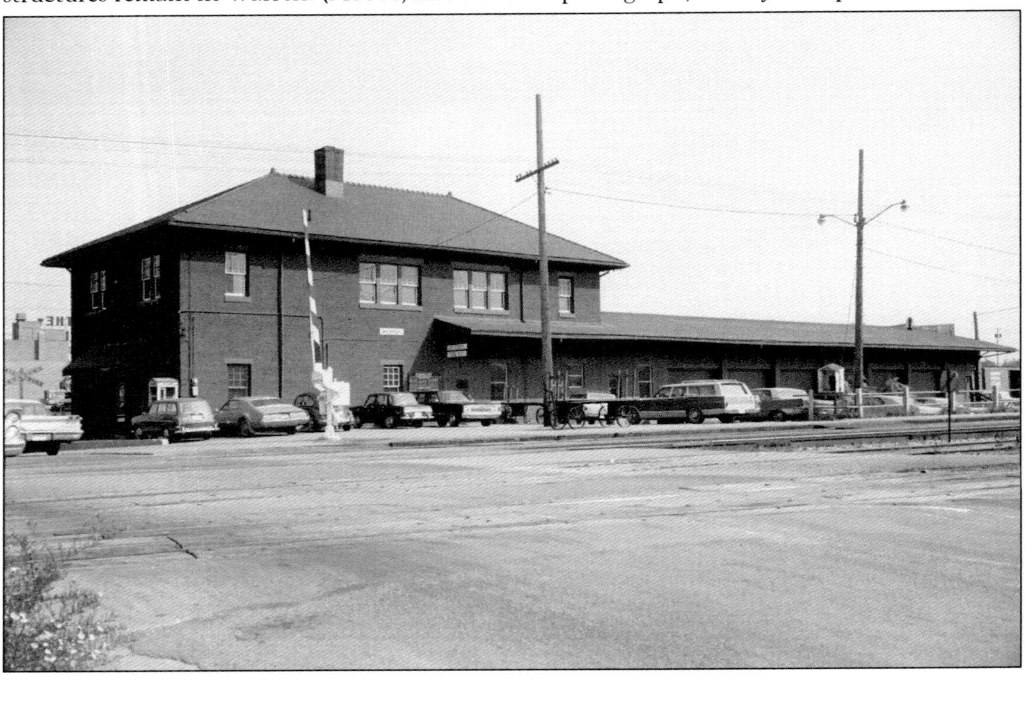

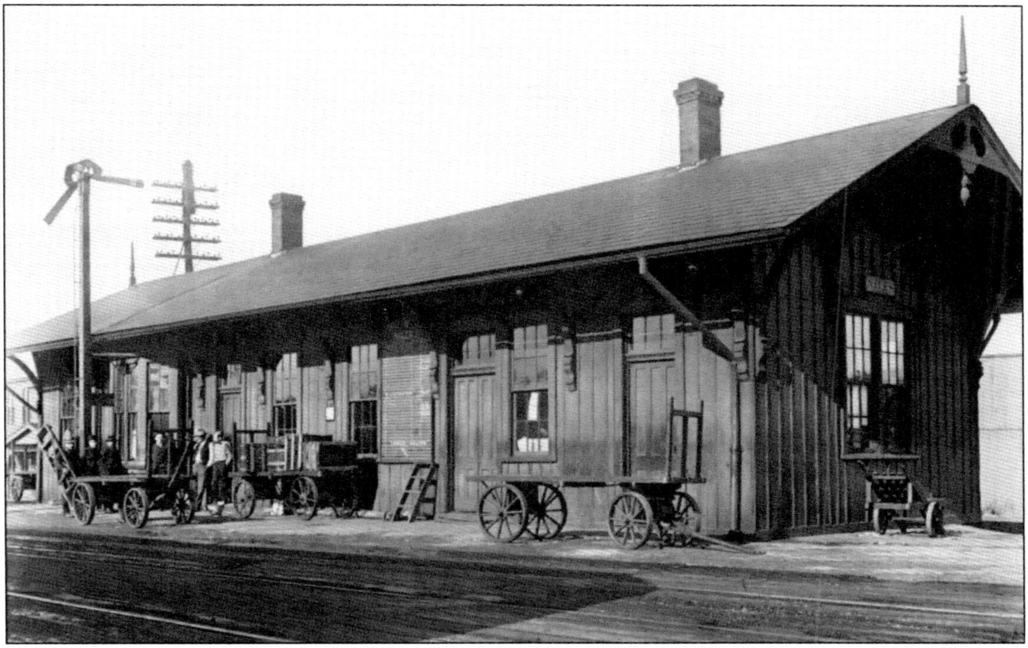

Old and new depots of the Erie Railroad at Niles were strikingly different. The train board mounted on the wall of the older depot lists not only main line trains but those on the Lisbon branch, which begins here. A nearly identical structure once served nearby Girard. The below depot was an architectural gem, and it is sad to say it no longer exists. (Above, Erie Railroad photograph, Mark J. Camp collection.)

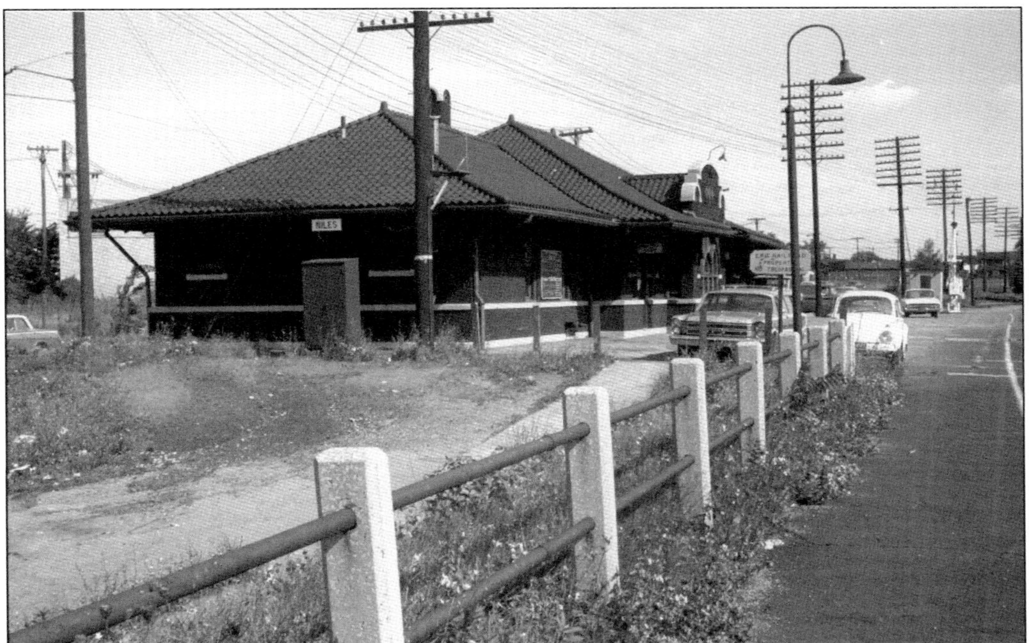

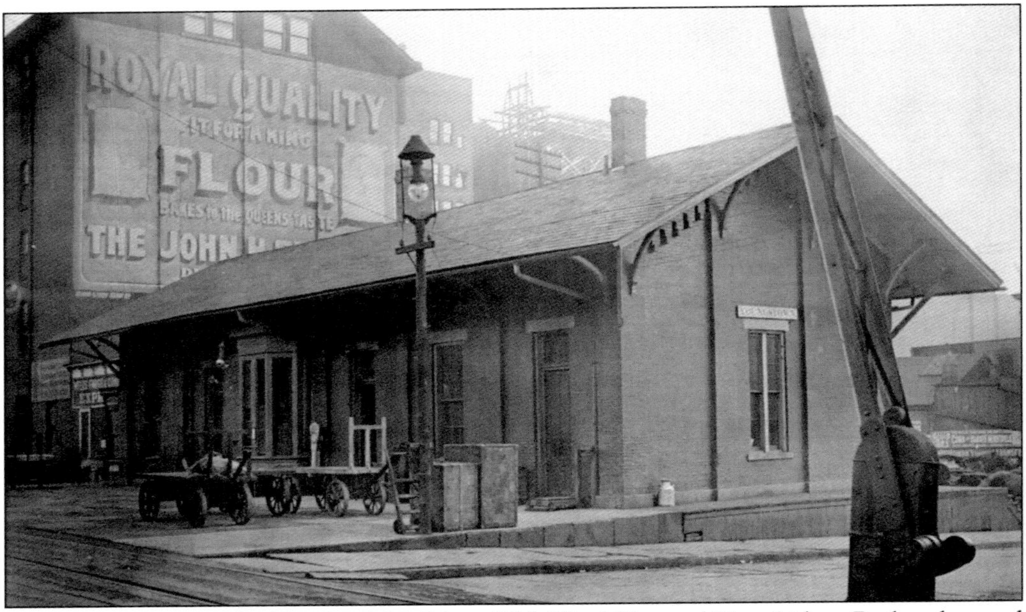

Youngstown was reached by the C&MV in 1856. The Niles and New Lisbon Railroad passed through in 1869. The above photograph shows the 1875 NYP&O depot at Youngstown around 1910. A large freight house was nearby. This building was plagued by four fires but survived until being demolished in 1926. June 1922 marked the opening of a six-story depot-office building near the intersection of Phelps and West Commerce Streets. This was one Ohio depot that just did not look like a depot. The site of the old depot became a parking structure. (Above, Erie Railroad photograph, Mark J. Camp collection.)

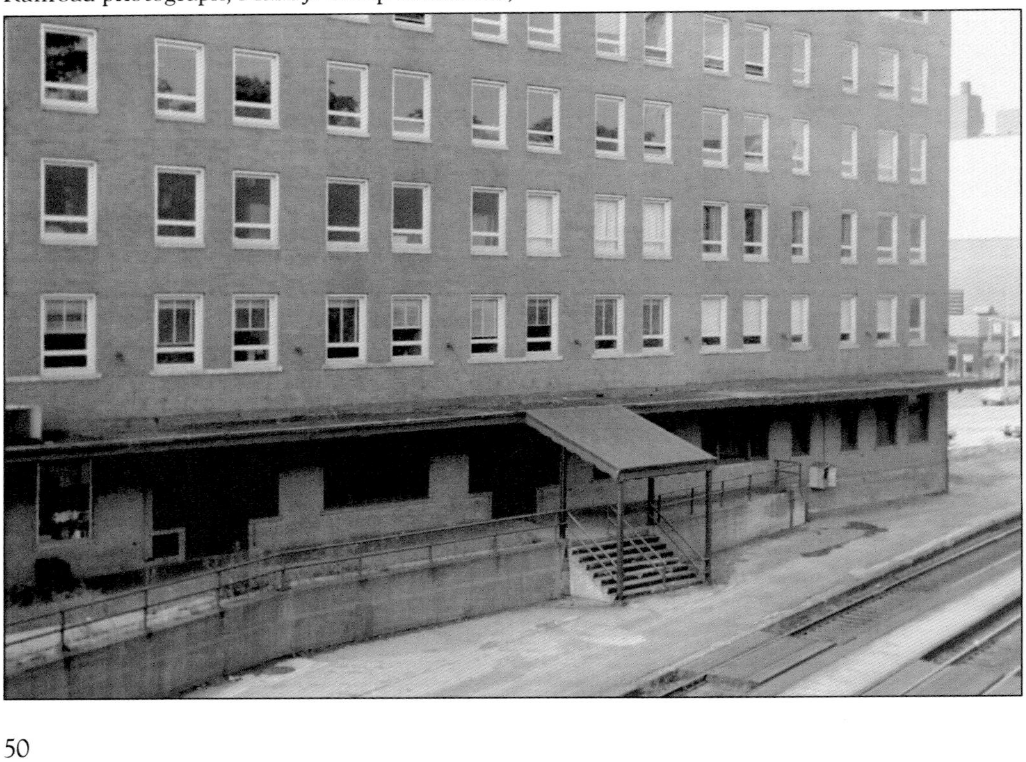

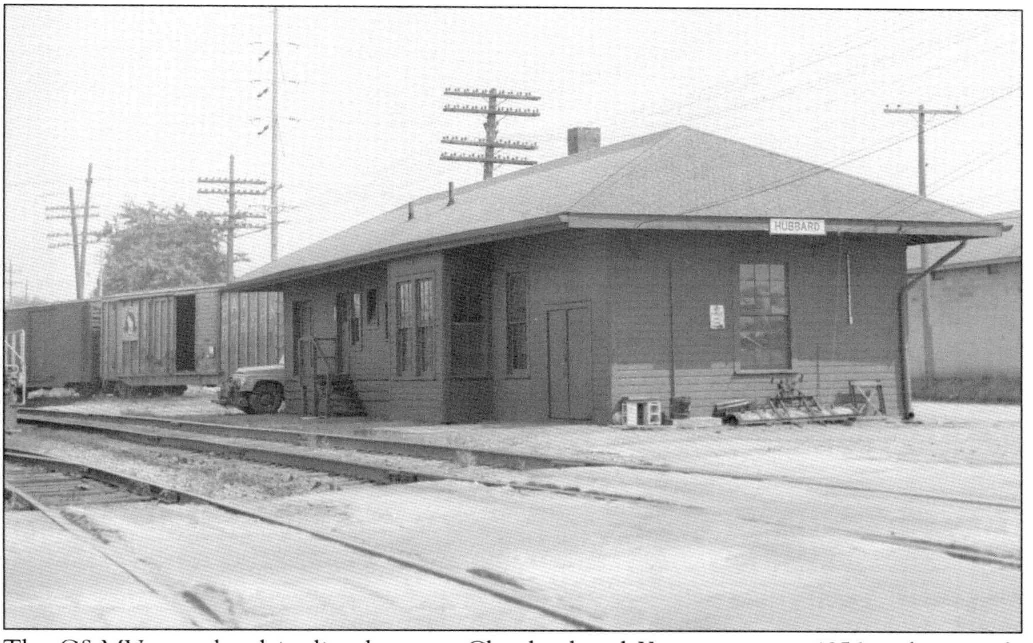

The C&MV completed its line between Cleveland and Youngstown in 1856 and promptly built a branch through Hubbard. The Erie Railroad built this combination depot at Hubbard to the same plans as Freedom, just varying the position of the vestibule and door and window placement. The above 1972 view shows it in the maroon paint scheme of the EL.

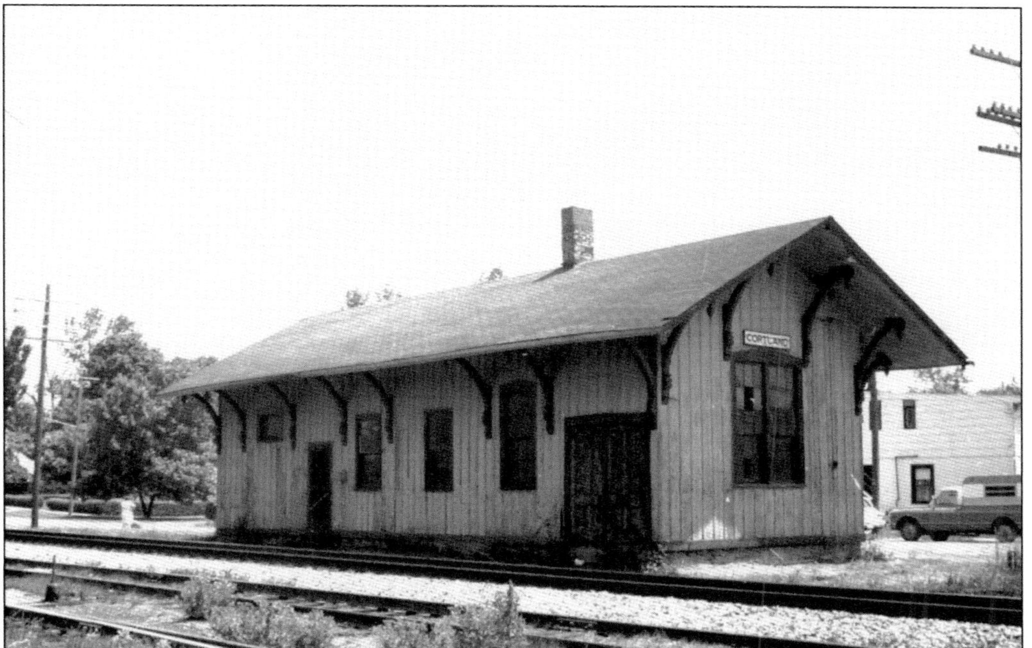

Cortland was incorporated in 1874. Cortland's Erie depot was about twice as long when originally built. Being on the bypass around Youngstown, the depot mainly handled freight. It was removed after the 1960s.

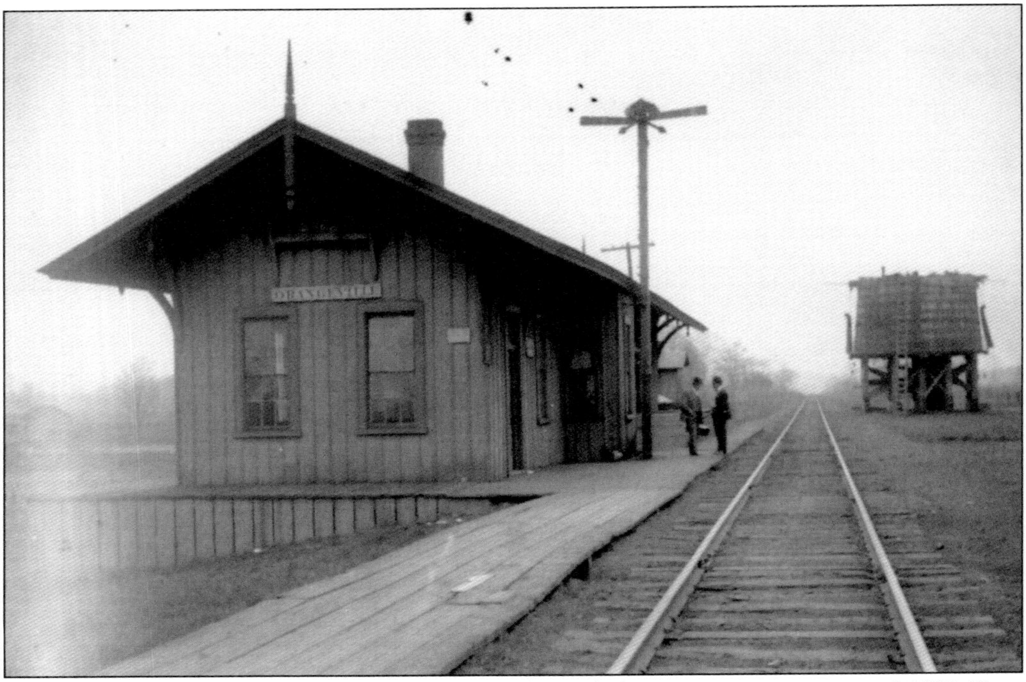

Orangeville, also on the Youngstown bypass, had two daily passenger trains around 1910. Note the double-spouted water tank and the plank platform. By the 1960s, the above depot was long gone and the town board had been hung on a section car building. (Above, Erie Railroad photograph, Mark J. Camp collection.)

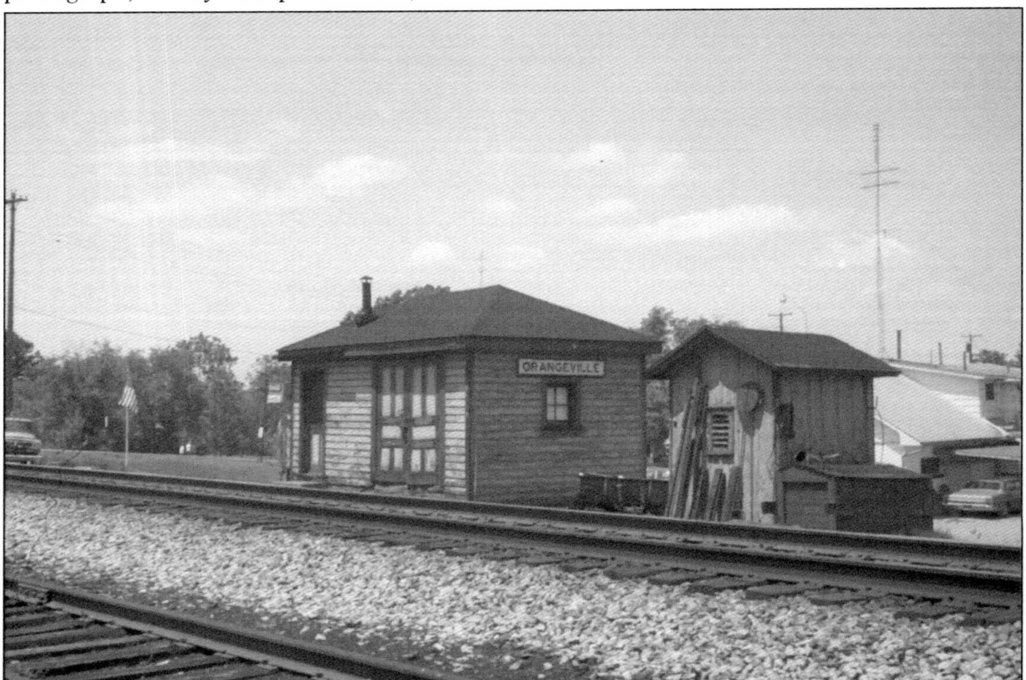

Three

New York Central Lines

Northeast Ohio's first railroad was the Cleveland, Columbus and Cincinnati Railroad. The line opened between Cleveland and Columbus in February 1851. After a series of purchases of other lines and corporate name changes during the 1860s–1880s, the line by 1889 evolved into the Cleveland, Cincinnati, Chicago and St. Louis Railroad, popularly known as the Big Four. The Big Four slowly fell under NYC control and was leased in 1929.

The Junction Railroad was chartered in 1846 to connect Cleveland and other lakeshore communities with Toledo. A competitor, the Toledo, Norwalk and Cleveland (TN&C) was chartered in 1850 to connect Cleveland and Toledo by passing through the more inland towns of Wellington, Norwalk, and Fremont. Both entered Cleveland over the Cleveland, Columbus and Cincinnati; the Junction Railroad connecting at Berea and the TN&C joining at Grafton. After mergers and name changes the lines became part of the Lake Shore and Michigan Southern Railroad (LS&MS) in 1869.

East of Cleveland, the Cleveland, Painesville and Ashtabula Railroad (CP&A) was completed between Cleveland and Painesville in 1851, and it opened to Erie, Pennsylvania, in November 1852. In 1863, the CP&A began construction of a branch from Ashtabula to Jefferson. The lines became known as the Lake Shore Railway in 1868. In 1869, the line became part of the LS&MS. The LS&MS completed a branch leaving the main line at Ashtabula and heading southeast to Jamestown, Pennsylvania, in 1872. The Mahoning Coal Railroad was leased to the LS&MS and opened a line from Andover to Youngstown to tap the rich coal fields in 1873. The LS&MS opened a short branch from Ashtabula to Ashtabula Harbor in 1873. In 1903, the LS&MS built a line with lower grades from Carson on the Jamestown branch to Brookfield, essentially parallel to the Mahoning Coal line.

Another eventual part of the LS&MS was the narrow-gauge Alliance and Northern Railroad completed between Alliance and Phalanx in 1877. After reorganization the line was extended to Mount Union as the Alliance and Lake Erie Railroad in 1878. After more financial problems, consolidations, and a conversion to standard gauge in 1880, what was by then known as the Lake Erie Alliance and Wheeling Railroad reached its southern terminal at Dillonvale in 1902. The LS&MS acquired the line in 1903.

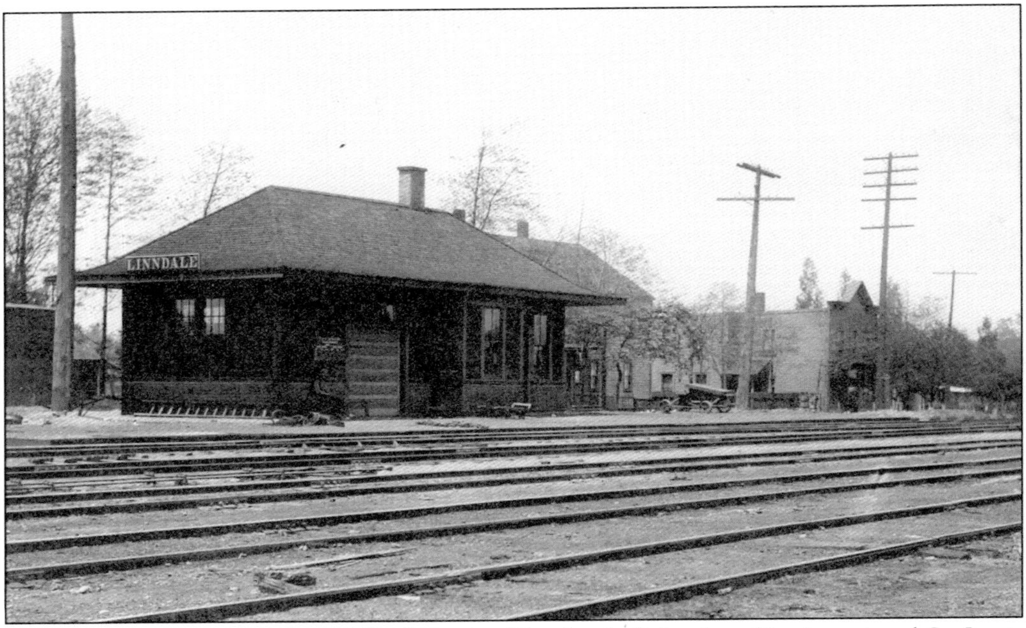

Linndale was incorporated in 1902 along the Cleveland, Columbus, Cincinnati and St. Louis Railroad (CCC&StL). This combination depot served until about 1930. Linndale was rewarded with a new larger passenger facility (below) upon the opening of Cleveland Union Terminal in 1930. It was the western station of the complex where Cleveland Terminal electric locomotives coupled to passenger trains for their trip to the terminal. A large yard and roundhouse complex was across the tracks from the depot. Electrified trackage was adjacent to the depot. The closing of Union Terminal brought an end to this once-busy transfer station. (Above, Mark J. Camp collection; below, 1949 Robert Runyan photograph, Bruce Young collection.)

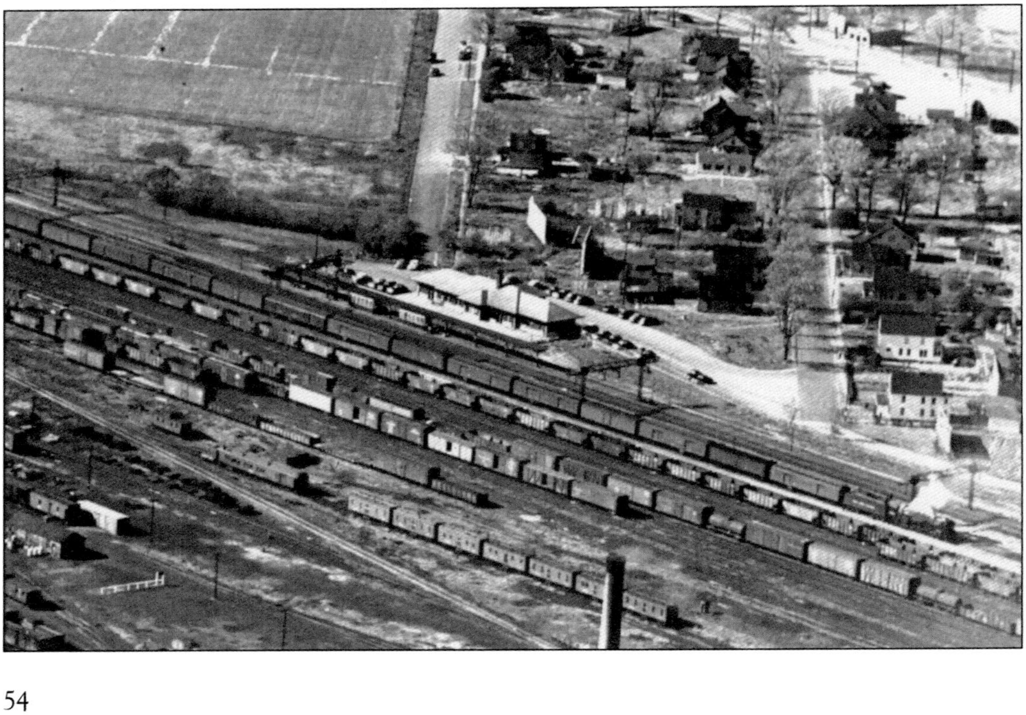

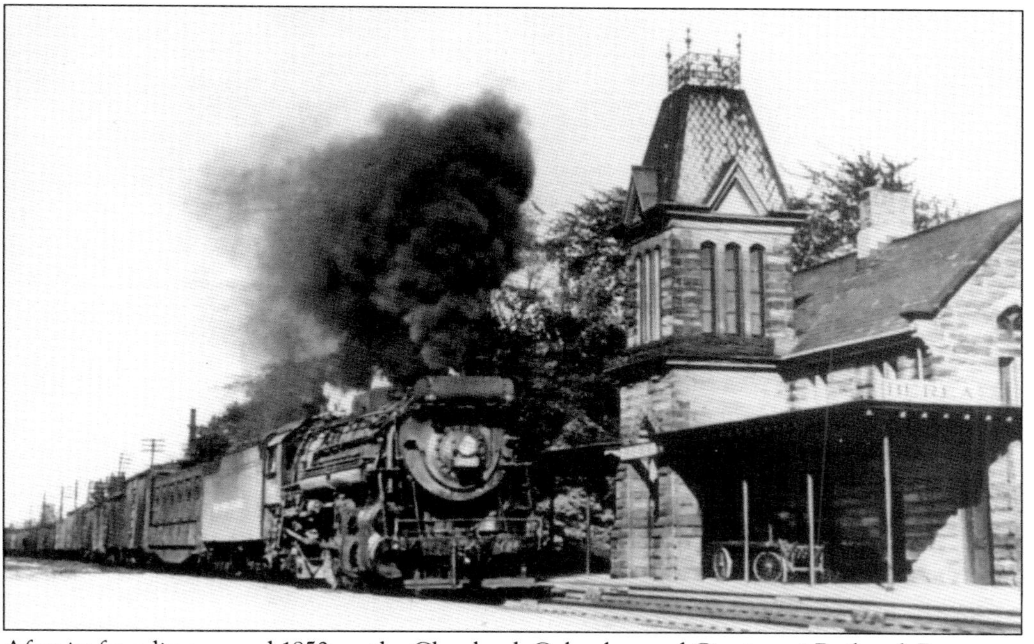

After its founding around 1850 on the Cleveland, Columbus and Cincinnati Railroad, Berea was served by a small frame depot; adequate in the early years but soon overtaxed. Sandstone shipments from local quarries led to the rapid growth of the community, and the railroad completed this impressive union passenger depot composed of Berea sandstone in May 1876. The former depot was relocated between the Big Four and LS&MS tracks and made into a freight house. After the opening, a horse-drawn trolley line connected the depot to downtown Berea. The mansard roof of the tower was removed sometime in the 1950s. By the mid-1960s, Railway Express used the depot. It then sat vacant for a few years until being opened as a restaurant in 1980. The tower was rebuilt as part of a later remodeling of the restaurant. Down the tracks is BE tower, built in 1929 by the NYC to replace an earlier frame CCC&StL tower. (Mark J. Camp collection.)

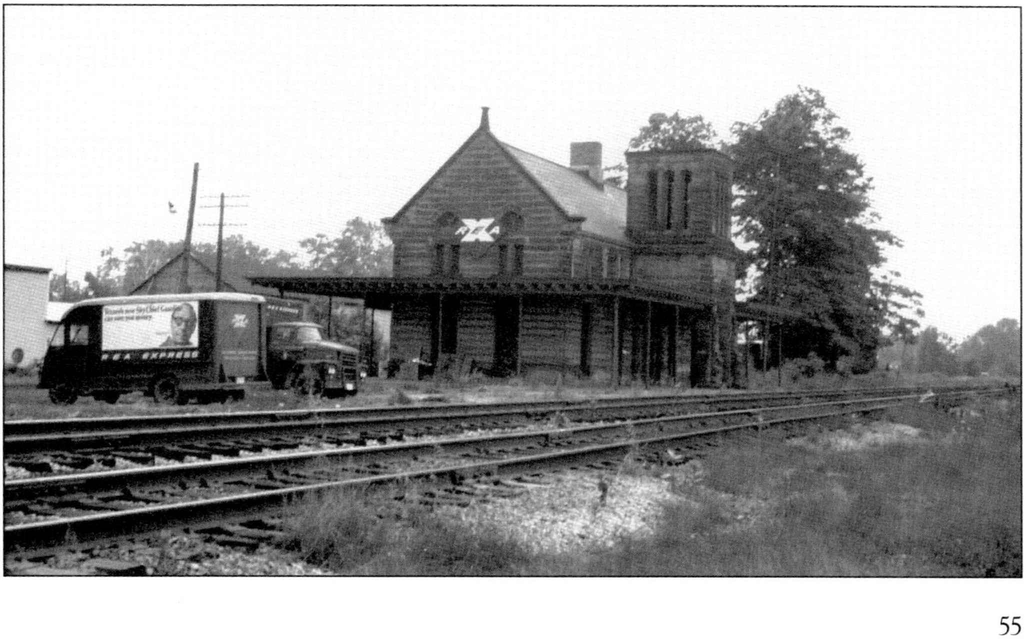

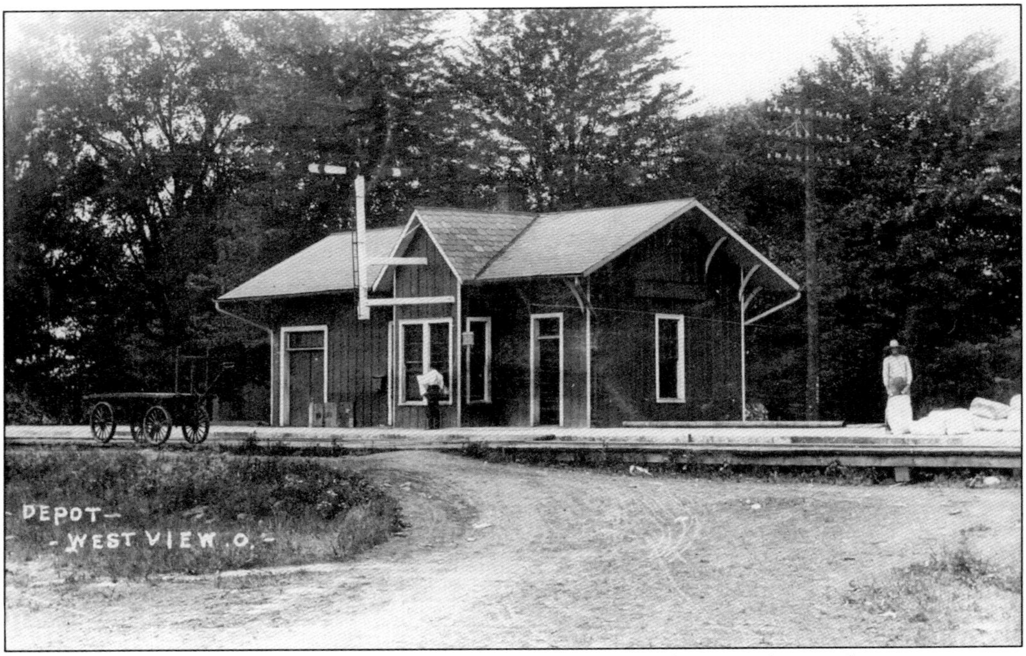

The Big Four depot at West View is of early design. This was also a sandstone shipping point in the late 1800s. Note the older style of order board projected from the vestibule. This depot was gone by the 1960s. (Mark J. Camp collection.)

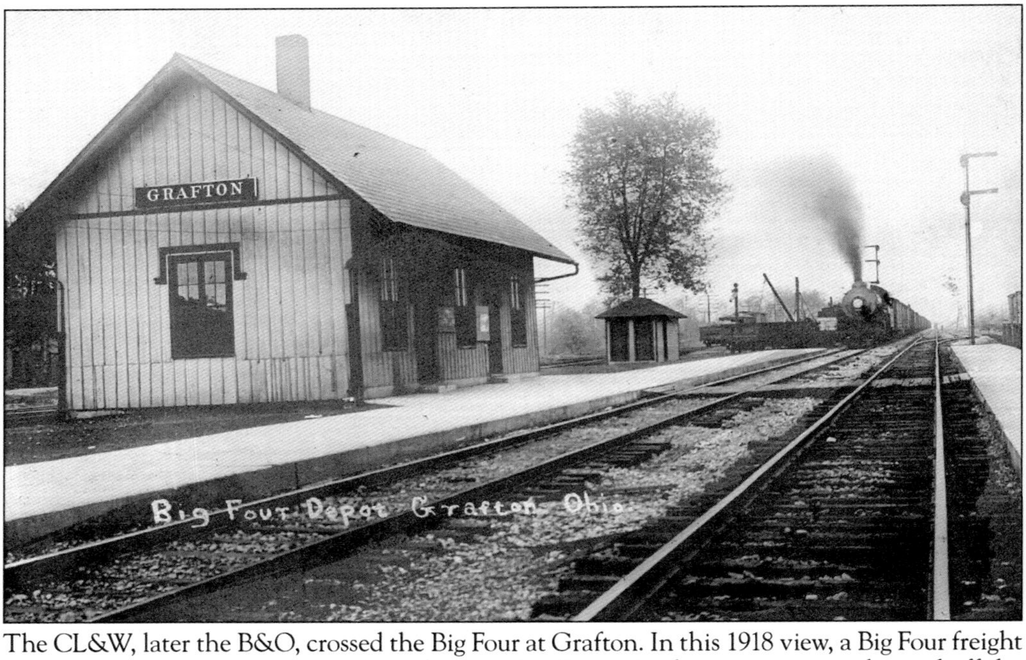

The CL&W, later the B&O, crossed the Big Four at Grafton. In this 1918 view, a Big Four freight approaches the passenger depot. Out of view is Big Four's Grafton tower, now relocated off the diamond and restored. (Mark J. Camp collection.)

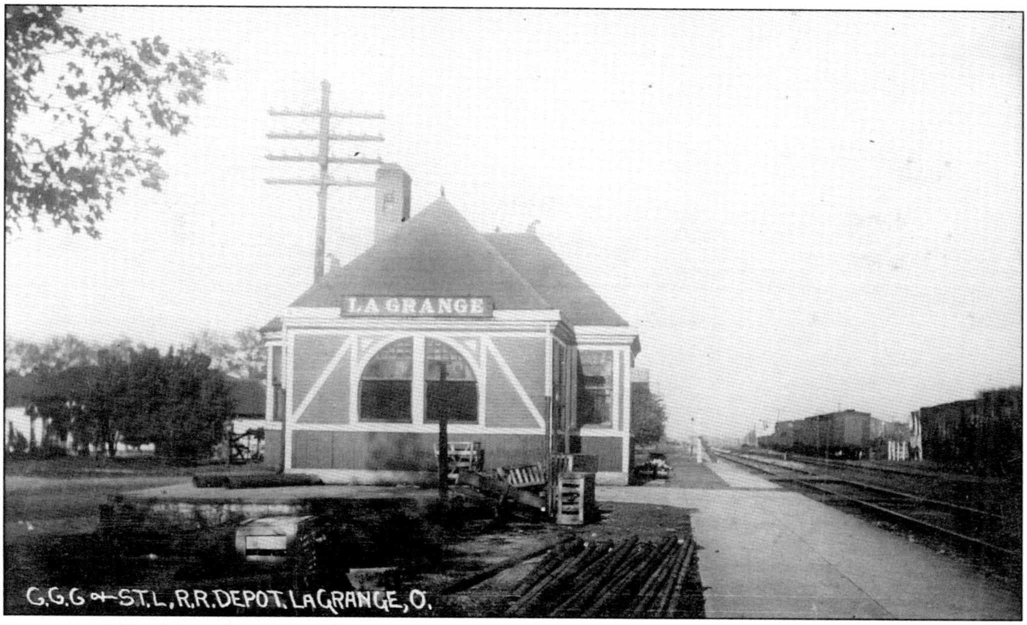

Lagrange's Big Four depot was distinguished by its semirounded double window on the passenger end, shortened eaves, and vestibules on both the trackside and street side of the structure. It was the third and final depot in Lagrange, built around 1898 after a town fire destroyed the previous depot. It closed in the late 1950s when passenger service to the community ended and disappeared by the late 1960s. (Mark J. Camp collection.)

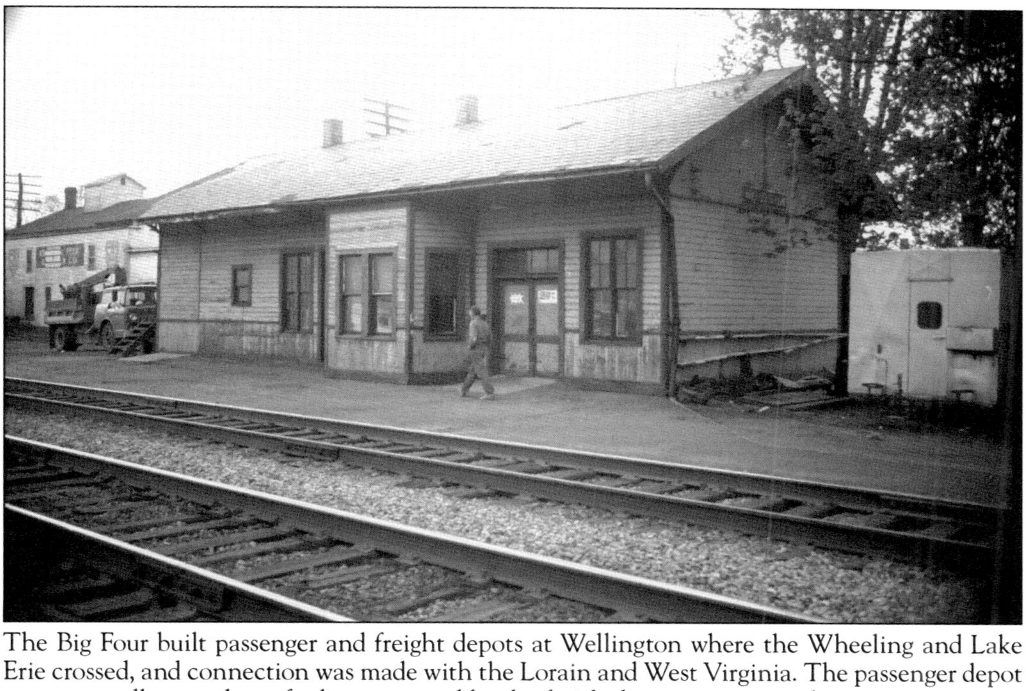
The Big Four built passenger and freight depots at Wellington where the Wheeling and Lake Erie crossed, and connection was made with the Lorain and West Virginia. The passenger depot was reportedly torn down for later reassembly; the freight house remains in business use.

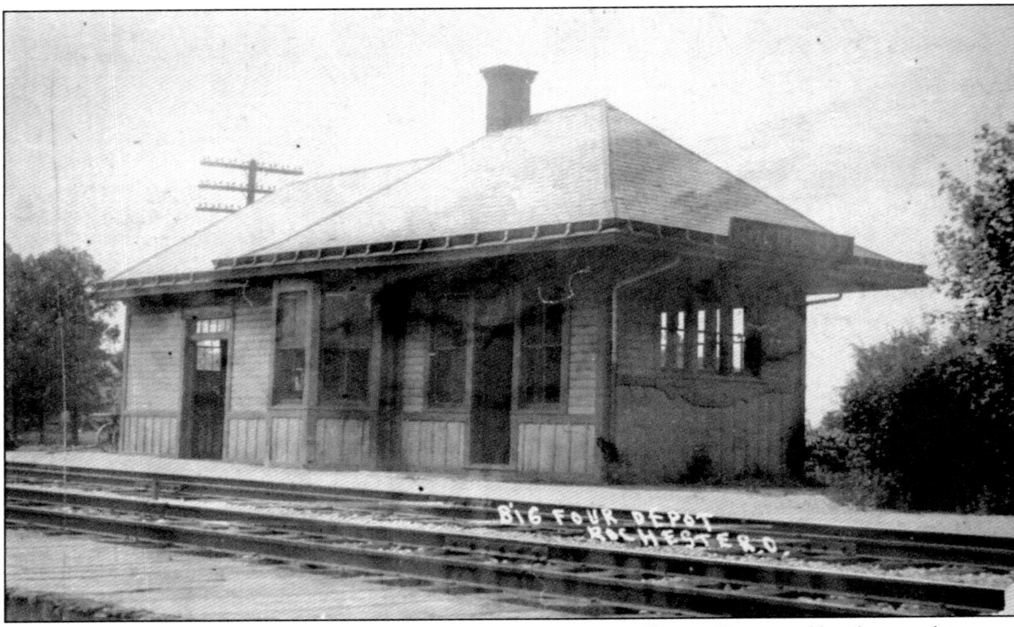

Another pleasing design issued by the Big Four engineering office is illustrated by the combination depot at Rochester. The depot was saved after its closing and relocated to become a historical museum. (Mark J. Camp collection.)

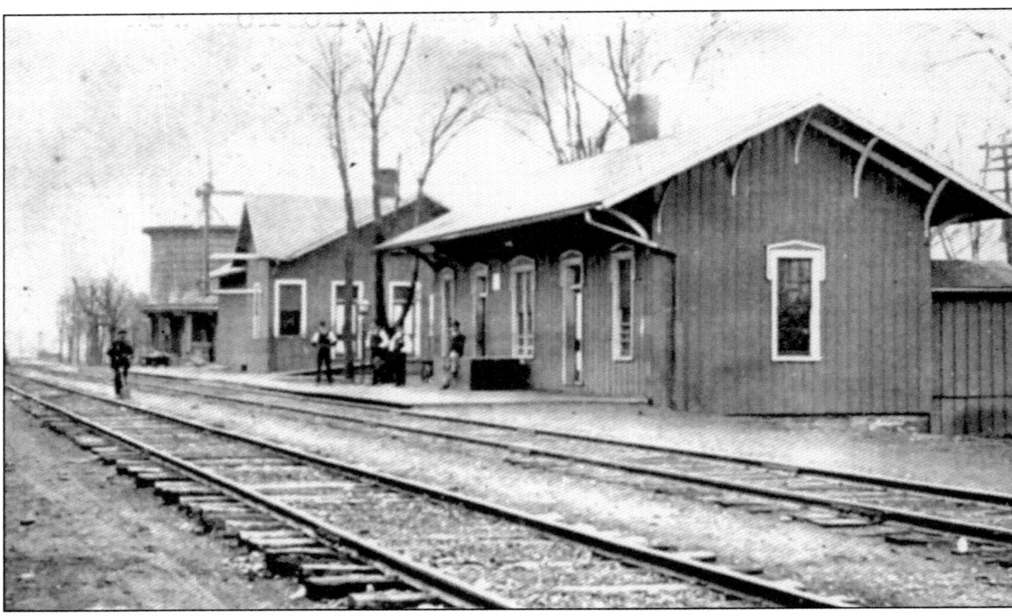

The Big Four had several structures at its station in New London in 1896. The passenger depot is in the foreground, with the waiting room for men separated from the waiting room for women and children by a ticket office. Adjacent was the telegrapher's office and freight house. By the 1960s, only a modified version of the passenger depot remained. (*Pictorial Atlas of Huron County, Ohio*, Charles Garvin collection.)

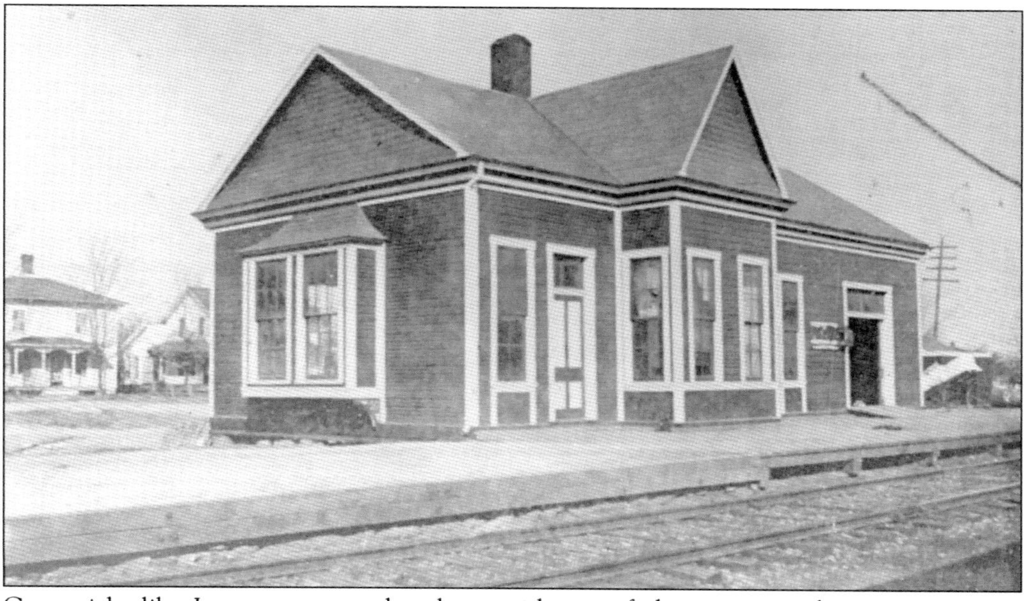

Greenwich, like Lagrange, sported a depot with a roof that terminated in gutters rather than overhanging eaves. A unique feature was the bay window on the passenger end of the building. This building was demolished around 1962. (*Pictorial Atlas of Huron County, Ohio*, Charles Garvin collection.)

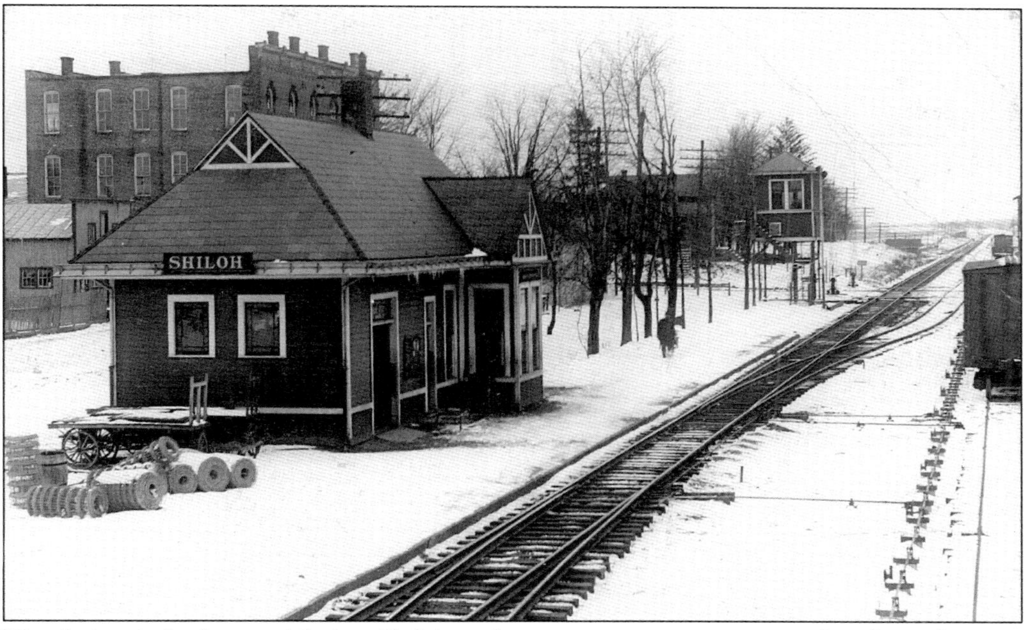

The design is further modified at Shiloh with narrow eaves, a steeper roof pitch, and ornate gutters and eaves. Down the track is a small standard-design Big Four interlocking tower. The tower man also controlled the crossing gates. No railroad structures remain at Shiloh. (Mark J. Camp collection.)

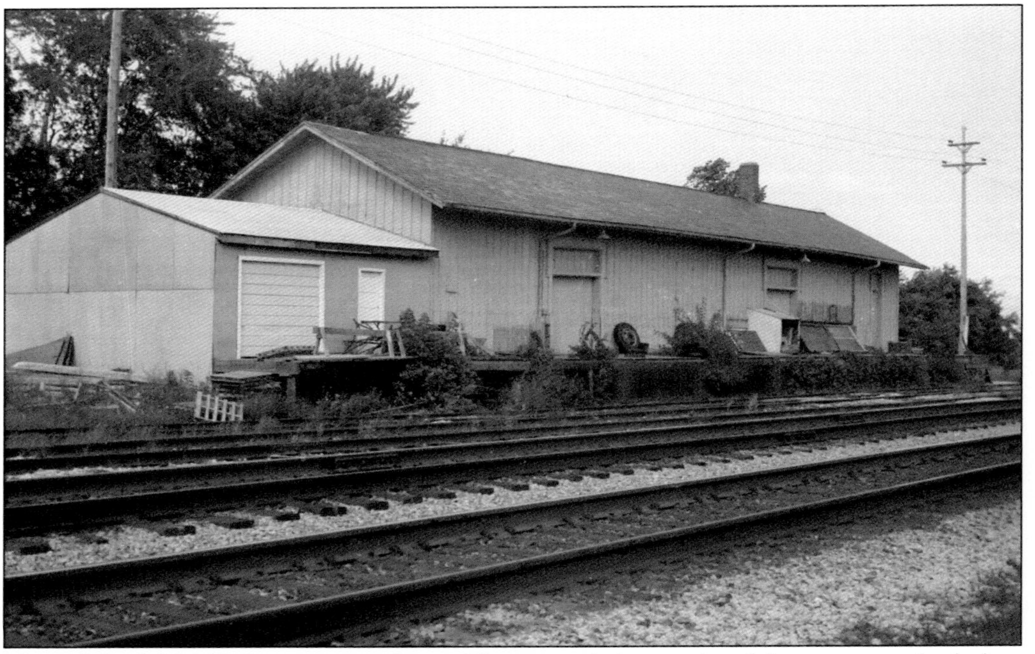

Most of the LS&MS depots in northeast Ohio were slight tweaks of the same standard plan. This building at Huron served as a freight depot until its closing. It remains in business use. (Charles Garvin photograph, 1966.)

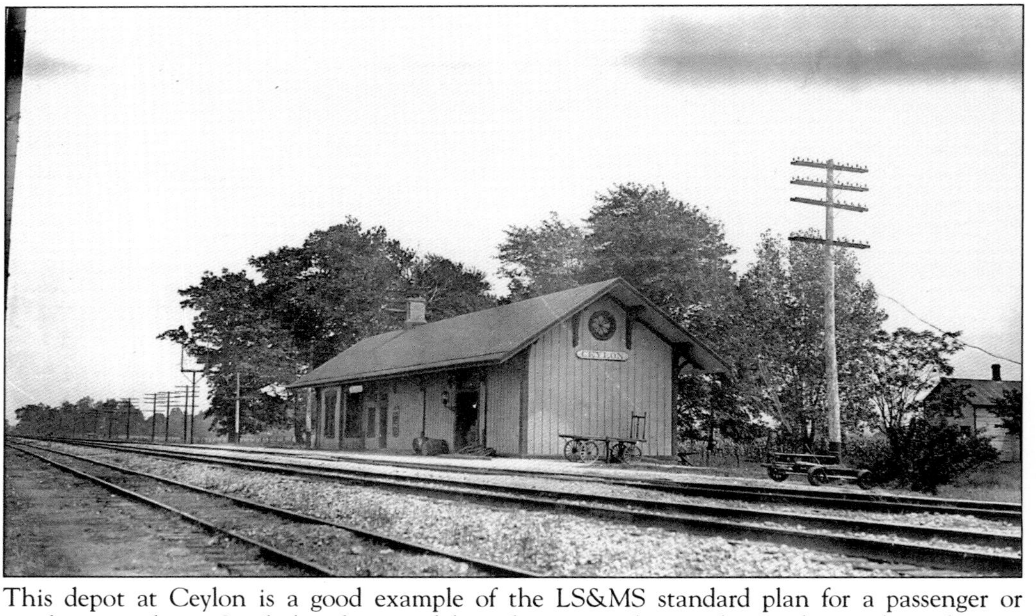

This depot at Ceylon is a good example of the LS&MS standard plan for a passenger or combination depot. Symbolic of many of these depots was the circular window in the end eaves, ornate lintels, and rectangular bay windows. This *c.* 1872 depot was gone by the late 1960s. (NYC Railroad photograph, Allen County [Ohio] Historical Society collection.)

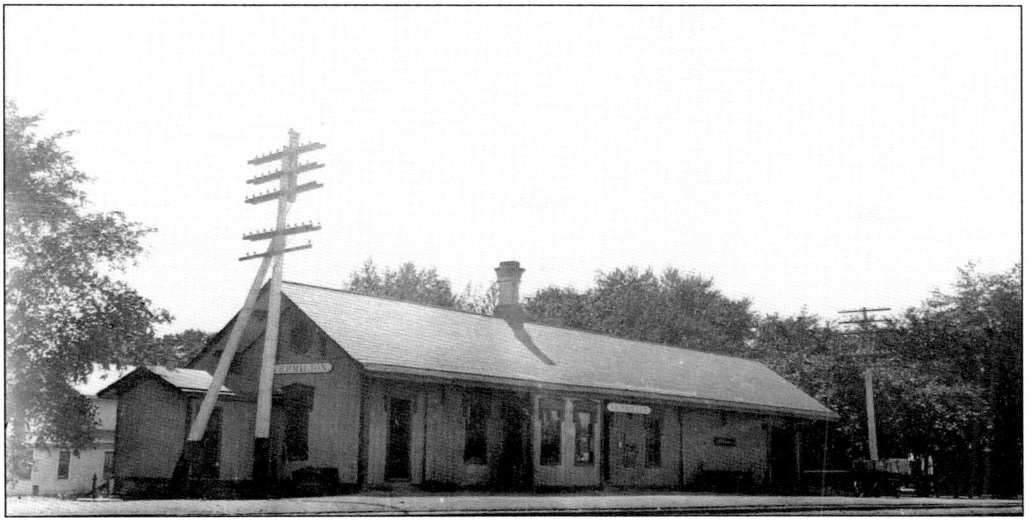

Vermilion's 1872 LS&MS depot differs little from Ceylon but does have a larger office area marked by the four windows in the vestibule. The small addition on the passenger end contains the washrooms. Out of view down and across the tracks is a freight house. Both depots remain today, the passenger depot used by a church and the freight house thoroughly disguised as a place of business. (NYC Railroad photograph, Allen County [Ohio] Historical Society collection.)

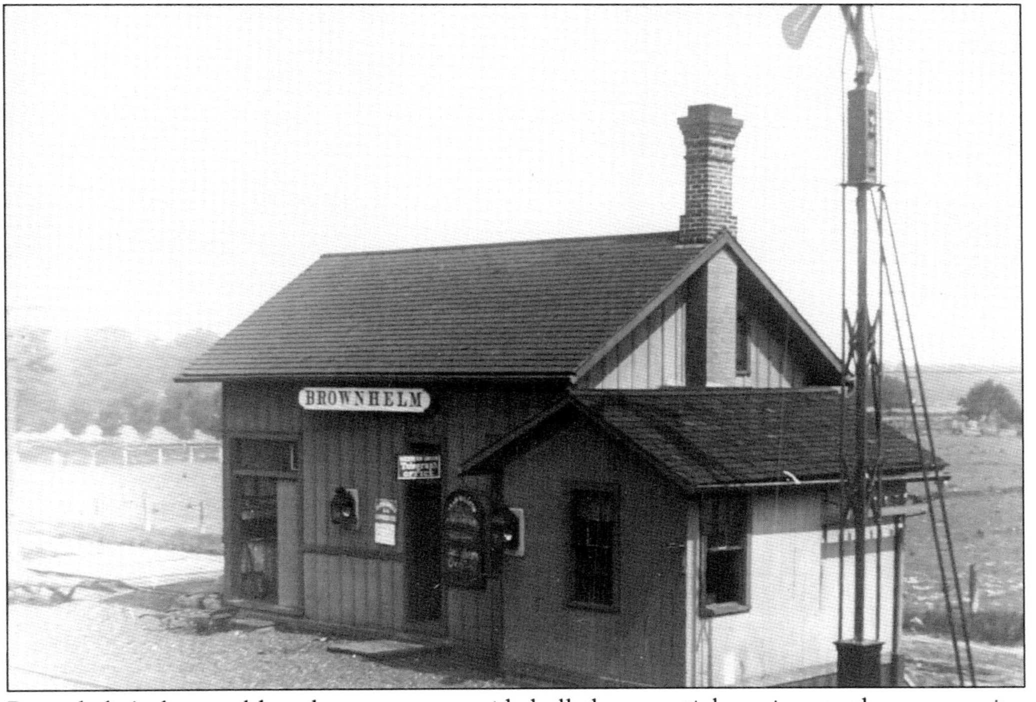

Brownhelm's depot, although compact, provided all the essential services to the community. Structures of this size were sometimes relocated to other stations after the closing of the agency, to be used as yard offices and storage buildings. They could be easily transported on a flat car. This depot was once an important sandstone shipping point but has been gone since at least the mid-1900s. (Bob Lorenz collection.)

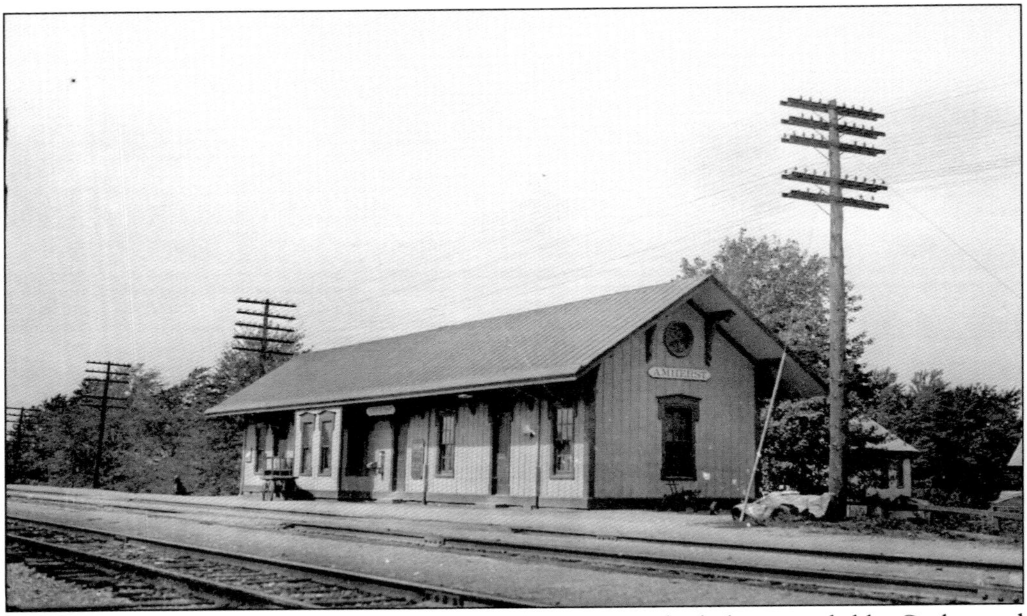

In 1872, the LS&MS built the above Amherst depot to standard plans, much like Ceylon and Vermilion. Note that the depot has separate waiting rooms and no facilities for freight handling. A standard plan freight house was also erected. The tracks through Amherst were elevated in the 1890s. Around 1902, a brick freight house was built on Franklin Street, replacing the earlier one. The local sandstone quarries kept the passenger and freight depots very busy in the early 1900s, but with declining local stops of NYC passenger trains in the late 1940s, business declined. The passenger depot was reportedly torn down for its lumber in 1946. By 1979, the freight house had been renovated and continues to serve as a meeting room. (Above, NYC Railroad photograph, Allen County [Ohio] Historical Society collection.)

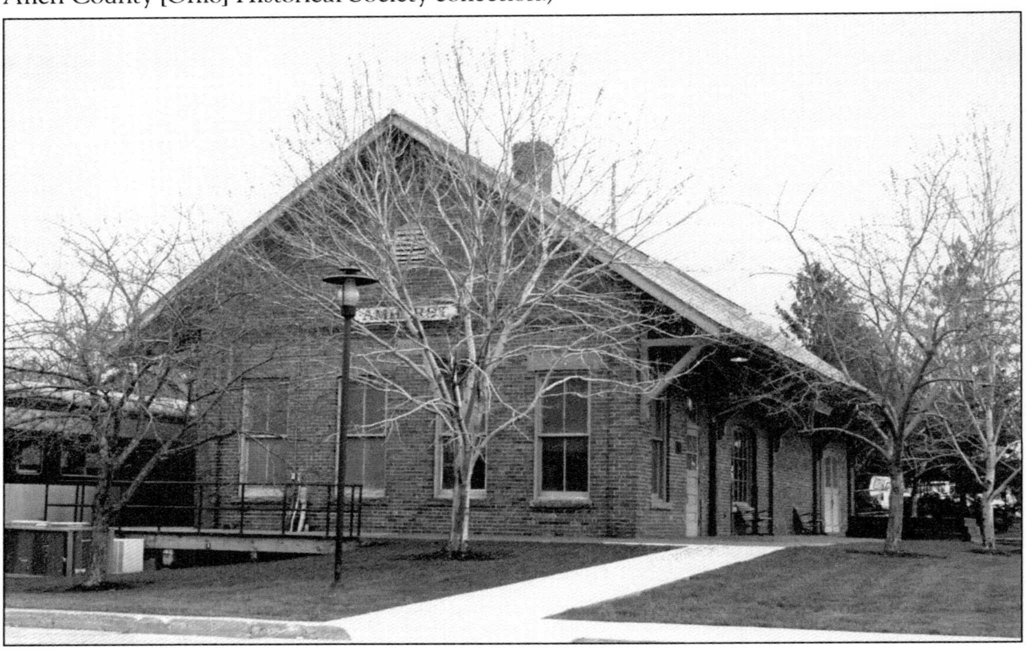

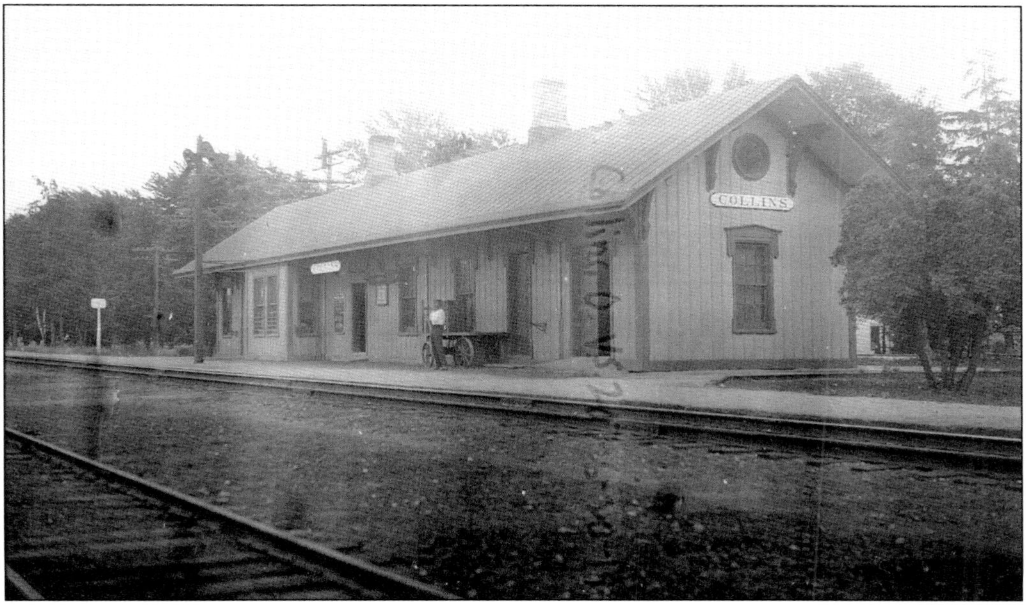

The more southerly route of the LS&MS followed the former TN&C joining the former Junction Railroad at Elyria. The passenger depots at Collins and Wakeman were both built in 1872 to similar standard plans. They differ in window and door arrangement. Collins has a bay window while Wakeman lacks one. Freight houses were nearby. Only the freight house remains at Wakeman as a storage building. The Collins passenger depot has been relocated in Collins and built into a feed and grain company; the freight house remains on site in use by the same company. For some years after being closed by the railroad, the Collins passenger depot was a rock shop. (Above, NYC Railroad photograph, Allen County [Ohio] Historical Society collection; below, 1947 Clyde Helms photograph.)

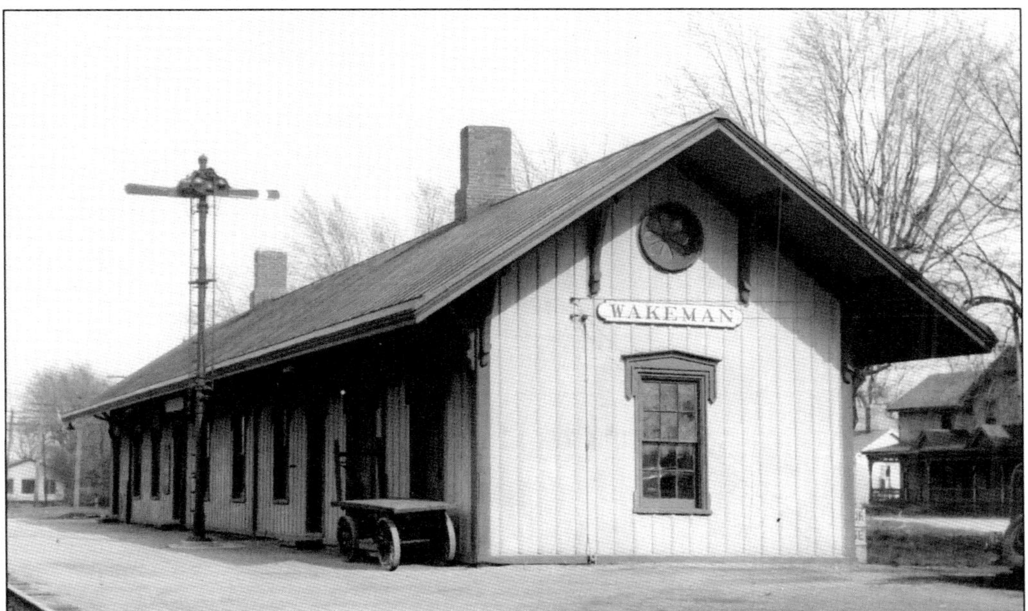

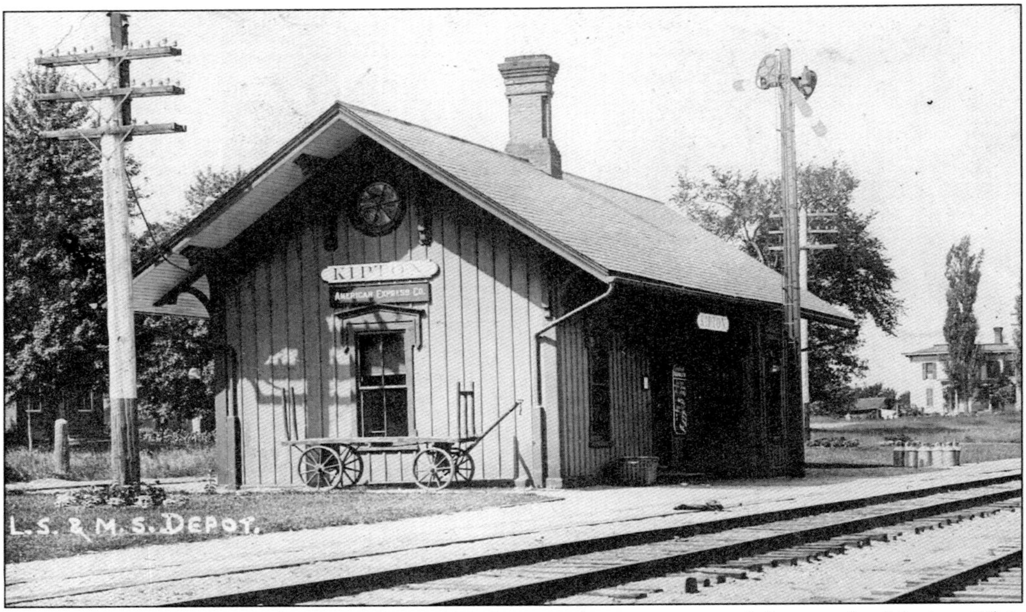

Kipton's passenger depot also dates from 1872. It was a shorter version of the standard design. This depot has been gone for decades, but the original TN&C depot, used after 1872 as a freight house, still stands along the abandoned roadbed. The college town of Oberlin has another version of the standard plan built in 1867. The building lacks the circular window below the end eaves and has rounded lentils, only three end roof supports, and a wider width. The freight house was the original TN&C combination depot built around 1852. Passenger service to Oberlin ended in 1949. The passenger depot continues to serve the community, but the freight house has been moved to Wellington. (Above, Mark J. Camp collection; below, 1947 Clyde Helms photograph.)

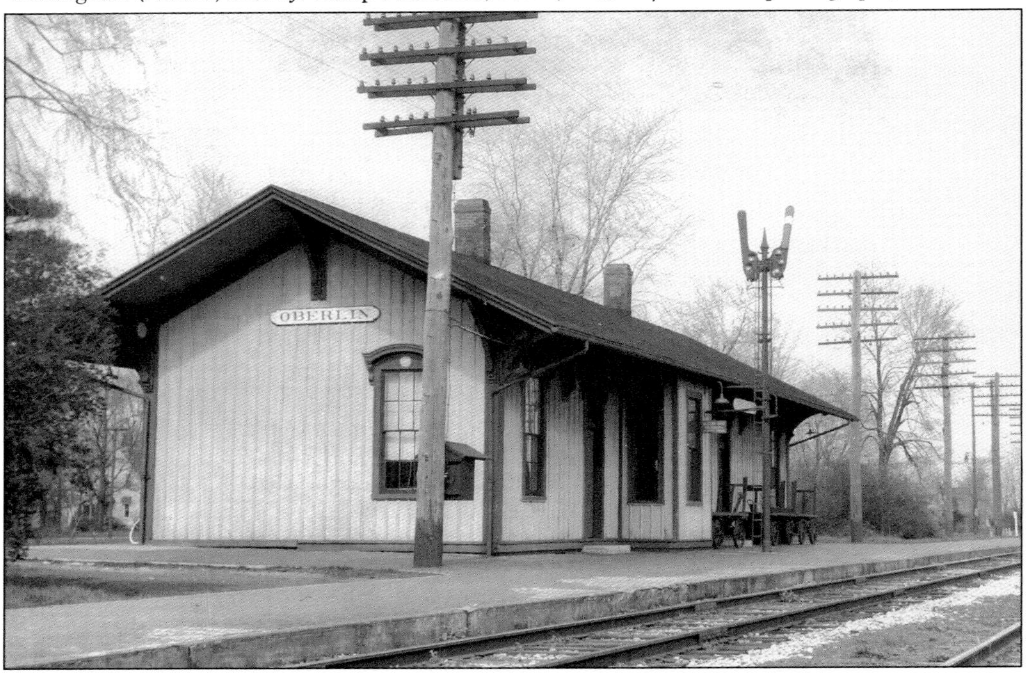

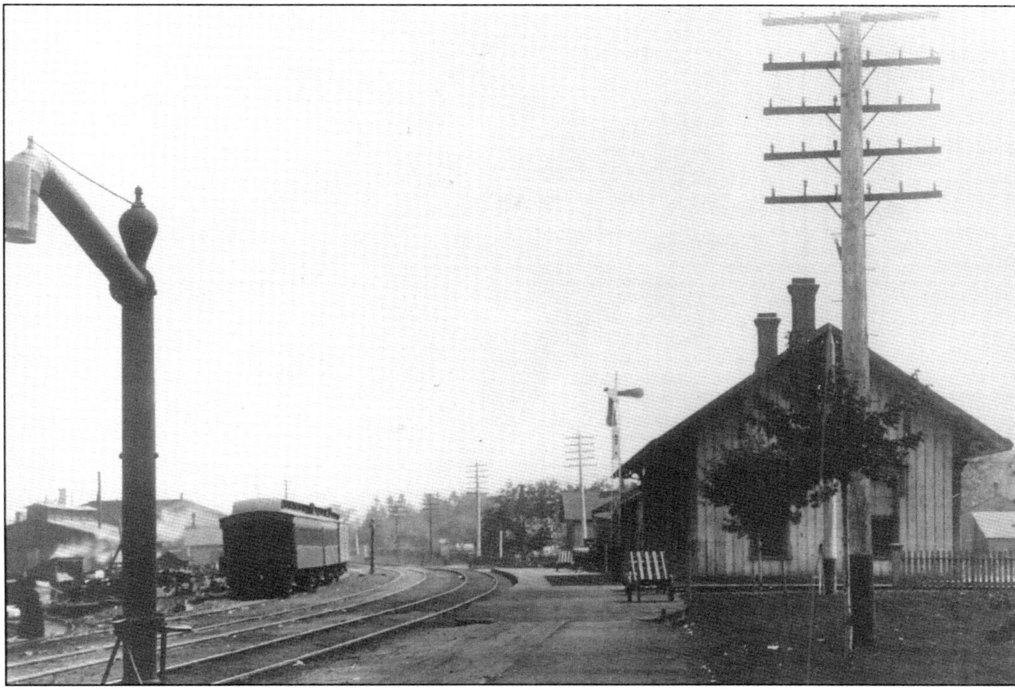

Elyria's LS&MS passenger depot, shown above, dates from the early 1870s. It is a slightly wider version of the standard plan with a lower pitch to the roof. In the early years the tracks ran through downtown Elyria at grade, causing increasing traffic problems. The elevation of the line through town solved these problems. In 1925, the NYC replaced the above depot with a new brick passenger depot of modern design. Although the depot has not been used by the railroad for sometime, it is currently under restoration. (Above, Bob Lorenz collection.)

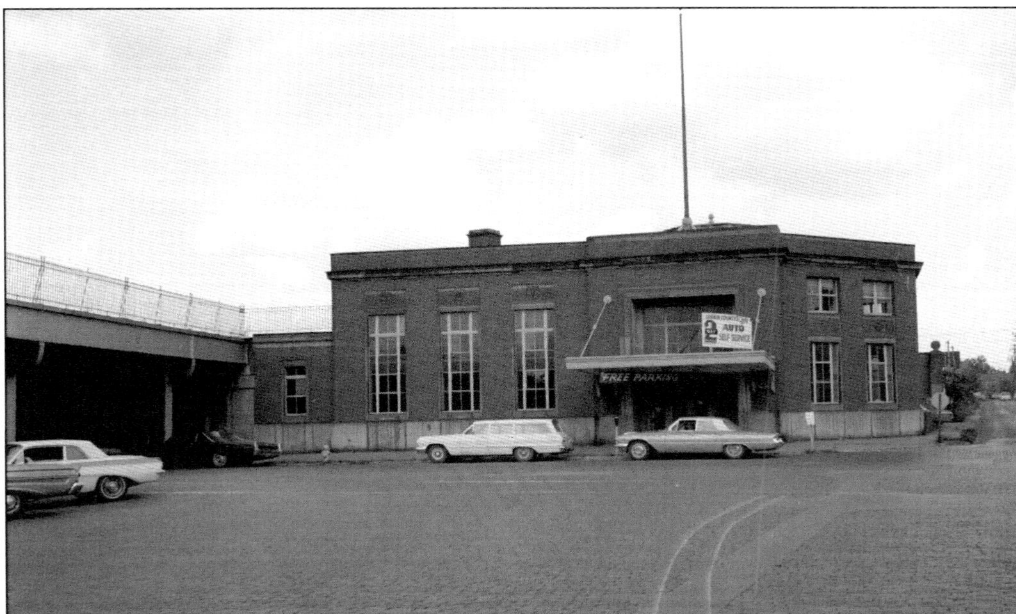

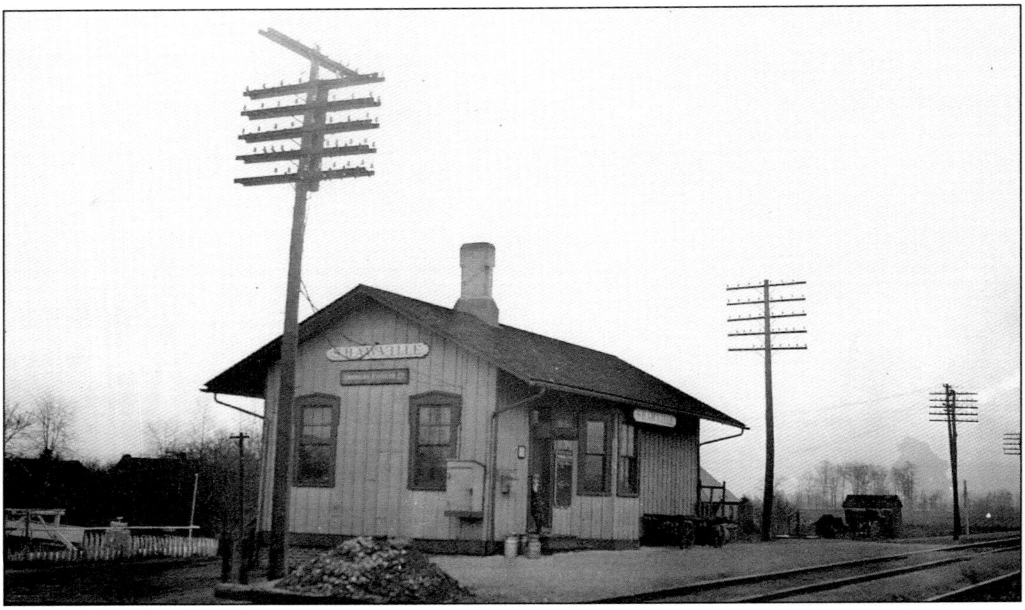

This November 1918 view shows the LS&MS depot at Shawville, now absorbed by Elyria. Soon will come the announcement that World War I is over. (NYC Railroad photograph, Allen County [Ohio] Historical Society collection.)

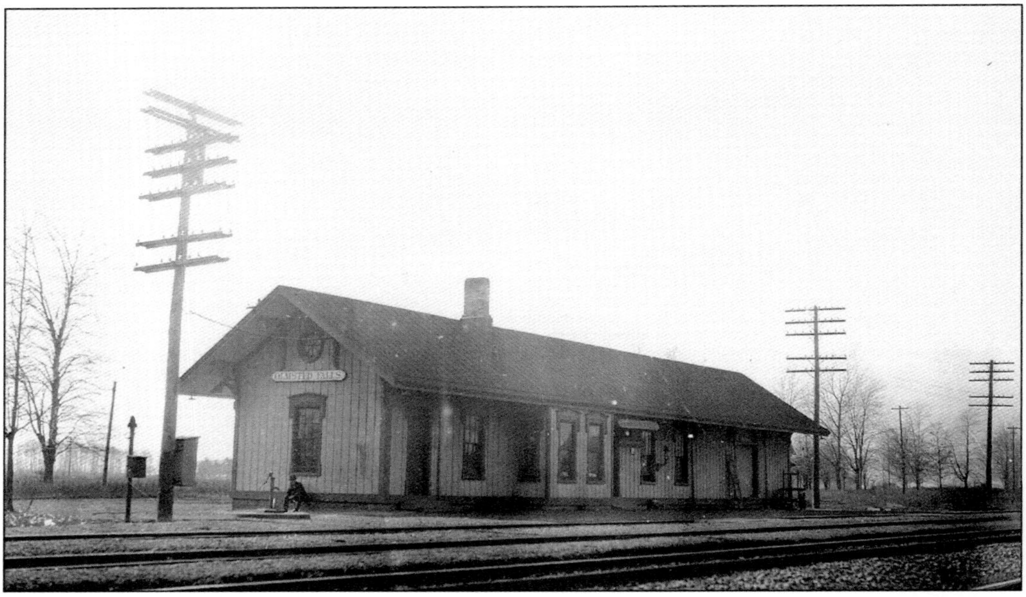

Olmsted Falls's LS&MS depot dates from 1877 and is similar to Ceylon and Vermilion. Although the open fields have been replaced with development the depot looks much the same today and serves as the headquarters of a local model railroad club. (NYC Railroad photograph, Allen County [Ohio] Historical Society collection.)

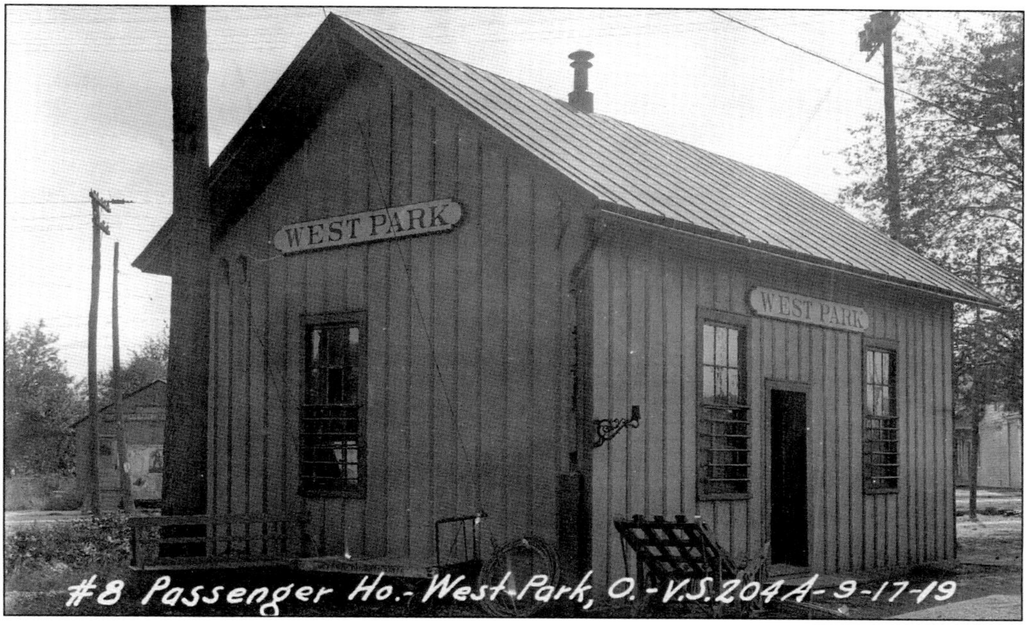

Passenger (shown above) and freight depots were built in West Park but were long gone by the 1960s. The first Union Depot, a brick barnlike structure, was opened by the Cleveland, Columbus and Cincinnati Railroad (CC&C) at the foot of Cleveland's Bath Street in 1851 or 1853. Cleveland's second Union Depot was built at a cost of $475,000 and dedicated on November 10, 1866. The south side of the depot included space for railroad offices, waiting rooms, a dining area, and baggage handling; the lakeside consisted of a large enclosed train shed with eight through tracks. A 96-foot clock tower was added the next spring. The depot originally served the CC&C; CP&A; Cleveland and Toledo; and Cleveland and Pittsburgh lines. (Above, NYC Railroad photograph, Allen County [Ohio] Historical Society collection; below, *c.* 1910 photograph, Bruce Young collection.)

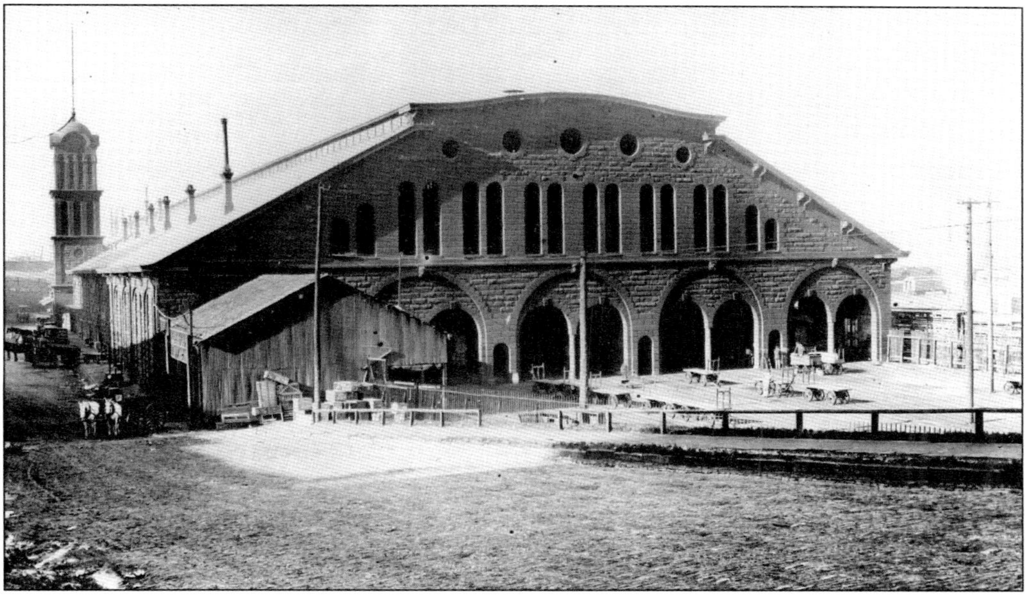

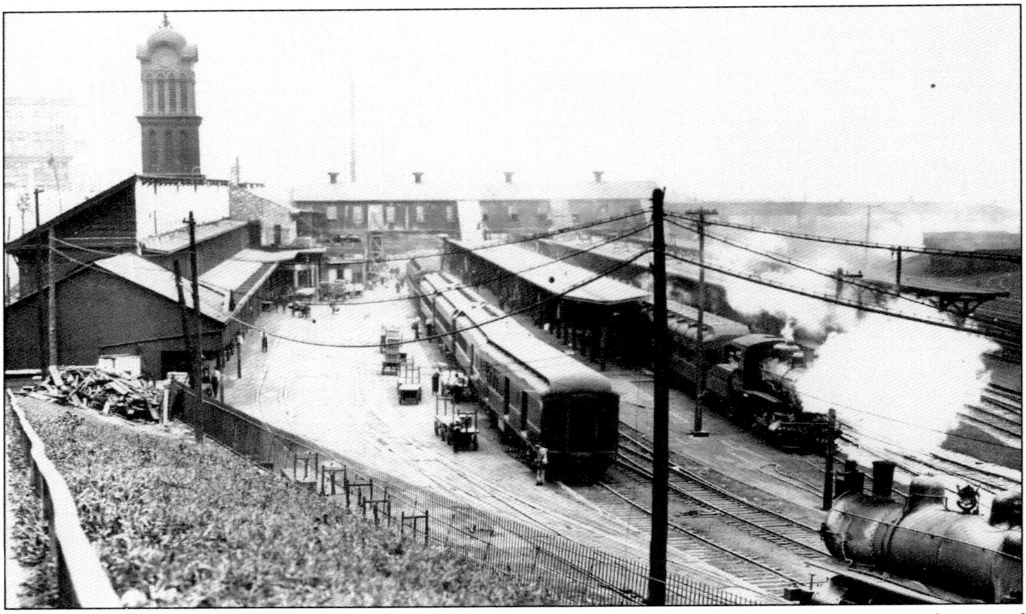

By 1915, Union Depot (above) had been significantly modified with the replacement of most of the barnlike train sheds with three umbrella sheds and a covered overhead concourse. Back in 1902, Cleveland, following the lead of other cities, formed a commission to look at the general pattern of growth of the downtown business and government district. The result was a civic center mall surrounded by seven public buildings stretching toward Lake Erie. At the far north end was a monumental union station to replace several older depots, including Union Depot. This union station was never built, but instead replaced by the Terminal Tower complex of the Van Sweringen Brothers built on Public Square between 1924 and 1934. The 1929 view below shows the elevated western approach to the terminal under construction. (Above, Bruce Young collection; below Cleveland State University Library Special Collections.)

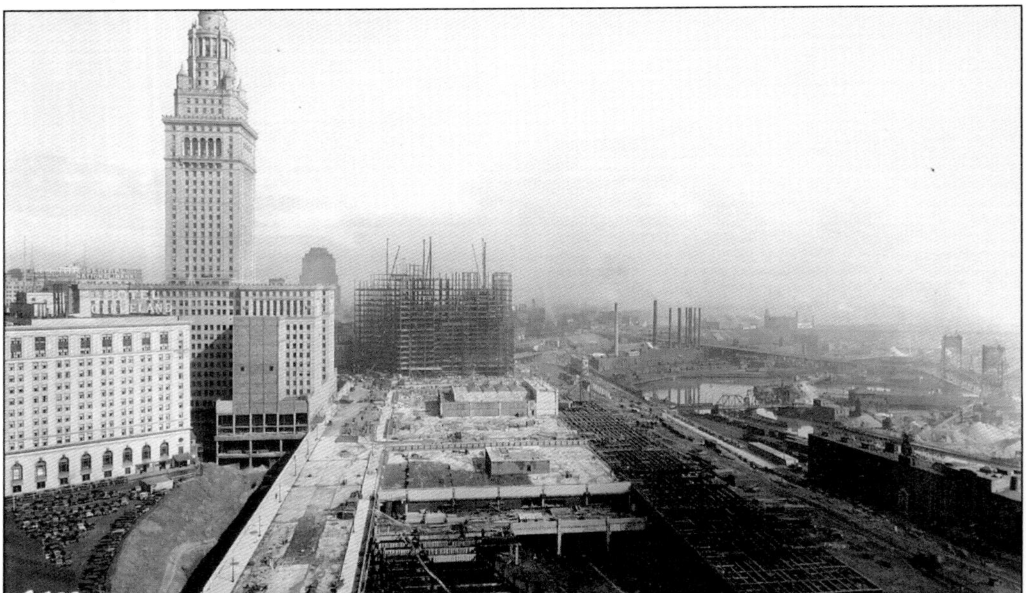

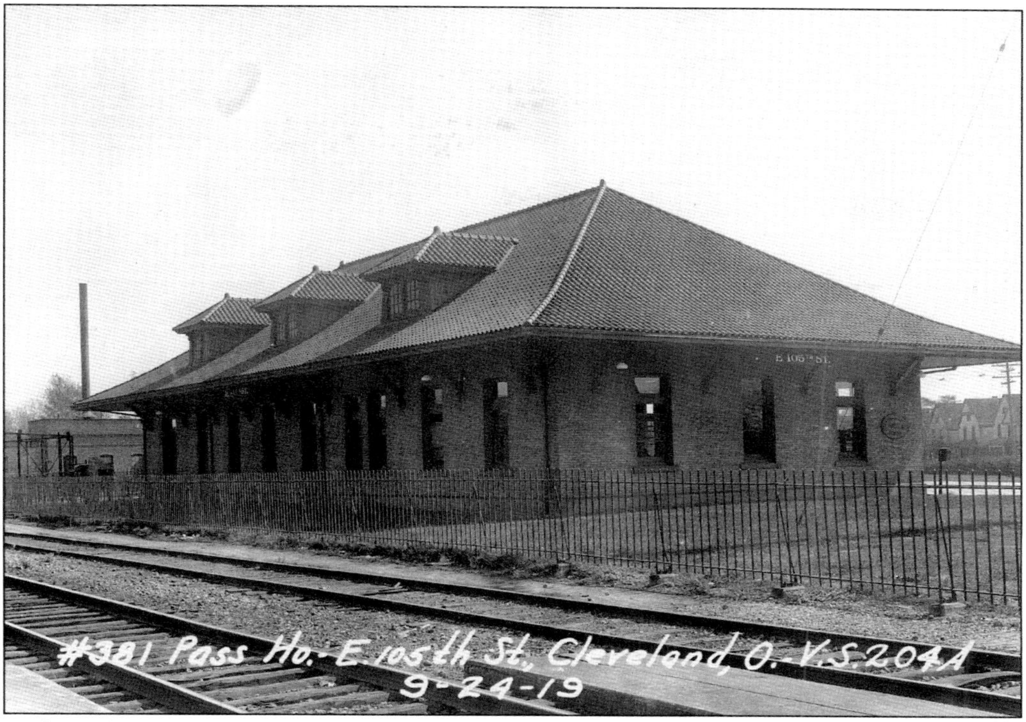

In the early 1900s, the NYC erected the above suburban passenger depot at East 105th Street in Cleveland. Nearby was a brick freight house. Both are now gone. LS&MS built the depot below to serve another suburb of Cleveland—Glenville. The bicycle is most likely for delivering telegrams. The Glenville depot was probably gone by the mid-1900s. (Above, NYC Railroad photograph, Allen County [Ohio] Historical Society collection; below, Mark J. Camp collection.)

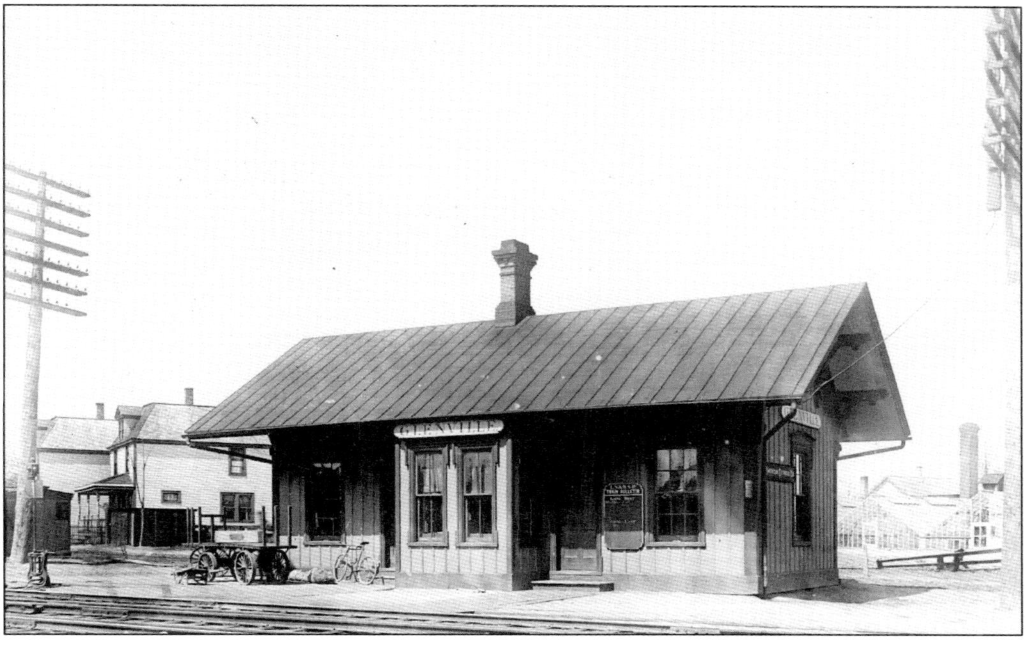

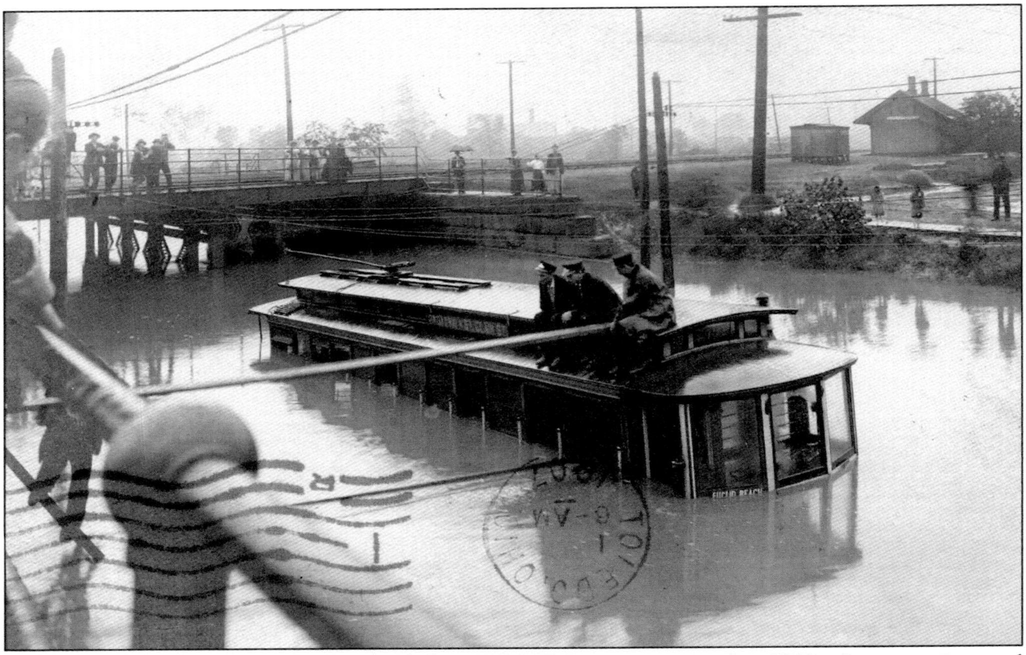

Collinwood was a major terminal of the LS&MS beginning in the 1890s. Locomotive and car repair facilities and a huge freight yard covered many acres. The elevated right-of-way kept the LS&MS running during summer rainstorms of 1907 that flooded the underpasses and stranded this hapless streetcar and its crew. People watch the rescue. In the background is the small c. 1870 depot and freight shed. Below is a 1919 view of the brick replacement depot at Collinwood, probably of NYC design. After Collinwood yard was rebuilt in 1929, it contained around 120 miles of track and could handle 2,000 cars per day. Little remains at Collinwood, just a few yard buildings, the huge shop buildings, roundhouses, and these depots have fallen victim to development and railroad modernization. (Above, Mark J. Camp collection; below, NYC Railroad photograph, Allen County [Ohio] Historical Society collection.)

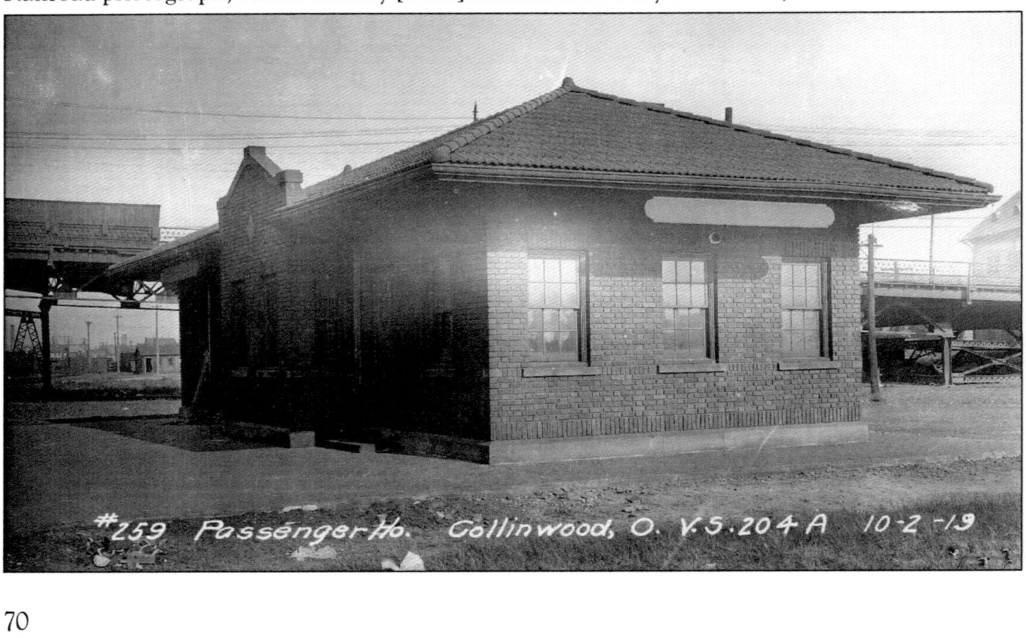

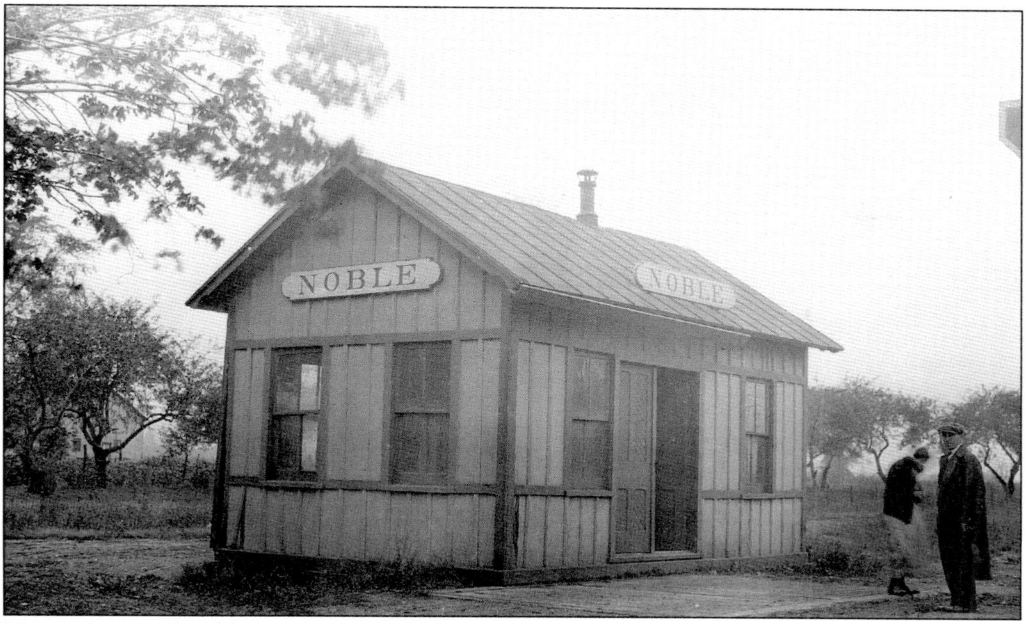

Nottingham and Noble were stations east of Collinwood, now absorbed by Greater Cleveland. The NYC built a small semienclosed passenger shelter at Nottingham in the early 1900s. The 1918 view above shows the facilities at Noble. Two passengers wait the arrival of the next local to take them into the city. (NYC Railroad photograph, Allen County [Ohio] Historical Society collection.)

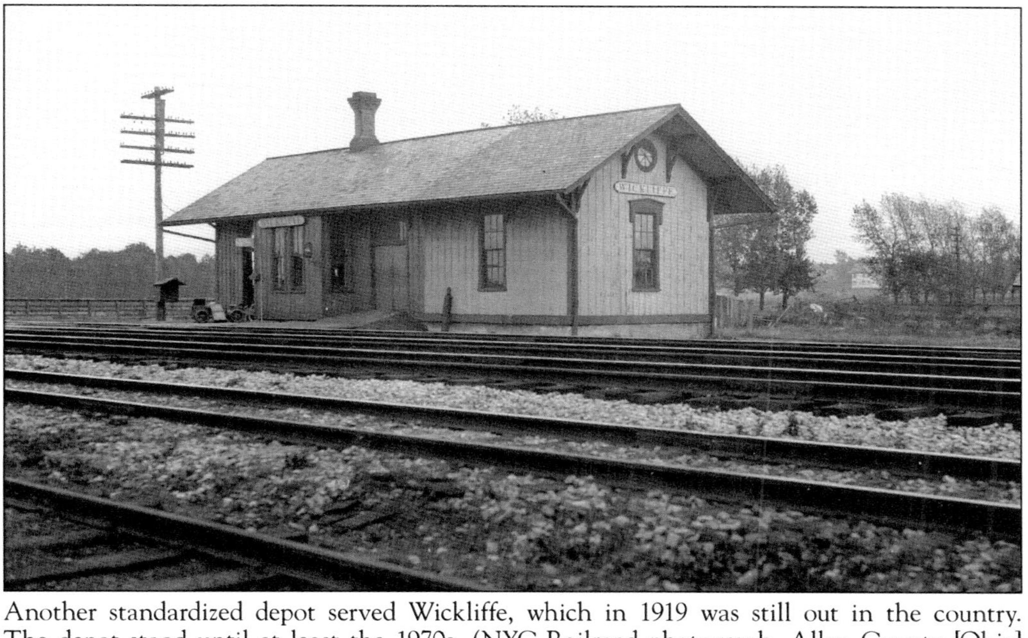

Another standardized depot served Wickliffe, which in 1919 was still out in the country. The depot stood until at least the 1970s. (NYC Railroad photograph, Allen County [Ohio] Historical Society collection.)

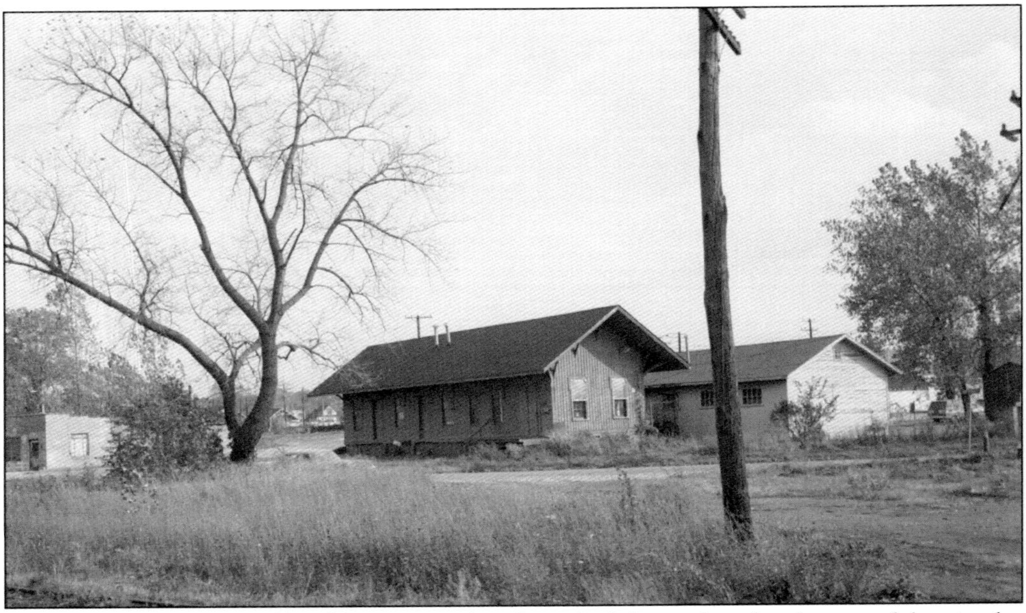

The LS&MS depot at Willoughby seems to be of standard design, but the absence of the circular window in the end eaves and roof supports makes it different from most. Nearby were a freight house and SW tower. Although relocated, the Willoughby passenger depot survives in business use. Between Willoughby and Mentor the LS&MS maintained a small enclosed passenger shelter at Reynolds. (Charles Garvin photograph, 1966.)

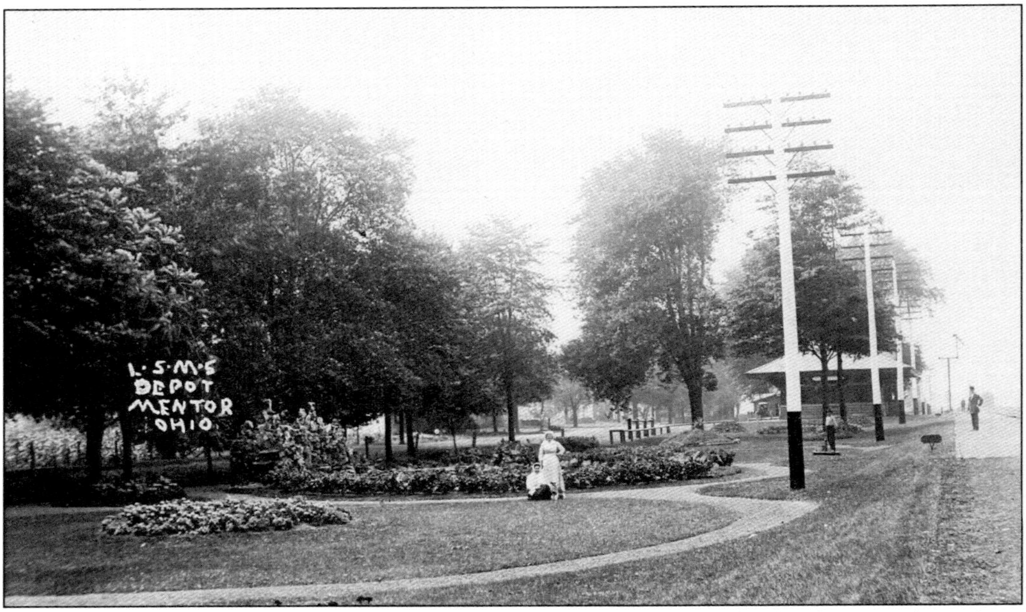

Mentor was the site of the LS&MS greenhouse that supplied plants for the depot gardens along this stretch of the main line. Obviously the gardens at Mentor's LS&MS depot were well kept and an enjoyable welcome to the city for all arriving by train. The passenger depot in the background replaced a frame one in the 1890s. Across the tracks was a 1909 vintage brick freight house. (Mark J. Camp collection.)

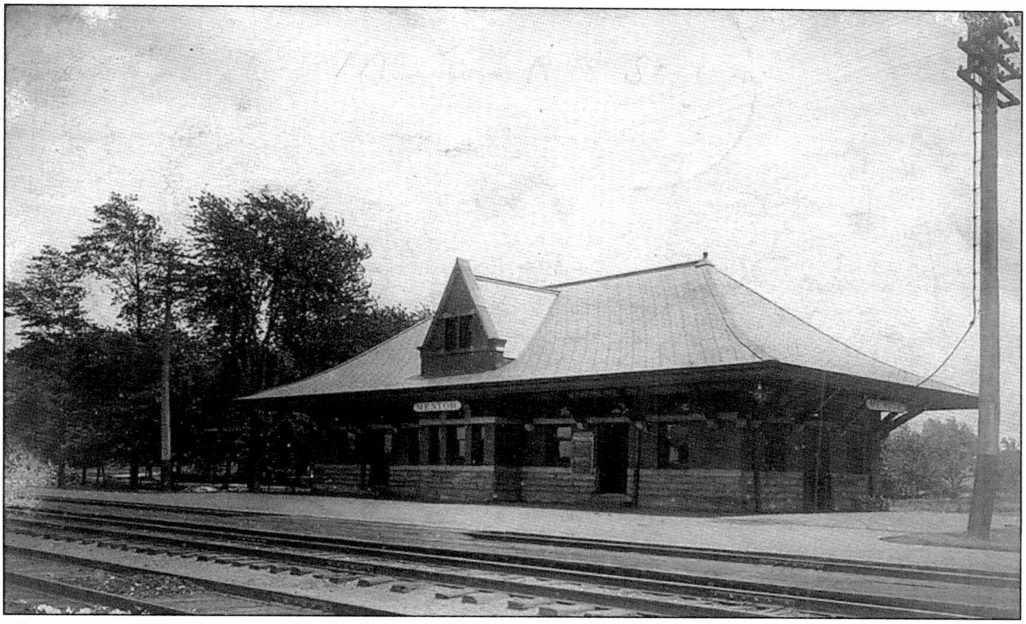

The postcard photographer picked a rather quiet time to record Mentor's 1890 vintage passenger depot. This depot was part of a depot upgrading program of the LS&MS that resulted in many new brick and stone depots between Buffalo and Chicago. Today the depot is a restaurant. (Phil Moberg collection.)

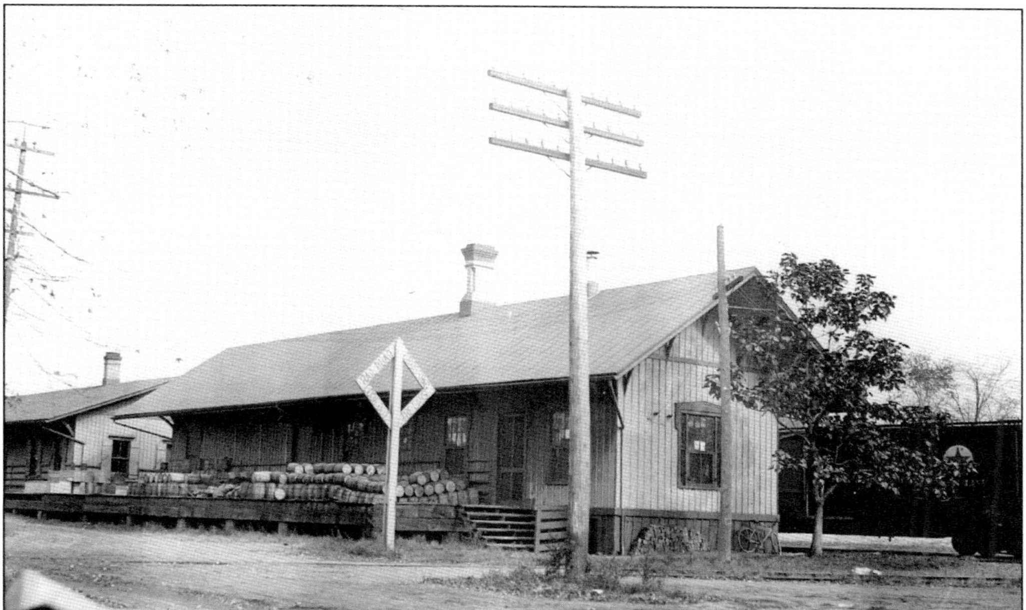

Built to the same plan as Willoughby is the earlier LS&MS passenger depot at Painesville shown in 1918. Adjacent is the freight house. (NYC Railroad photograph, Allen County [Ohio] Historical Society collection.)

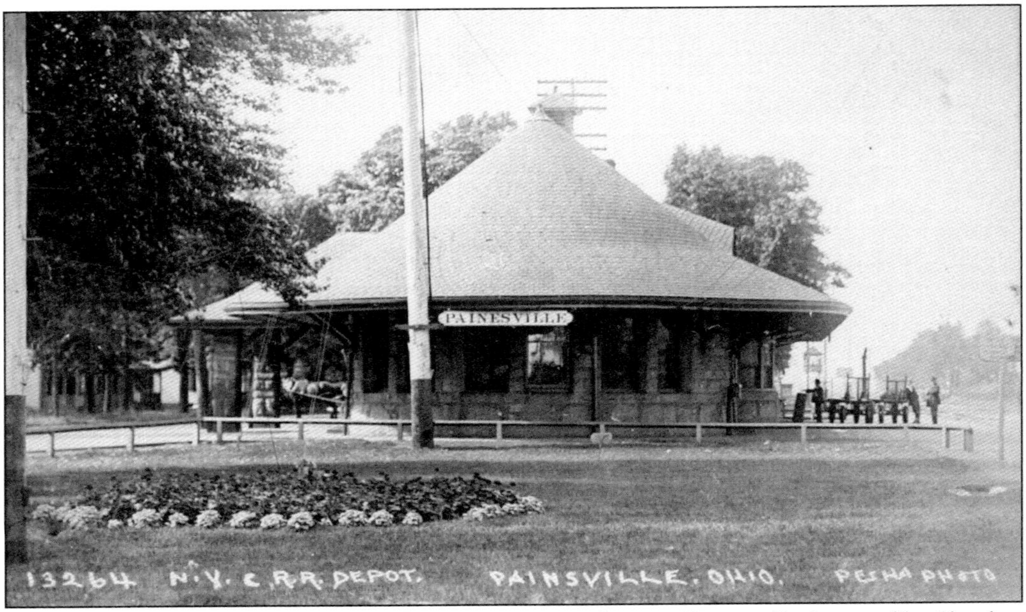

In February 1893, the LS&MS opened a new passenger depot at Painesville designed by Shepley, Rutan and Coolidge of Boston. In later years the depot also served as a bus terminal. The depot sat unused for several years before passing under the care of the Western Reserve Railroad Association. (NYC Railroad photograph, Allen County [Ohio] Historical Society collection.)

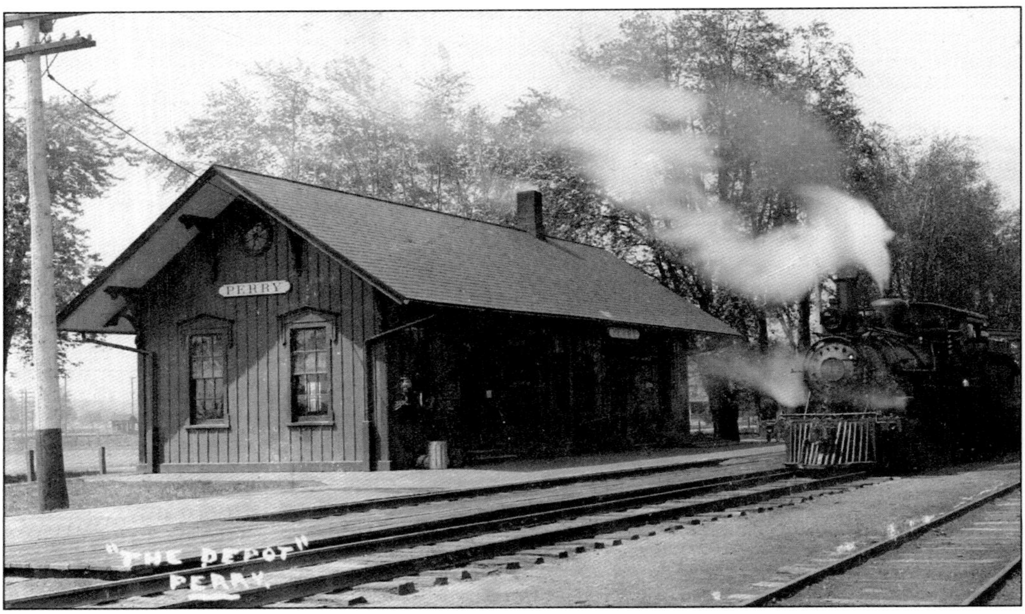

Between Painesville and Perry the LS&MS maintained an enclosed unmanned shelter at Lane into the 1930s. At Perry a LS&MS switcher shuffles cars around 1907. The standard-design passenger depot probably dates from the 1870s. Nearby was a standard freight house. In the distance behind the left side of the depot is a small waiting shelter of the Cleveland, Painesville and Eastern interurban. Nothing remains in Perry. (Mark J. Camp collection.)

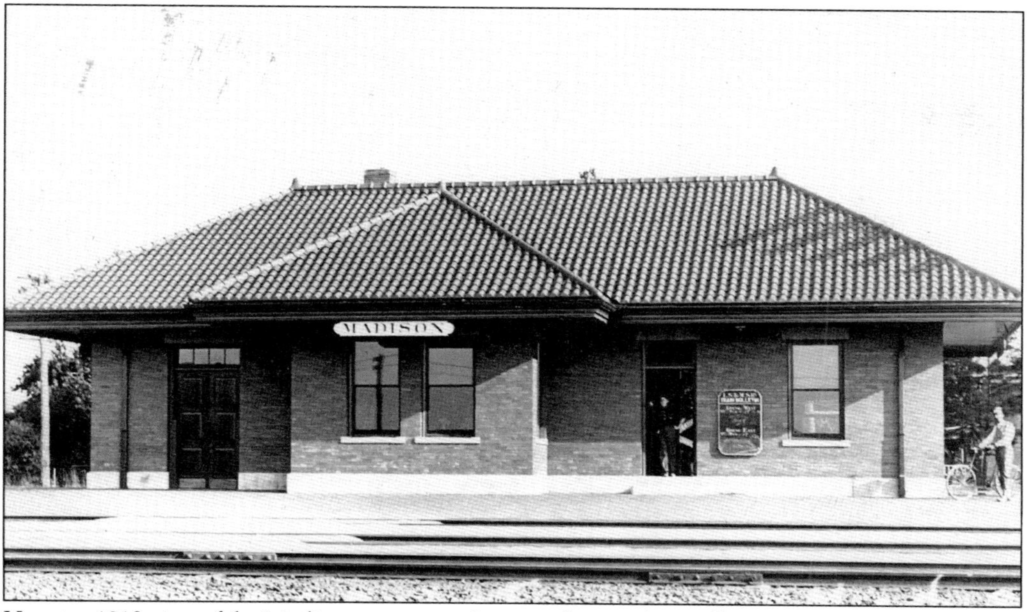

Here is a 1913 view of the Madison passenger depot with two of its staff posing for the photographer. The man with the bicycle may just have returned from delivering a telegram. Across the tracks was a frame freight house, a portion of which was the old passenger depot. All Madison railroad structures have been removed, but they existed into the late 1990s. (Mark J. Camp collection.)

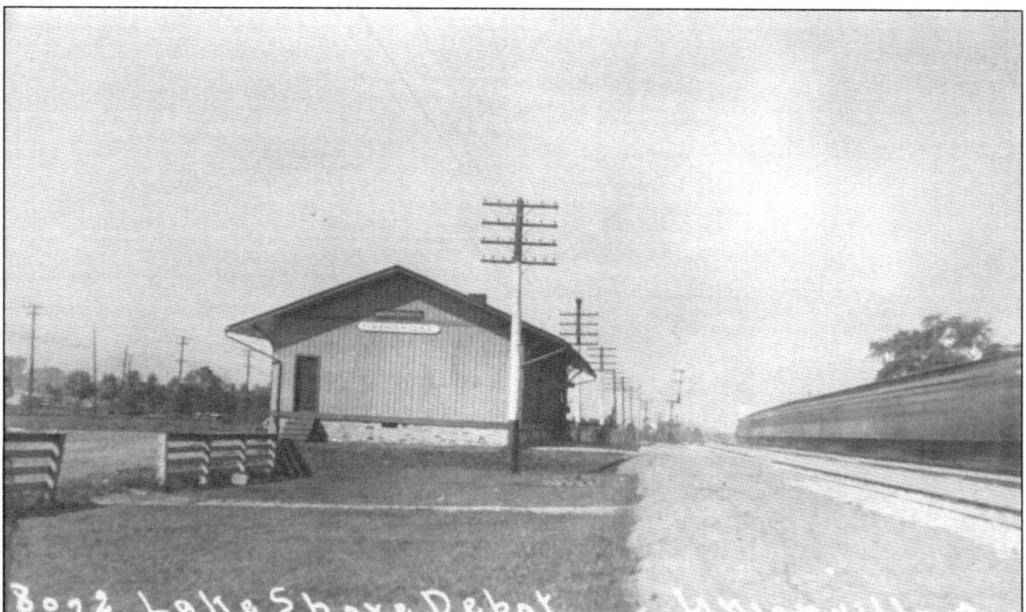

Unionville's combination depot is shown in this 1919 view. A nearly identical depot was built farther east at Saybrook. (Phil Moberg collection.)

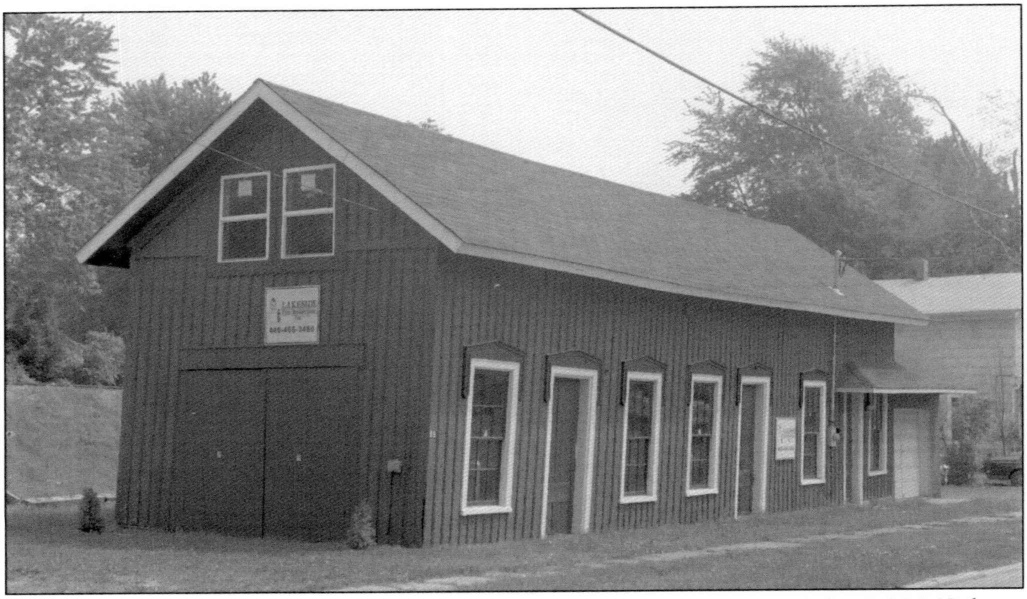

The CP&A reportedly reached Geneva from the west in late 1851. Geneva's first LS&MS depot was constructed in 1886. During the *c.* 1900 depot rebuilding plan of the LS&MS, Geneva was scheduled for replacement. The 1886 depot was cut into two sections; the passenger end was winched across the tracks, and the baggage-freight part was moved south of the tracks. The passenger end was purchased and moved further along Railroad Street to a local lumber mill. The above view shows the depot in 1968. August 1901 marked the opening of the new $8,000 passenger depot at Geneva, located just west of the old depot. A long brick freight house was built opposite the brick and stone depot. Oddly the older passenger depot is the only Geneva depot remaining today. The 1901 depot was demolished around 1967 for valuable parking space. (Below, 1918 NYC Railroad photograph, Allen County [Ohio] Historical Society collection.)

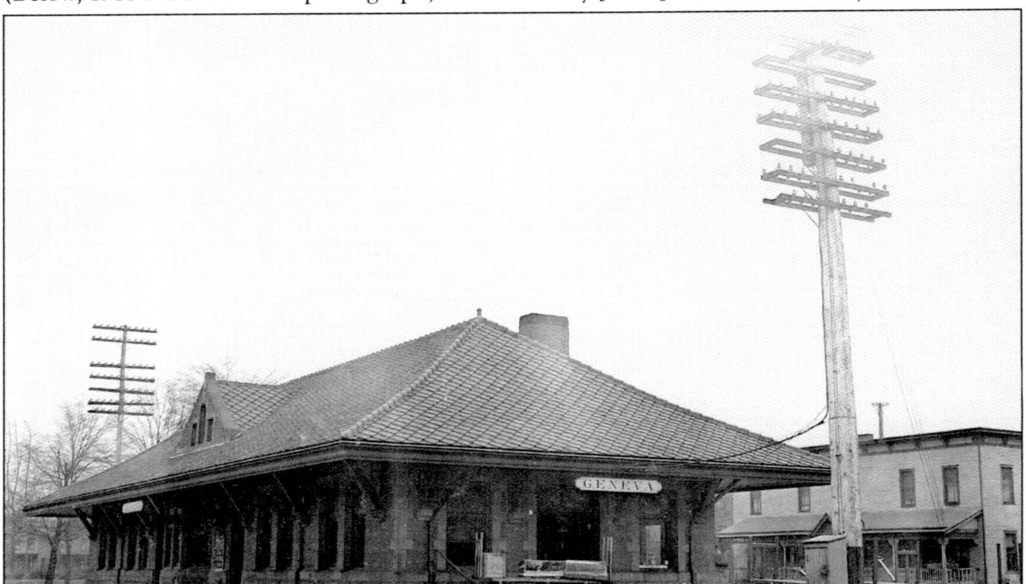

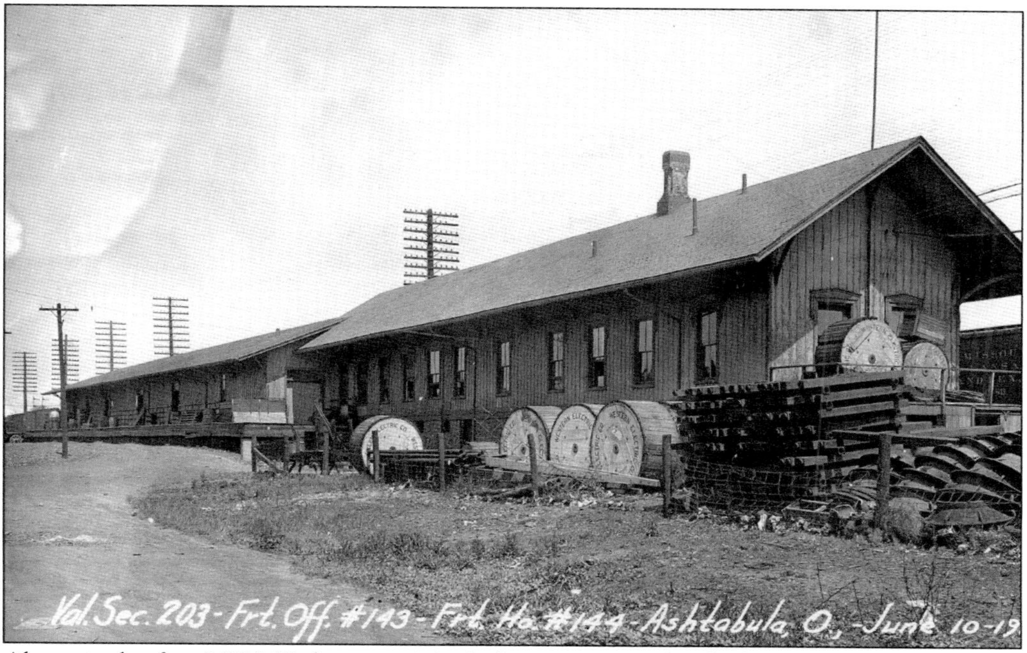

Above is the first LS&MS depot at Ashtabula, in use as a freight house in 1919. When the passenger depot below was completed in 1901, the old depot was converted to freight use. The freight house has disappeared along with most of the railroad buildings in Ashtabula's extensive yard. The passenger depot, located on West Thirty-second Street, is still used by the railroad. Nearby are storefronts that once served the many railroaders frequenting the depot and railroad yards. Unfortunately, the mention of Ashtabula still brings to mind the great railroad accident that took place just east of the passenger depot. On December 29, 1876, a high trestle bridging the Ashtabula River collapsed carrying some 100 people to their deaths. (Above, NYC Railroad photograph, Allen County [Ohio] Historical Society collection.)

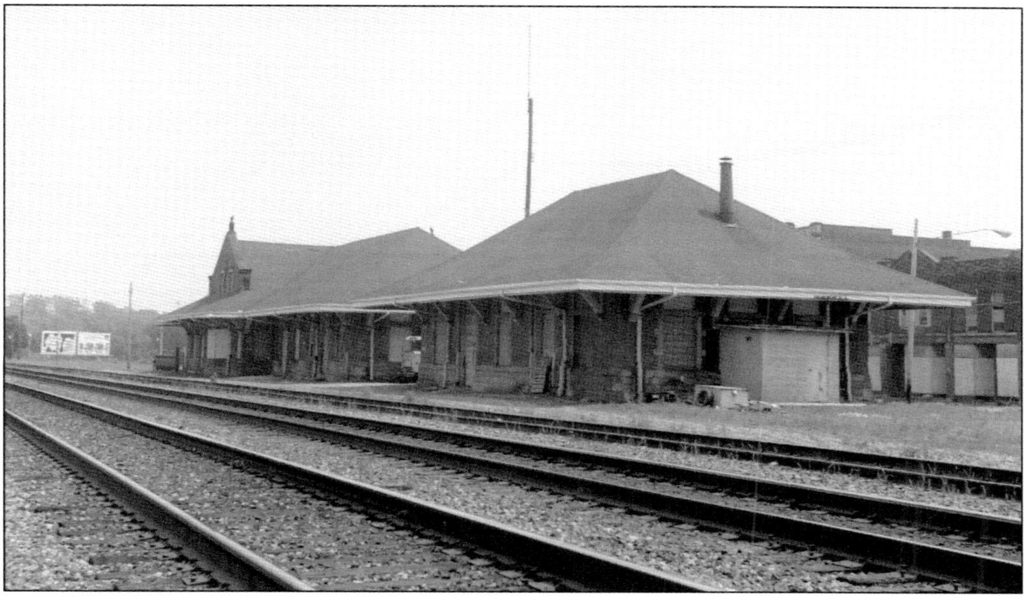

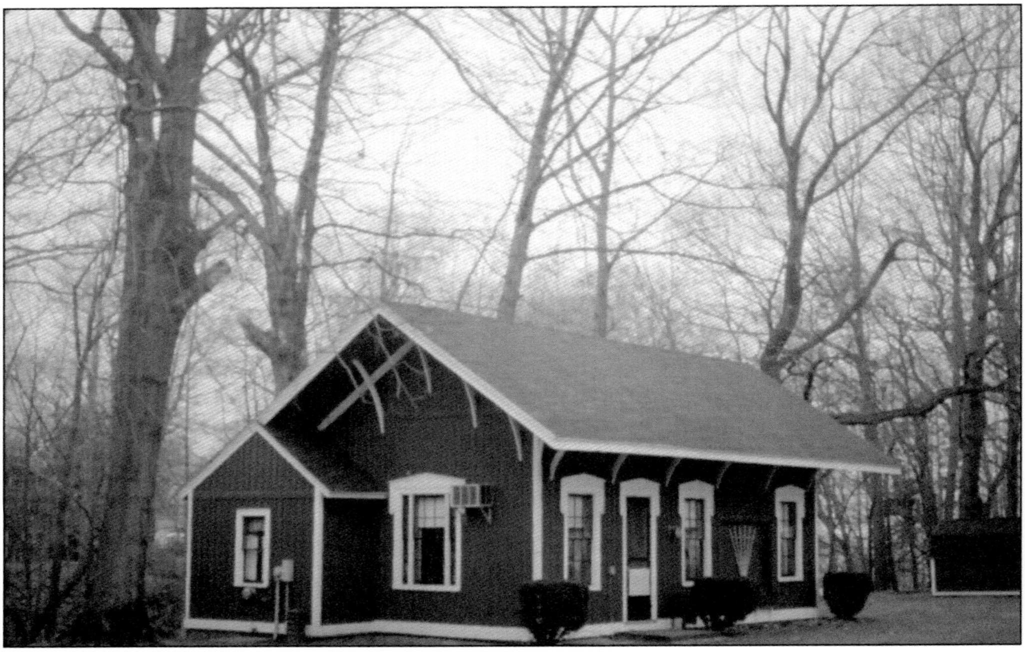

Kingsville's depot was moved and restored, and now serves as a cottage in a residential area between Kingsville and Conneaut.

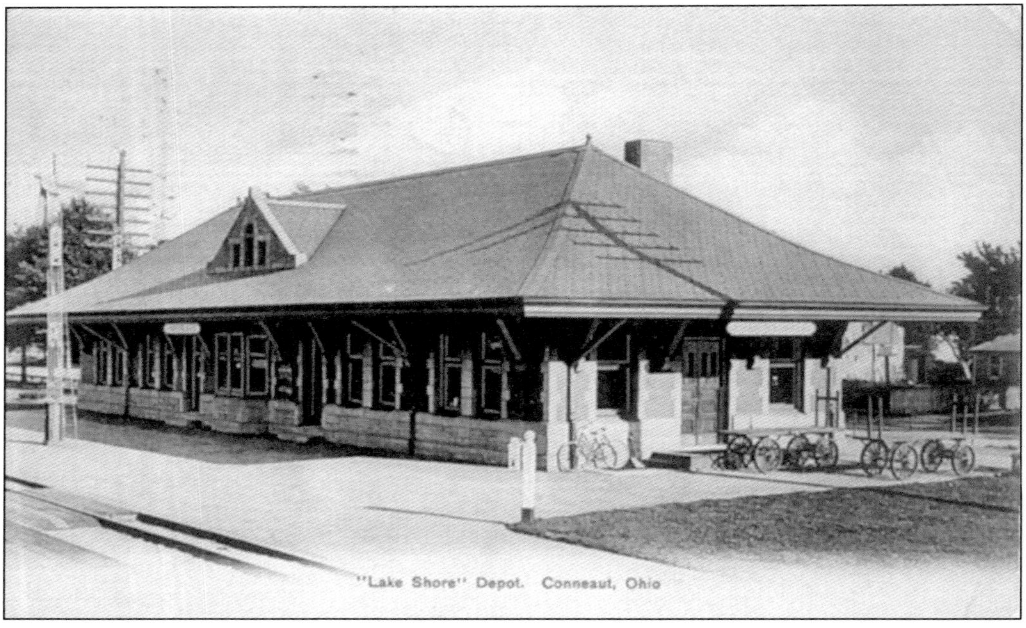

Conneaut also received a new depot in 1900 replacing an earlier LS&MS standard plan frame passenger depot. Out of view across the tracks is an 1873 freight house. Both depots have been restored. The passenger depot is the home of the Conneaut Historical Railroad Museum, and the freight house now houses the Conneaut Area Historical Society. (Phil Moberg collection.)

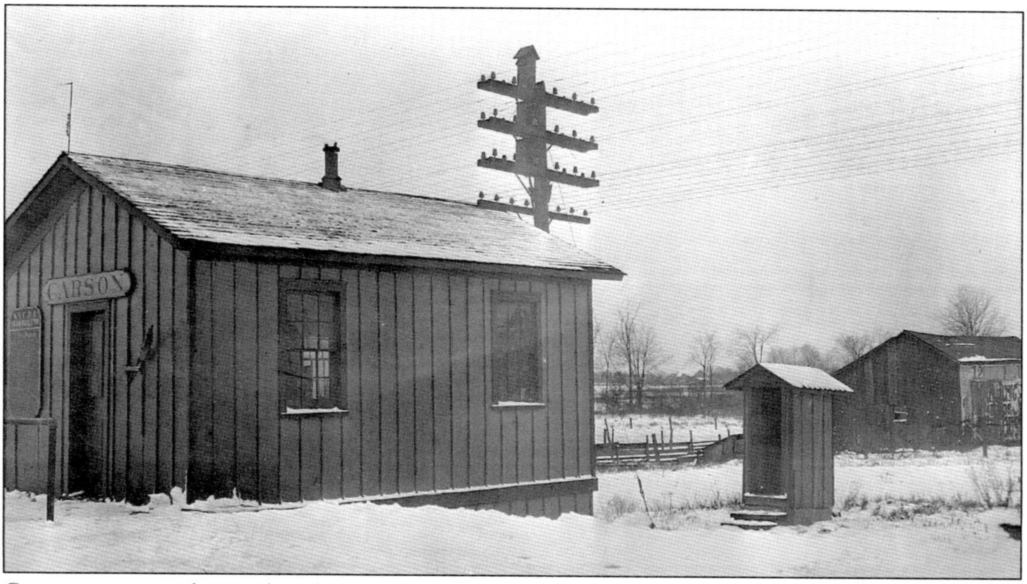

Carson was mainly a railroad station created in 1903 when the low-grade line from Ashtabula to Youngstown split off the line to Jamestown, Pennsylvania, by way of Jefferson and Andover. A large yard was constructed here to handle both coal trains to Ashtabula and iron ore trains to Youngstown. This small depot and single privy was all that was needed. (NYC Railroad photograph, 1919, Allen County [Ohio] Historical Society collection.)

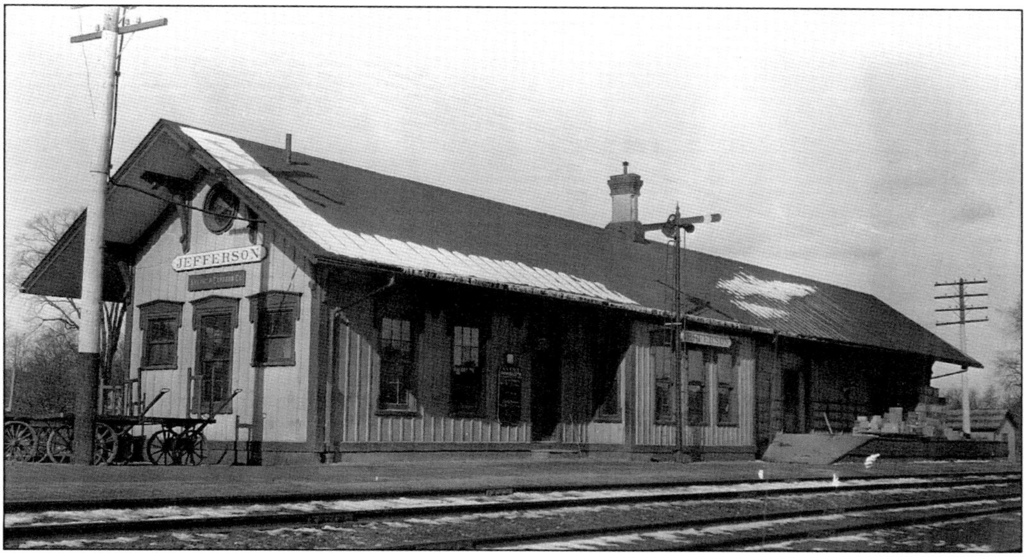

The standard plan LS&MS depot in Jefferson was built in 1872. The NYC last used the depot in 1961, and the depot sat vacant for many years. The East Jefferson Street depot currently serves the Ashtabula Carson and Jefferson Railroad and is the departure point for scenic train rides. Although never used as a depot, a lawyer's office building near the courthouse was built in the 1870s to LS&MS depot plans by a local lawyer that once represented the railroad when they were building the line to Jamestown, Pennsylvania. (NYC Railroad photograph, 1919, Allen County [Ohio] Historical Society collection.)

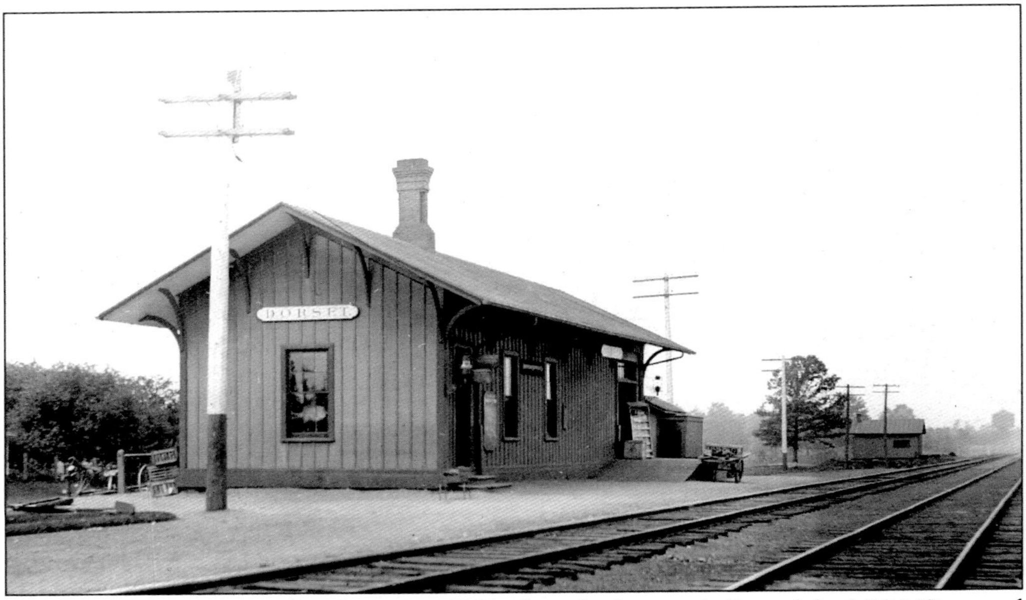

Dorset became a major railroad town in 1903 when the low-grade line of the LS&MS crossed the old line to Jamestown, Pennsylvania. This depot dates to 1872. In 1903, a frame interlocking tower was built at the junction. This was later replaced by a concrete block structure. In the yard was a locomotive coaling dock. Only the tracks remain today. (Mark J. Camp collection.)

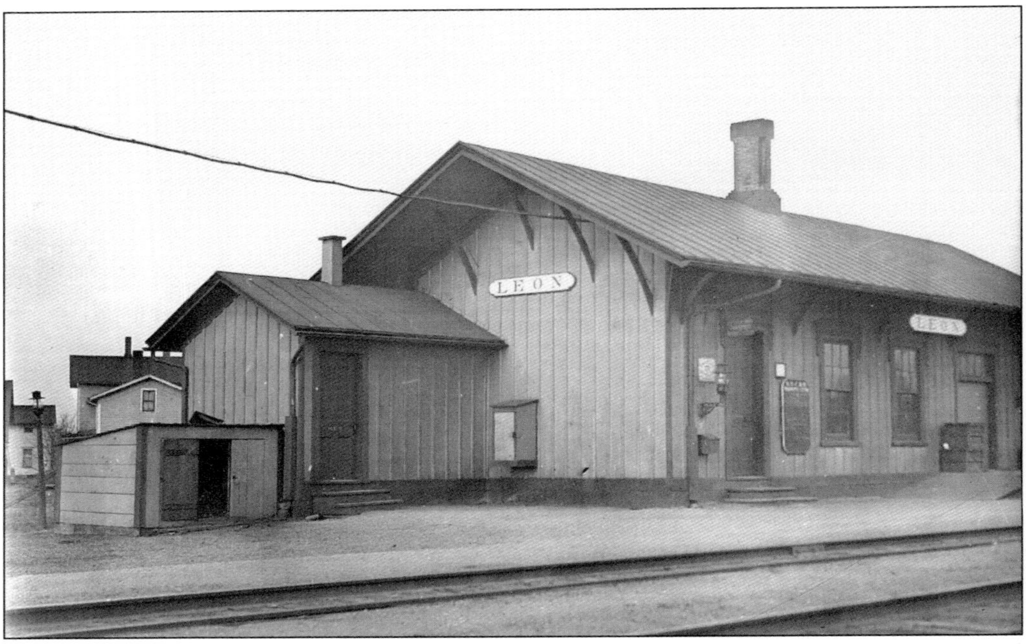

A smaller version of the standard plan was constructed at Leon in 1872. It also served the small crossroads of Padanaram. Note the restroom addition. No privies in Leon! The depot still exists, forming the second floor of a barn on Leon Road. (NYC Railroad photograph, 1919, Allen County [Ohio] Historical Society collection.)

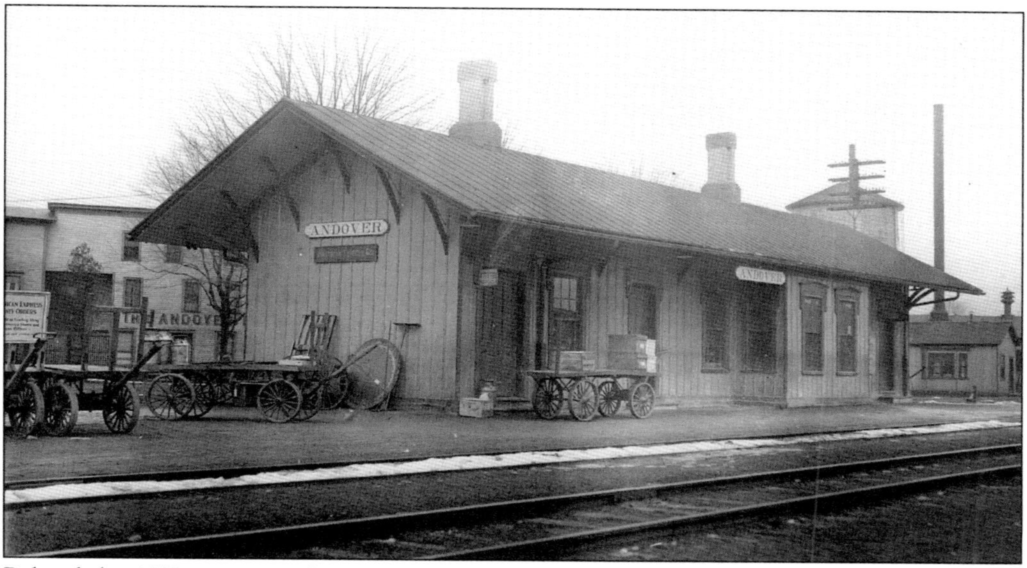

Behind the 1873 passenger depot in Andover is the Hotel Arlington, a water tank, and pump house—the building with the tall stack. Andover was a popular destination of travelers in the 1880s partaking in local mineral springs. Passenger service ended in the late 1950s. The depot served as village offices before being moved to the Wick area. (NYC Railroad photograph, 1919, Allen County [Ohio] Historical Society collection.)

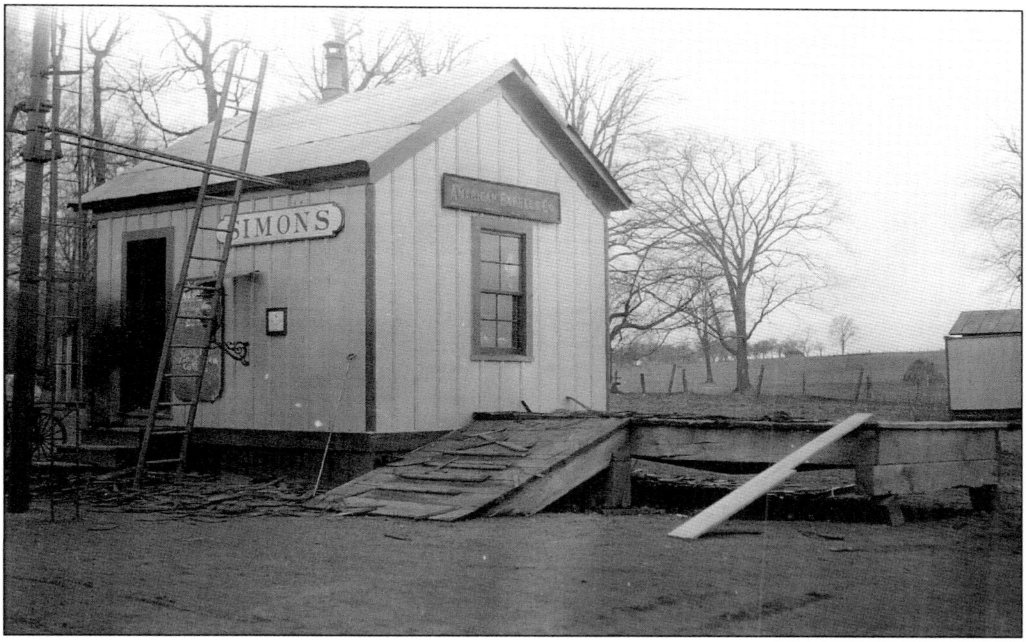

The last stop in Ohio on the LS&MS Jamestown line was at Simons. In 1919, the small depot was being reroofed. Unlike some of the other stops, restroom facilities were still out back. The depot was closed in 1931. This small building survives as part of a business near town. (NYC Railroad photograph, Allen County [Ohio] Historical Society collection.)

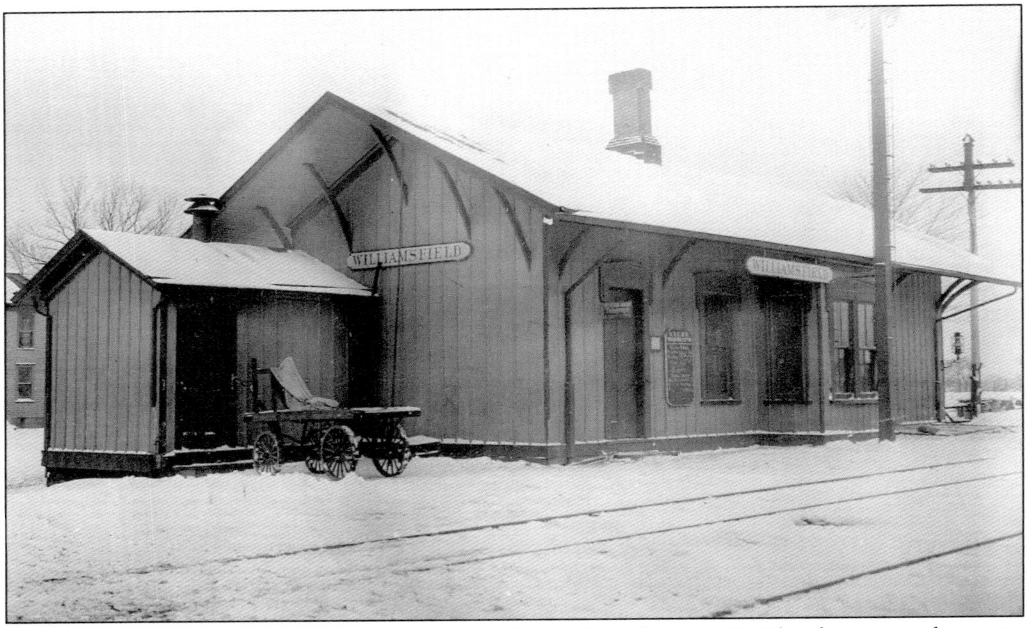

Williamsfield depot on the Mahoning Coal Railroad dates from 1873. The depot quietly awaits the next train on this overcast February 1919 day. Just to the west on the 1903 low-grade line at Wick was a wooden locomotive coaling station and small telegrapher's office. (New York Central Railroad photograph, Allen County [Ohio] Historical Society collection.)

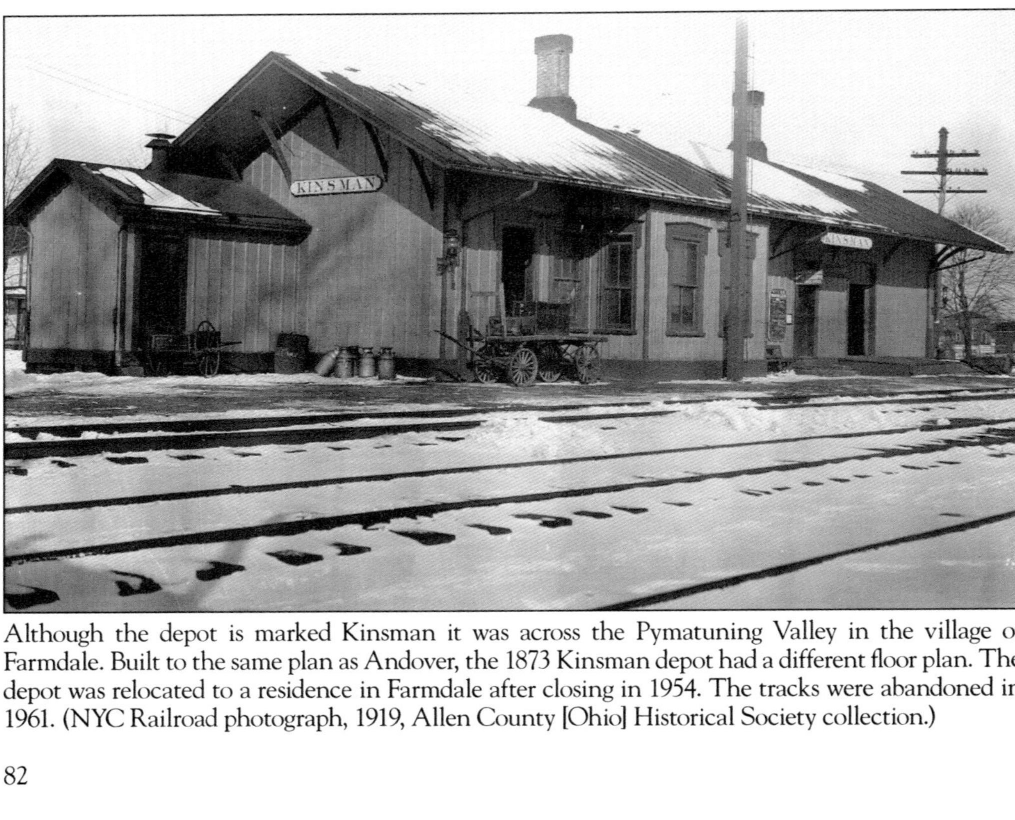

Although the depot is marked Kinsman it was across the Pymatuning Valley in the village of Farmdale. Built to the same plan as Andover, the 1873 Kinsman depot had a different floor plan. The depot was relocated to a residence in Farmdale after closing in 1954. The tracks were abandoned in 1961. (NYC Railroad photograph, 1919, Allen County [Ohio] Historical Society collection.)

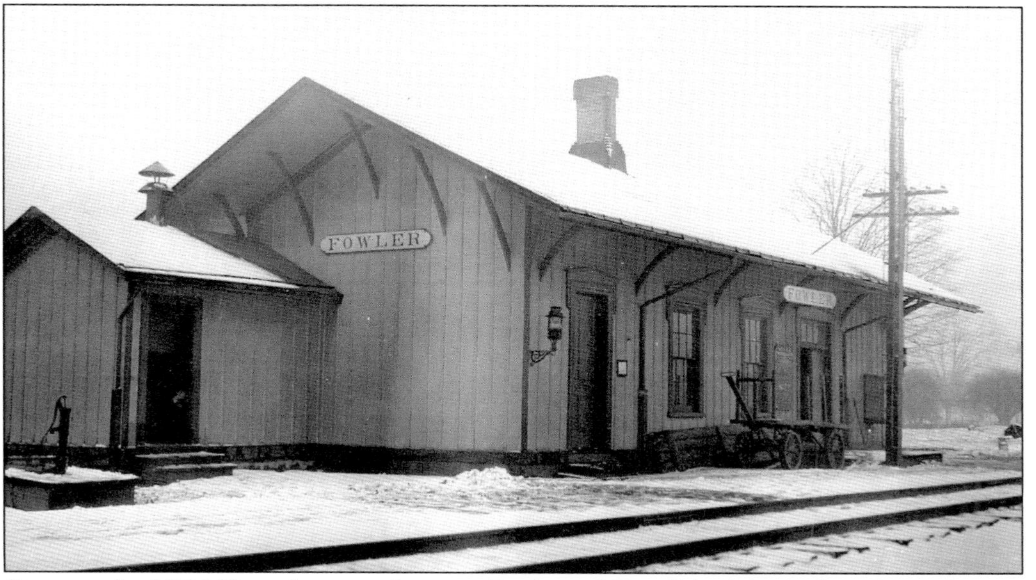

Compare the LS&MS combination depots at Fowler and Tyrrell, both built along the Mahoning Coal Railroad in 1873. Note the differences in length, floor plan, and roof composition. (NYC Railroad photograph, 1919, Allen County [Ohio] Historical Society collection.)

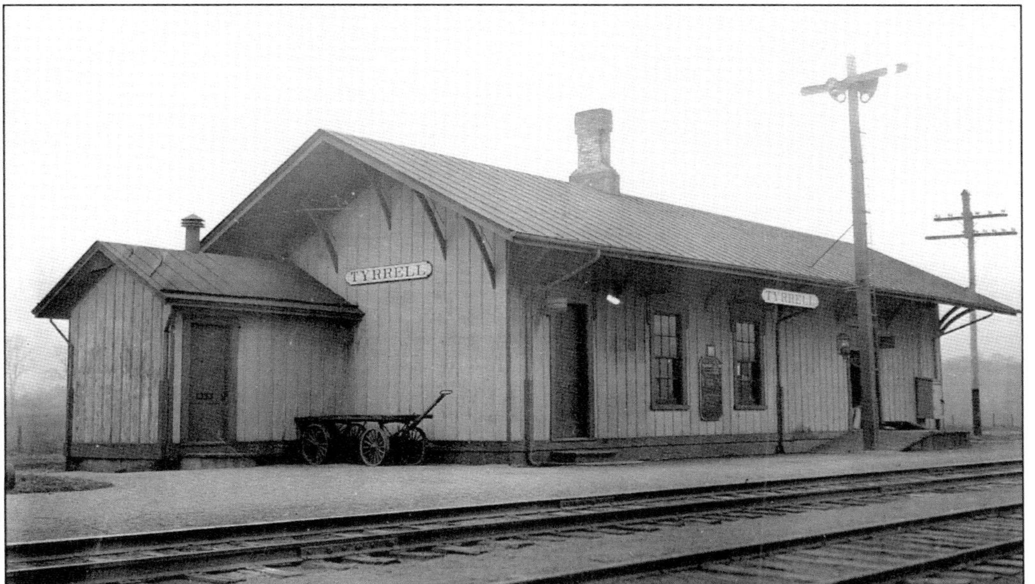

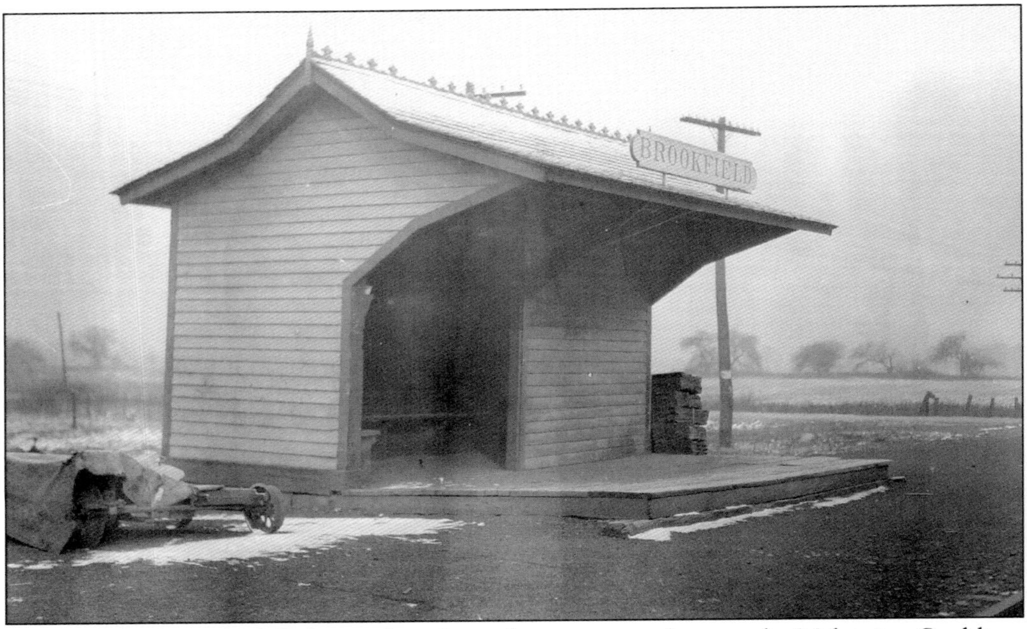

Brookfield had an LS&MS depot of similar architecture to others on the Mahoning Coal line. Today it is part of a local business. The three-sided shelter, pictured above in 1919, was apparently built for the convenience of passengers on the 1903 low-grade line. (NYC Railroad photograph, Allen County [Ohio] Historical Society collection.)

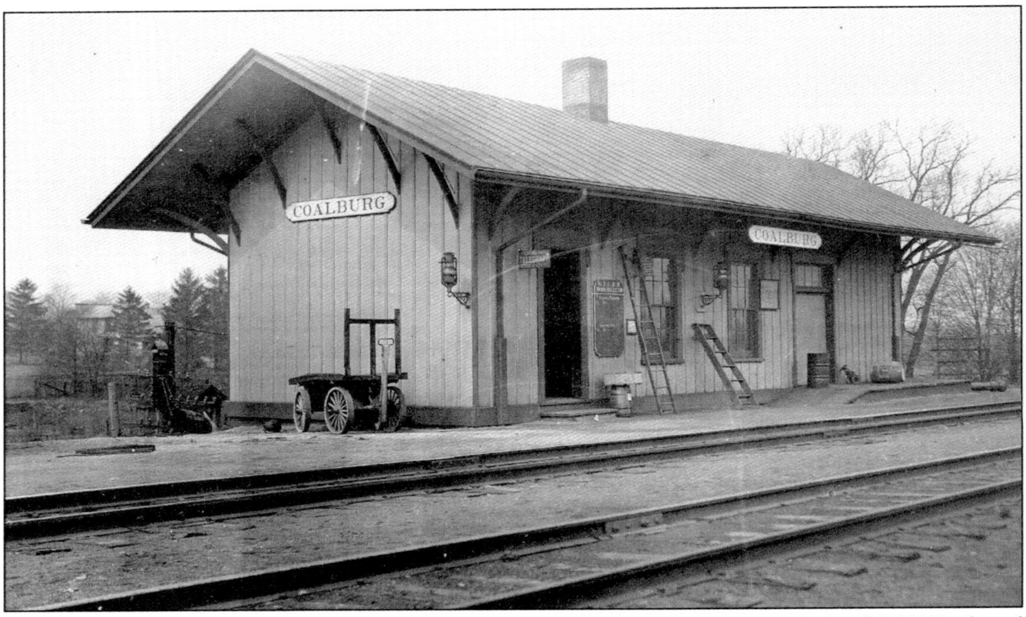

Coalburg, like Dorset, Fowler, Leon, and Tyrrell, was built without a vestibule. (NYC Railroad photograph, 1919, Allen County [Ohio] Historical Society collection.)

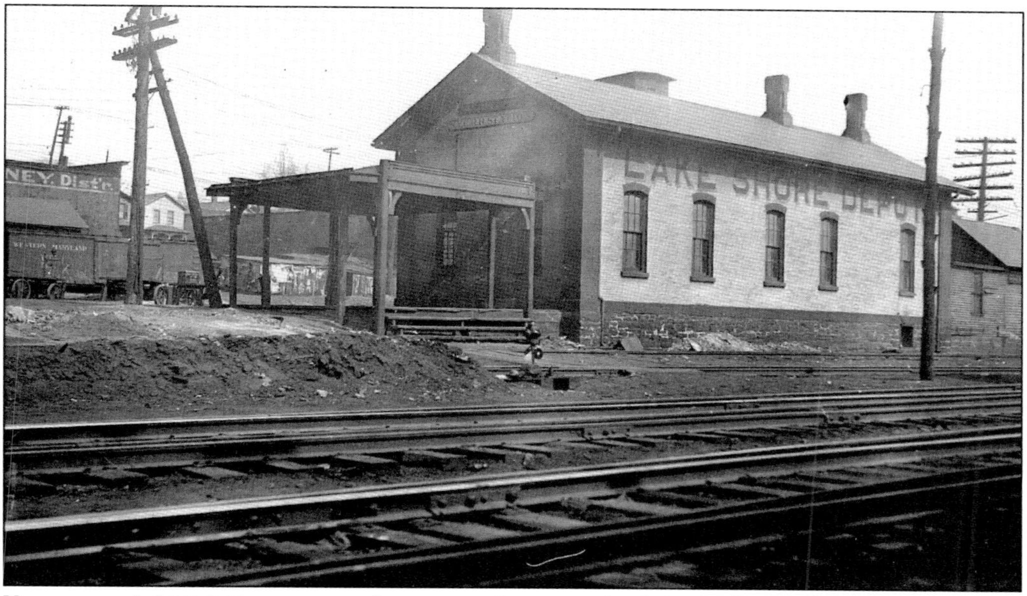

Youngstown's LS&MS passenger depot was of nonstandard design but still shows its ancestry in the above 1919 view. Nearby was a water tank and freight house. In the 1920s, these shabby facilities were replaced by the large NYC Railroad depot, shown below in 1971. The $500,000 brick-and-stone structure opened in the summer of 1926 near the intersection of Himrod and Wilson Avenues. The upper floor contained the waiting rooms and ticket office; the middle floor had the Franklin Division offices of the NYC; and the ground floor housed the baggage and express facilities. This depot was one of many NYC depots offered for sale in 1956. There were no takers, and by the late 1960s the depot had fallen into disrepair and eventually met the wrecker's ball. (Above, NYC Railroad photograph, Allen County [Ohio] Historical Society collection; below, Charles Garvin photograph.)

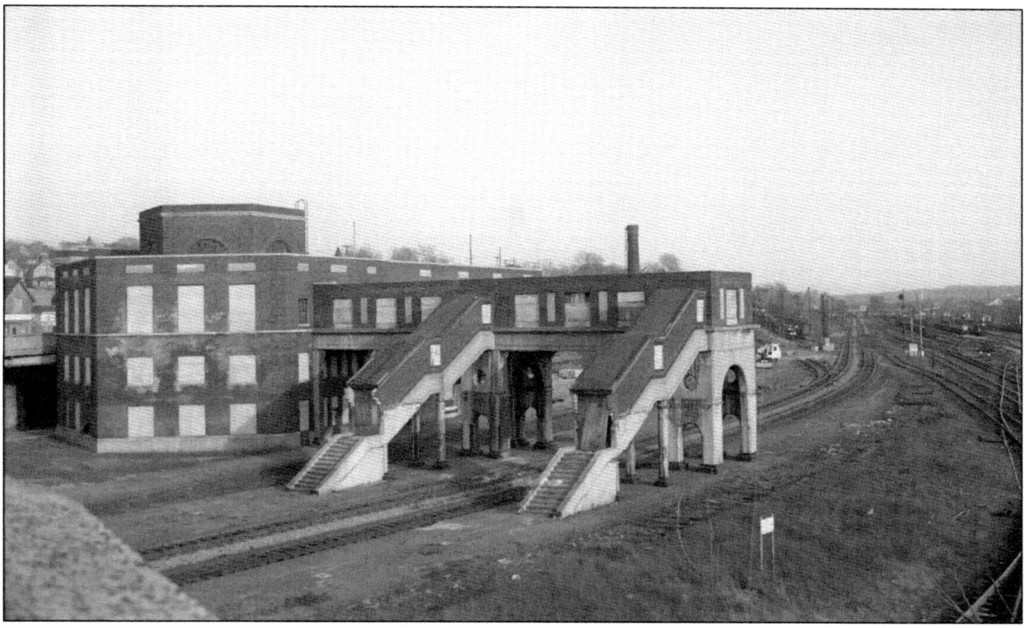

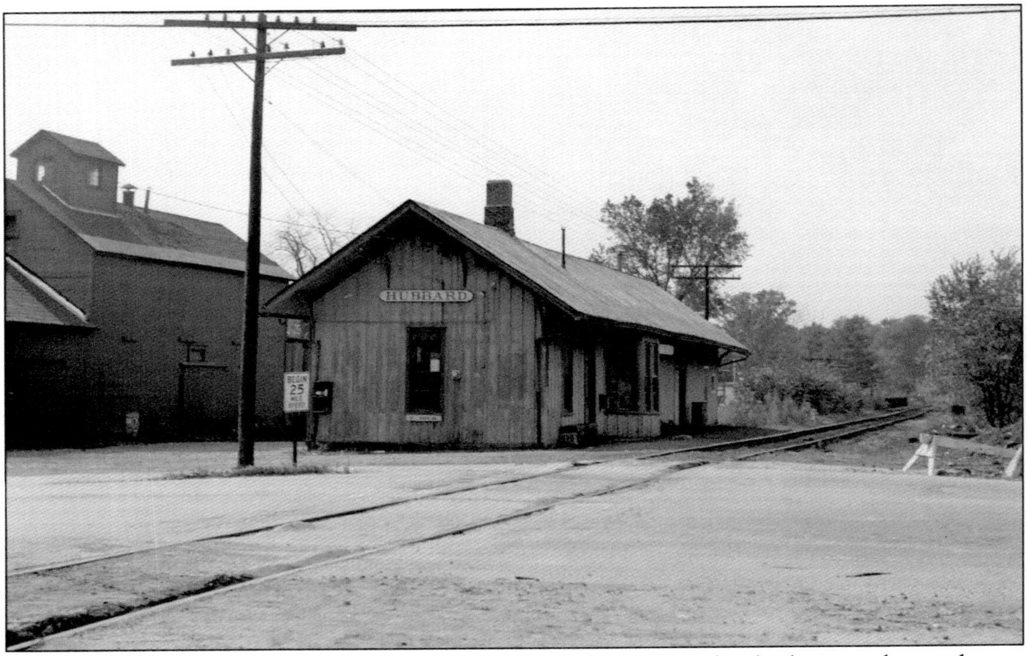

The LS&MS maintained the above combination depot at Hubbard. It had received sporadic use as early as 1919, but by 1971 was being used by railroad maintenance crews. It has since been torn down, although a depot replica exists nearby.

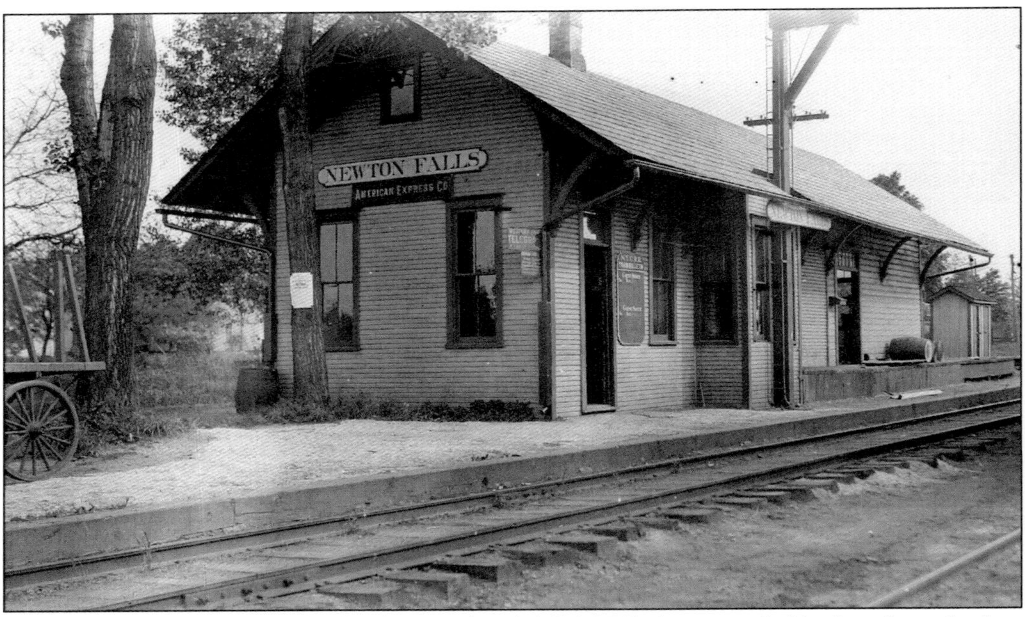

The Lake Erie Alliance and Wheeling Railroad (LEA&W) depots probably date from the late 1870s and follow several plans. Newton Falls was where the LEA&W crossed the B&O. This combination depot remains on site in business use along the abandoned roadbed. (NYC Railroad photograph, 1919, Allen County [Ohio] Historical Society collection.)

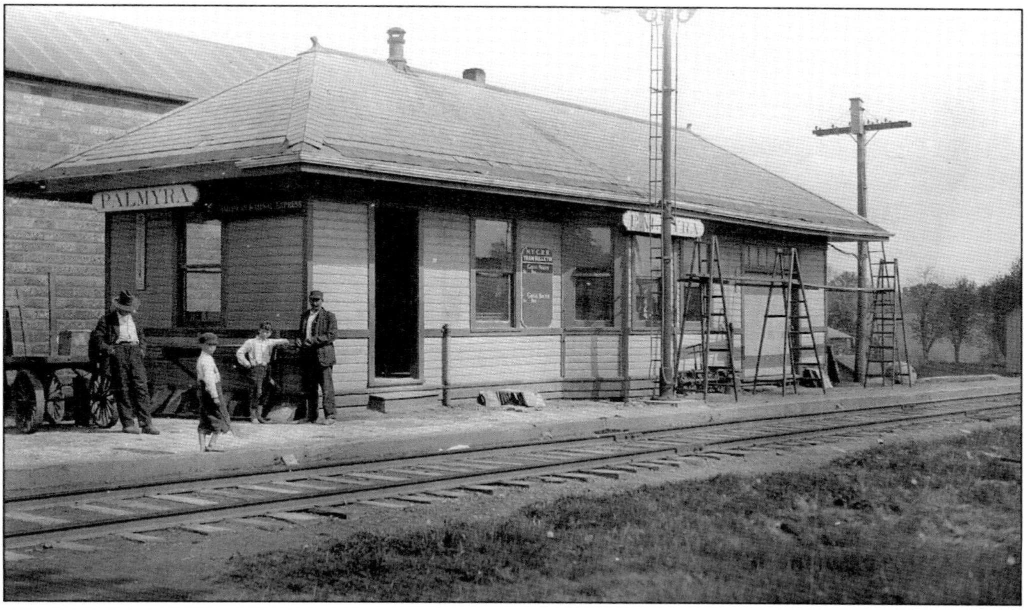

The LEA&W depot at Palmyra shows a resemblance to a common NYC design. It may be a later replacement built during NYC control. A new shingle roof is nearly completed in this 1919 view, replacing the original slate. This depot was actually east of town at Diamond, the former location of a large brick and tile plant. The depot is still extant. (NYC Railroad photograph, Allen County [Ohio] Historical Society collection.)

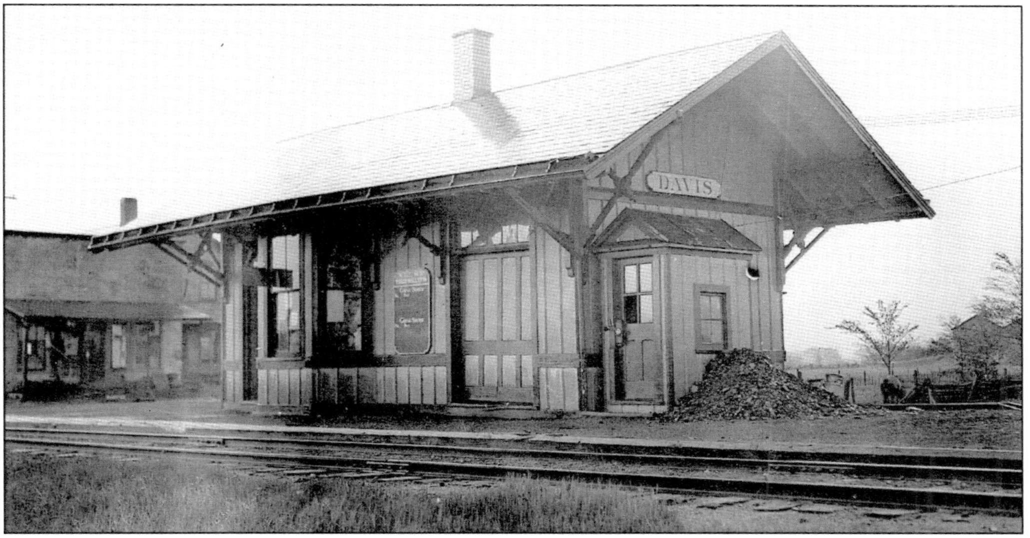

Another design was used at Davis. The small shed is a telephone booth. Although winter is a few months off, the agent has a ready pile of coal. The depot disappeared long ago. (NYC Railroad photograph, 1919, Allen County [Ohio] Historical Society collection.)

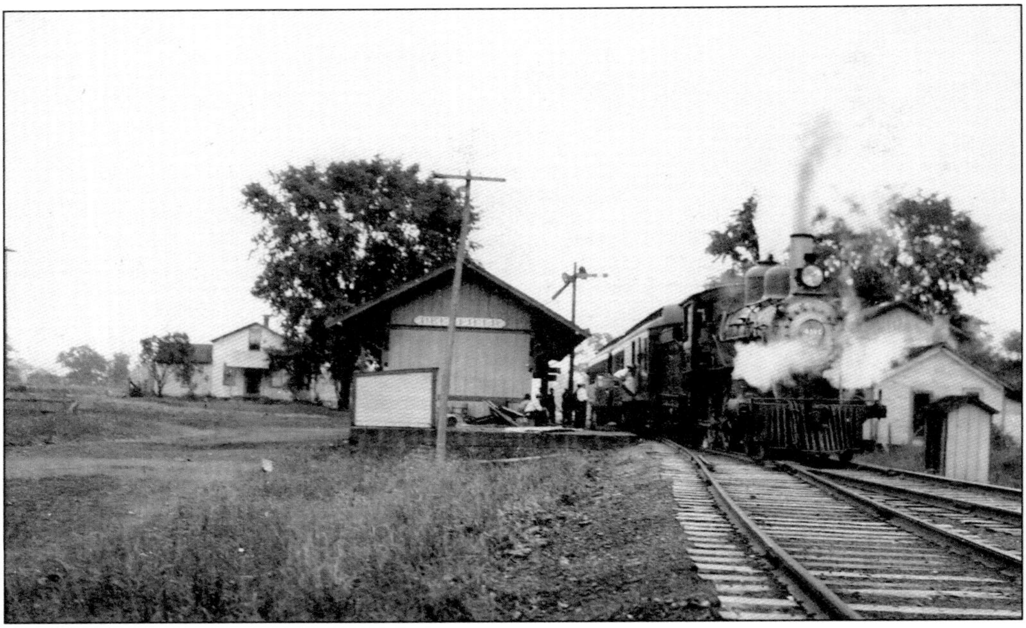

It is train time at Deerfield! Parcels and luggage are being loaded on the combination baggage-coach on this southbound two-car passenger train around 1907. Deerfield's depot no longer exists. (Mark J. Camp collection.)

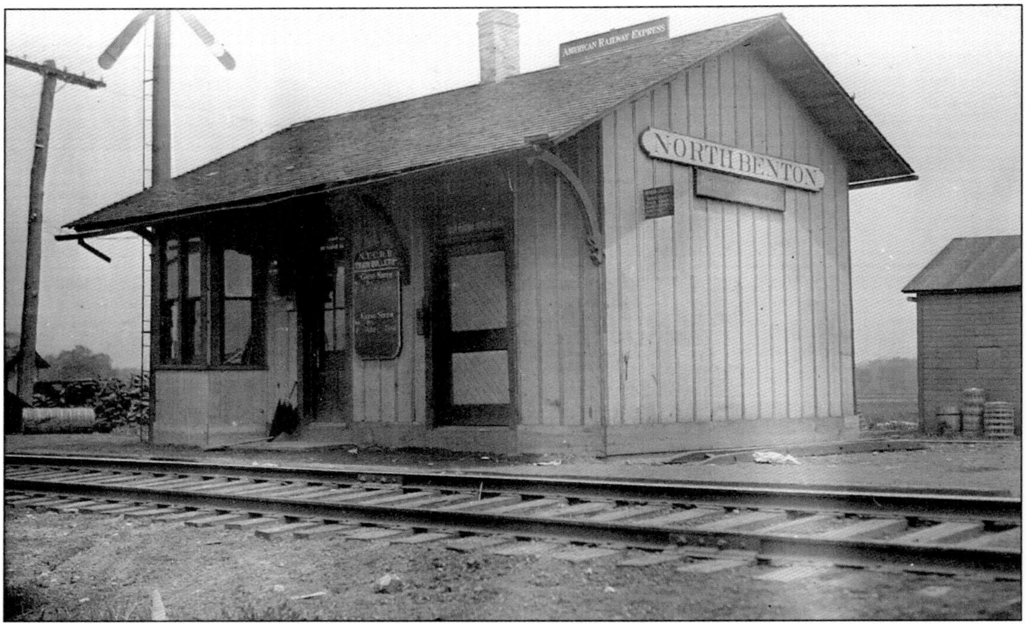

The LEA&W depot at North Benton is of still another design. By 1919, the structure was showing its years. It has been gone for many years. (NYC Railroad photograph, Allen County [Ohio] Historical Society collection.)

Four

Nickel Plate Lines

The New York Chicago and St. Louis Railroad (NYC&StL), commonly referred to as the Nickel Plate, completed its line from Buffalo to Chicago in record time during 1881–1882. Three days after its opening in October 1882, however, the Nickel Plate was taken over by the NYC and LS&MS, its direct competitor between Buffalo and Chicago. In 1916, the NYC was forced to divest itself of the Nickel Plate, and it was purchased by the Van Sweringen Brothers of Cleveland. After mid-1900 financial difficulties the NYC&StL leased the Wheeling and Lake Erie Railroad (W&LE) in 1949. The Nickel Plate became part of the Norfolk and Western Railroad in 1964. The line ran its last passenger trains along the former Nickel Plate on September 9, 1965.

The W&LE was chartered in 1871 to connect Lake Erie with the Ohio River and the coalfields of southeastern Ohio. The main line of the W&LE, completed in 1892, passed south of Akron and Cleveland, but the line obtained access to Cleveland's lake port by gaining trackage rights on the Cleveland, Terminal and Valley Railroad (CT&V) from Justus to Cleveland. In August 1899, the W&LE obtained an exclusive entrance to Cleveland by purchasing the Cleveland, Canton and Southern Railroad (CC&S). In the same year it also took over the Cleveland, Belt and Terminal Railroad, which opened in 1893 with tracks between the CC&S and the Big Four in Cleveland. August 1877 marks the chartering of the Youngstown and Connotton Valley Railroad, a narrow-gauge line originally projected to connect Youngstown with Bowerston on the W&LE mainline. By 1879, the line became the Connotton Valley Railroad. Financial difficulties beset the line in the mid-1880s, but by 1885 the main line stretched southward from Cleveland, the new northern terminus, to Coshocton. In November 1888, the railroad, then known as the Cleveland and Canton, was converted to standard gauge. In 1892, the railroad, by then known as the CC&S, expanded by taking over three smaller lines. One of the smaller lines was the Cleveland, Chagrin Falls and Northern, which opened between Solon and Falls Junction in July 1890 and connected with the old Painesville, Canton and Bridgeport Railroad, a former narrow-gauge line connecting Chagrin Falls with Solon. Receivership came for the CC&S in 1893.

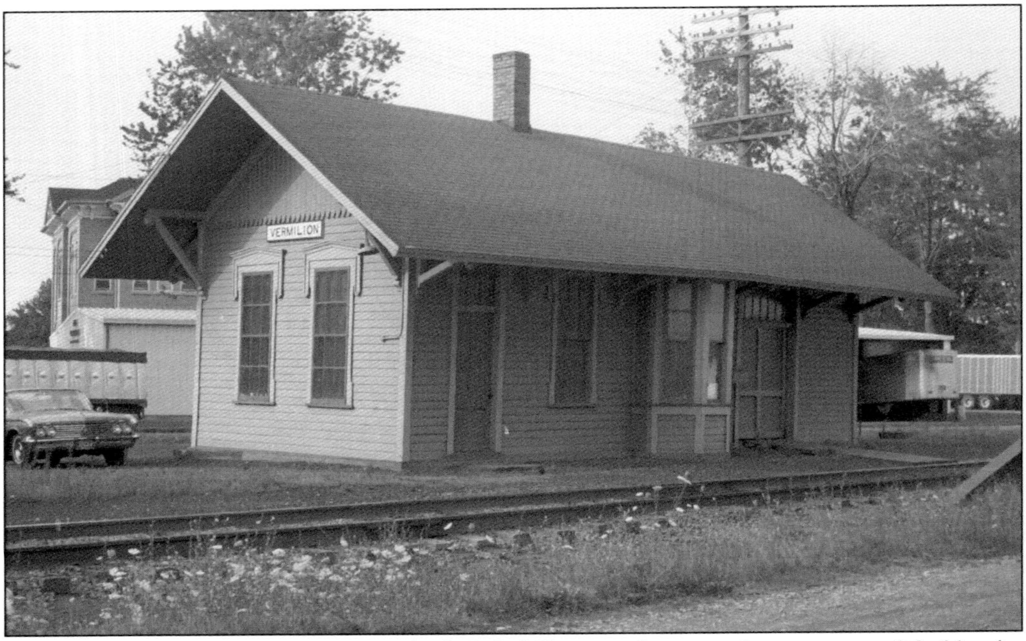

The basic plan of the 1881–1882 standard Nickel Plate combination depot is exemplified by the depot at Vermilion, seen here in 1966. Identifying elements include the scalloped boards under the end eaves, somewhat rounded bay windows, and ornate lintels. Vermilion has since been moved off the right-of-way and is under restoration. (Charles Garvin photograph.)

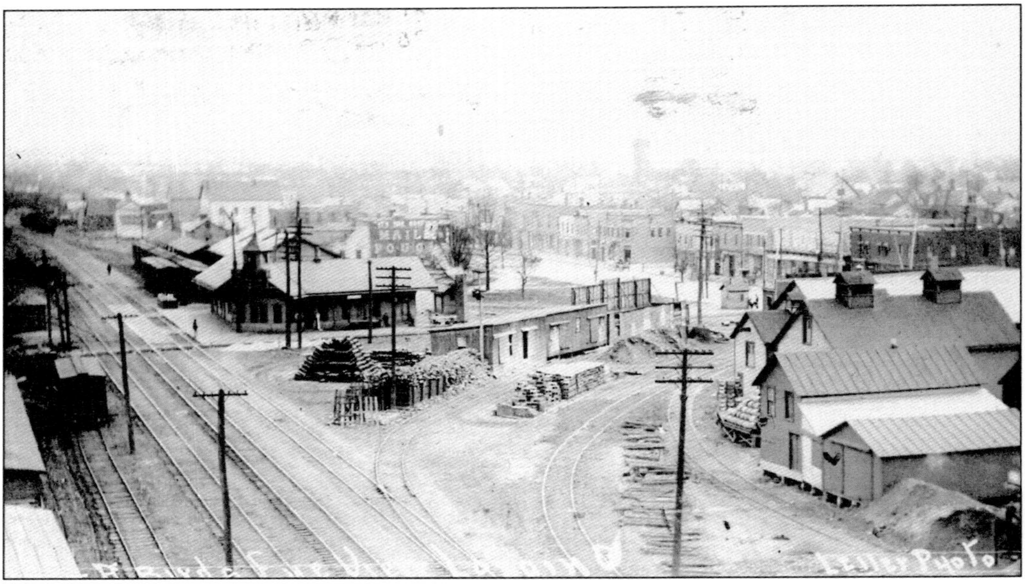

At Lorain the Nickel Plate (running right and left) crossed the former Cleveland Lorain and Wheeling Railroad. The lines shared this L-shaped passenger depot. The NYC&StL freight house is out of view to the right; the B&O freight house is behind the passenger depot. The depot was still there in the early 1970s, but all that remains today is a modified B&O freight house and the freight crane from the platform of the NYC&StL freight house. (Mark J. Camp collection.)

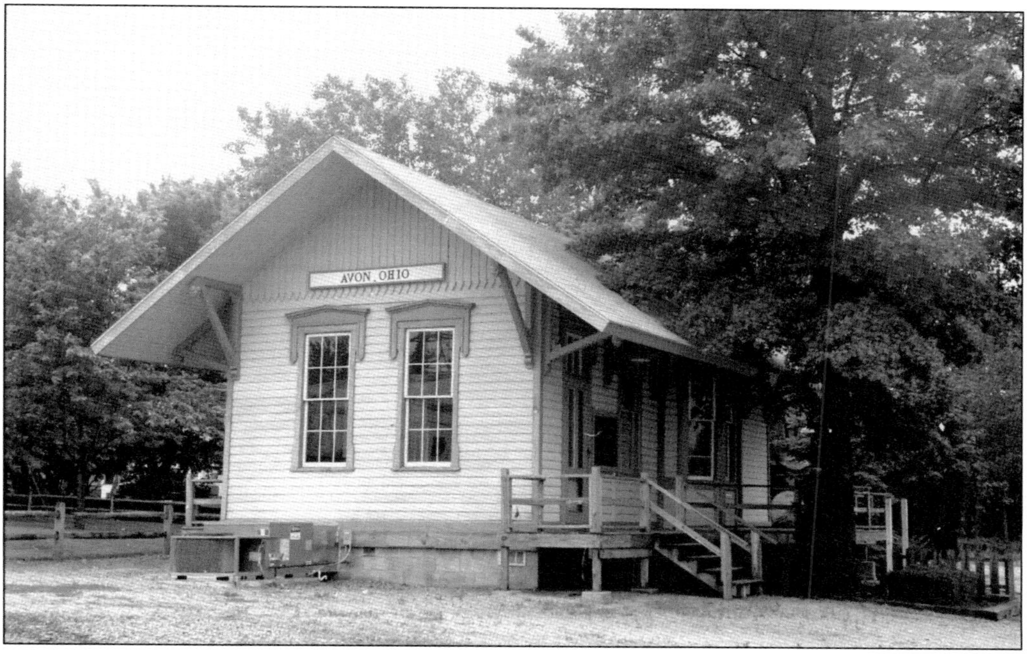

The Nickel Plate depots at Avon and Bay Village date from 1882. Bay Village's depot was originally called Dover. Both depots were relegated to freight service in 1940. The Bay Village agency closed in 1958. Both have been relocated, and their railroad motif has been preserved. Avon was for a while a hobby shop. Bay Village is now a community center.

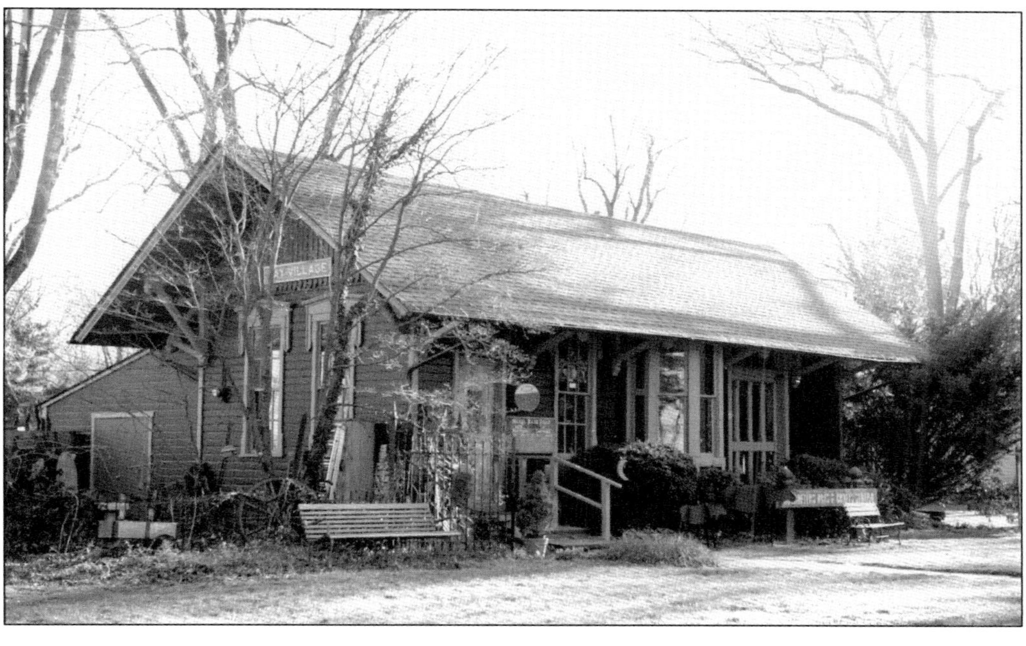

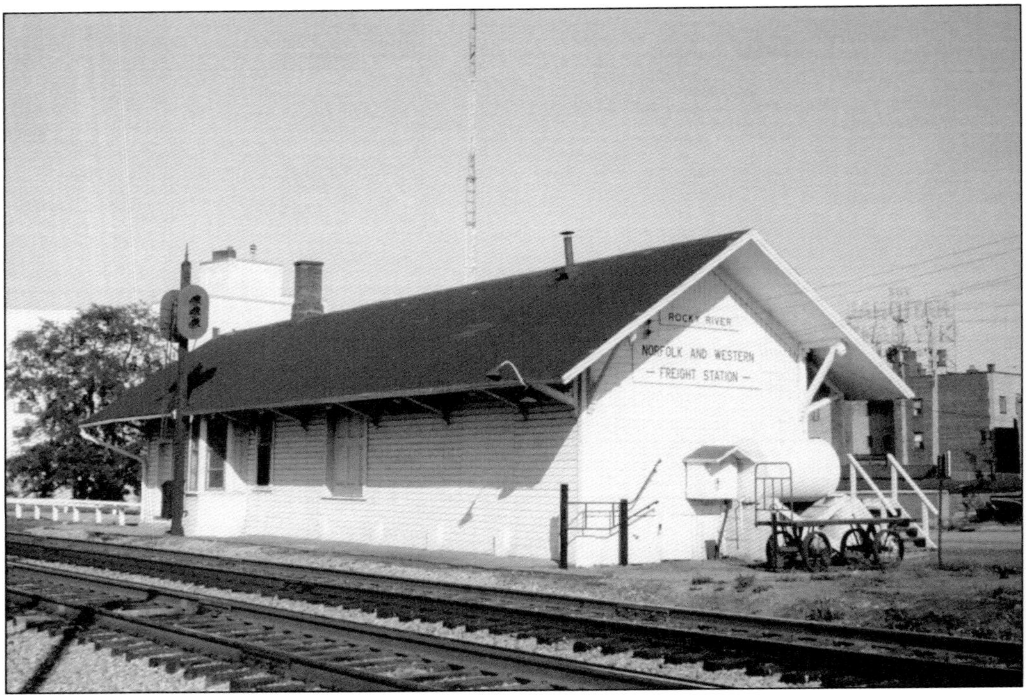

Rocky River's 1881–1882 Nickel Plate depot remains on site.

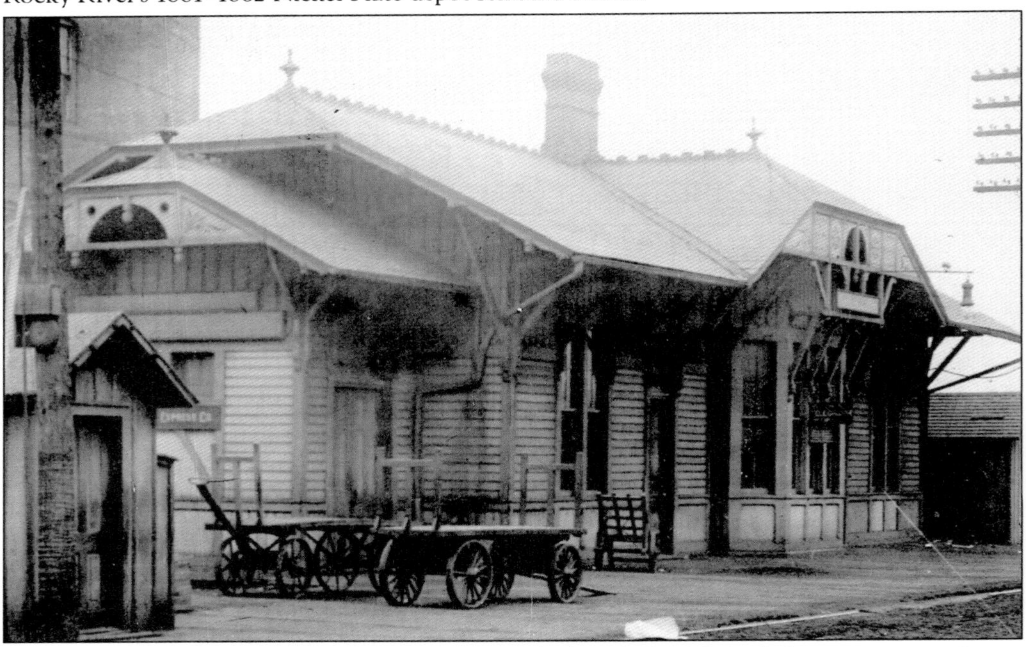

Before the opening of Cleveland Union Terminal, the NYC&StL had three passenger depots within Cleveland. On the west side of downtown was the West Twenty-fifth Street depot. Built in 1881, the blueprints of this gingerbread-adorned structure were also used at Fort Wayne, Indiana, and Erie, Pennsylvania. In 1905, the platform appeared a quiet place in between trains. (Photograph collection of Cleveland Public Library.)

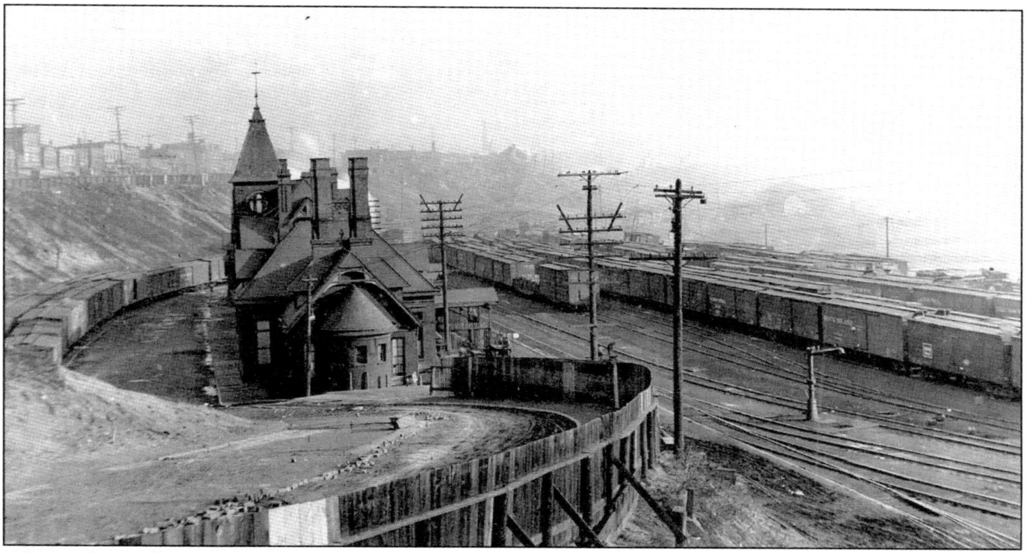

Along the valley of the Cuyahoga River was the 1881 Broadway Avenue depot. This was the main NYC&StL depot for Cleveland for 45 years. In 1922, the air pollution of the industrialized valley is plainly evident. Broadway depot was torn down to make way for the approach tracks of Cleveland Union Terminal. (Photograph collection of Cleveland Public Library.)

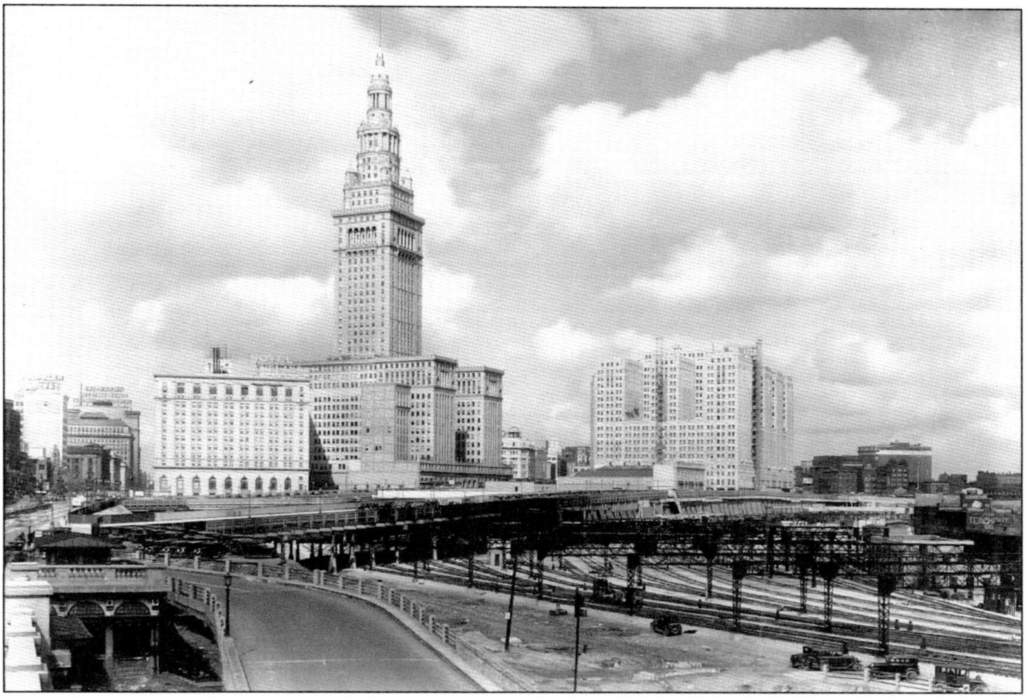

The 17-acre Terminal Tower complex was constructed on Public Square between 1924 and 1934. Cleveland Union Terminal hosted its first train on October 23, 1929, and formally opened on June 29, 1930. The terminal eventually served trains from the B&O, Big Four, Erie, NYC, and Nickel Plate and rapid transit. Last passenger service was in 1977. Tower City Center was developed in the old railroad concourse. (Cleveland State University Library Special Collections.)

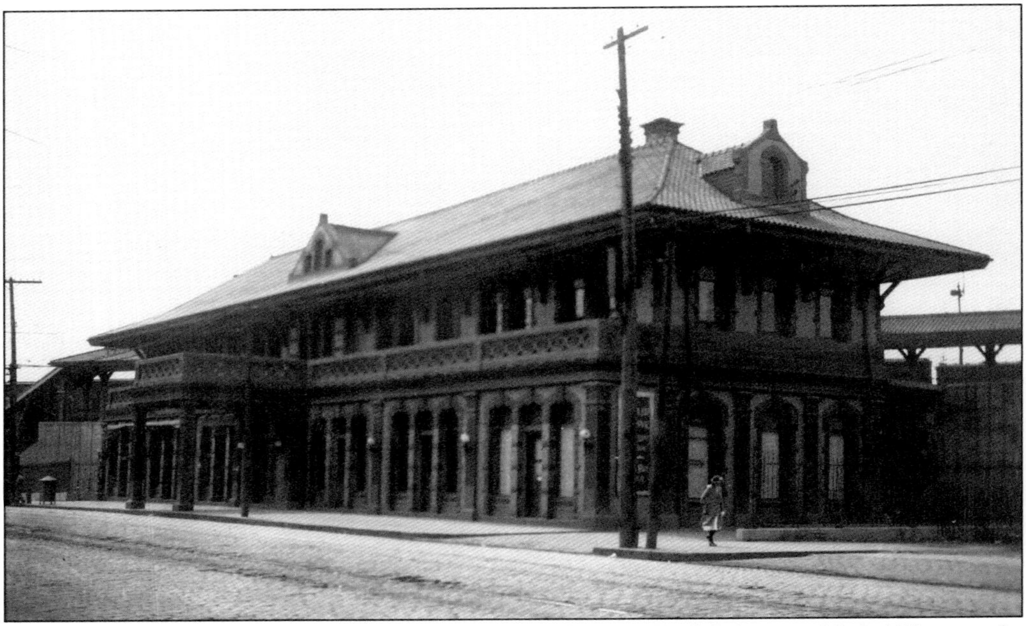

Another Cleveland Nickel Plate depot was the one above at Euclid Avenue. Nickel Plate tracks came into the second level of this structure, built in 1910, which like Broadway Avenue depot, is unique among Nickel Plate structures. This depot, located far from the grime of the Cuyahoga River valley, became the favored boarding spot for Clevelanders. August 19, 1929, was the last day of business because it was in the path of the electrified NYC tracks into Union Terminal. The depot below, a joint NYC-NYC&StL, facility opened on June 22, 1930, replacing the Nickel Plate's Euclid Avenue depot. Here steam locomotives yielded their coaches to the electric locomotives for the final distance into Union Terminal. The depot was there until the 1960s. (Above, photograph collection of Cleveland Public Library; below, Cleveland State University Library Special Collections.)

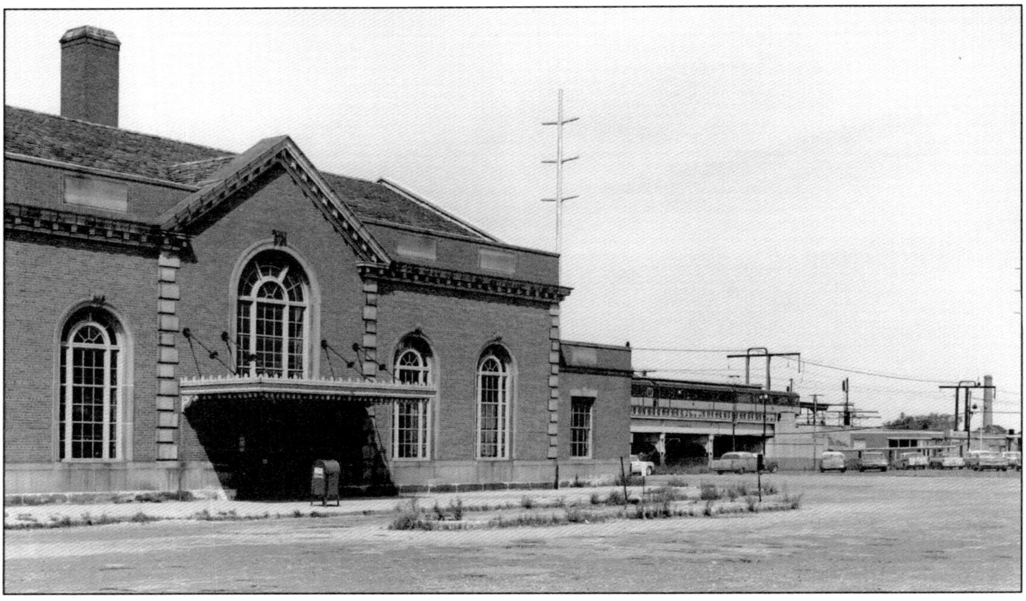

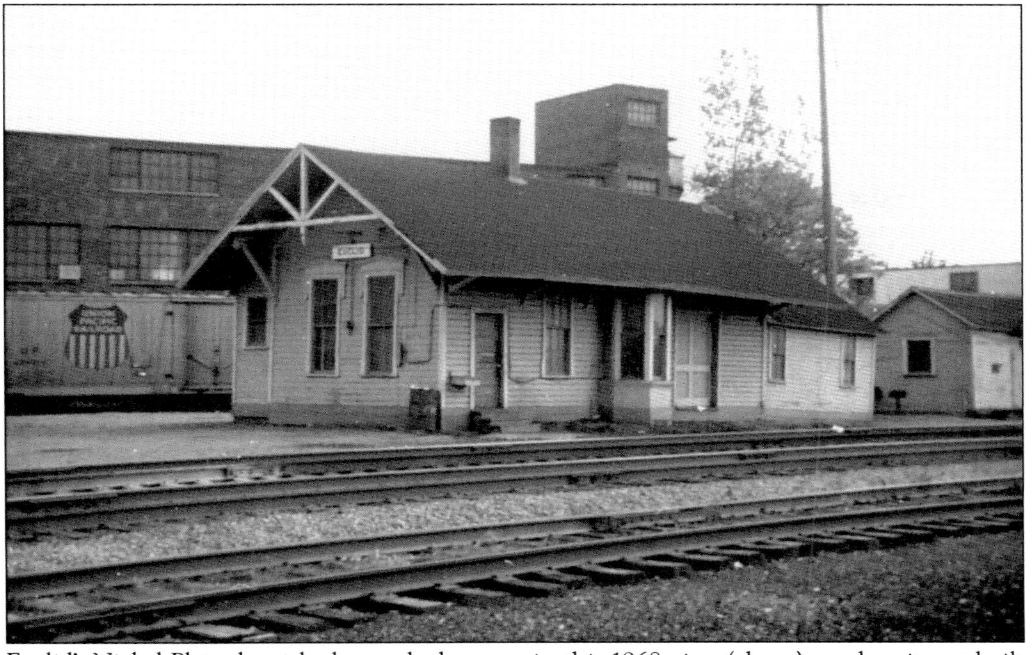

Euclid's Nickel Plate depot looks much the same in this 1968 view (above) as when it was built in 1881, except for the restroom addition on the back. Another standard combination depot was at Wickliffe. By the time of this 1965 photograph (below), passenger service and the Nickel Plate itself had disappeared. Both depots have since been retired.

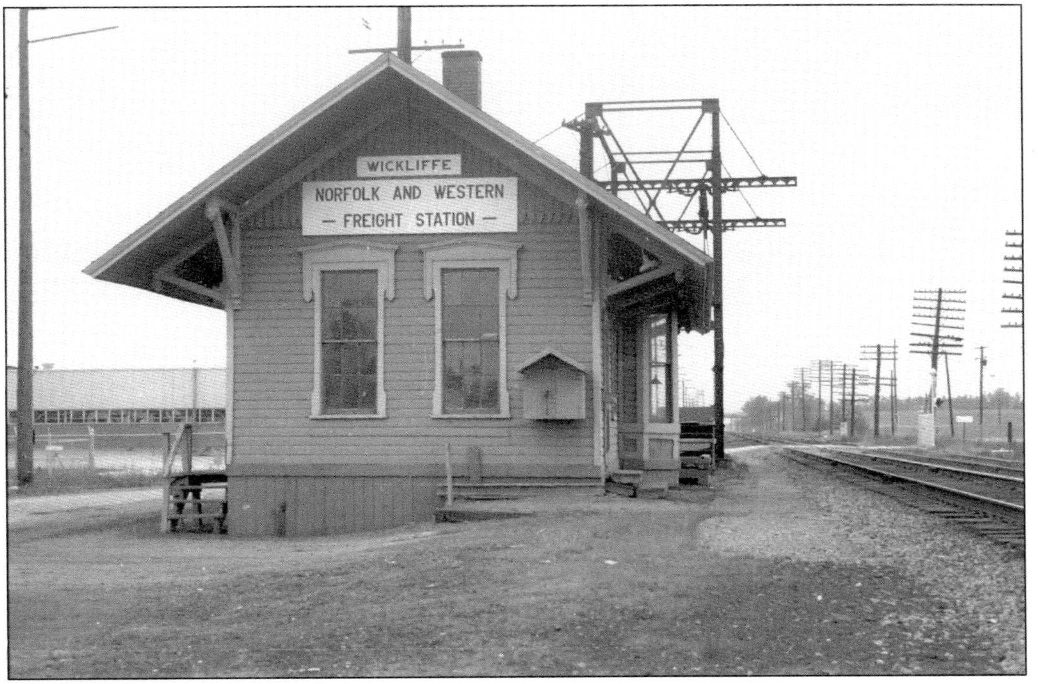

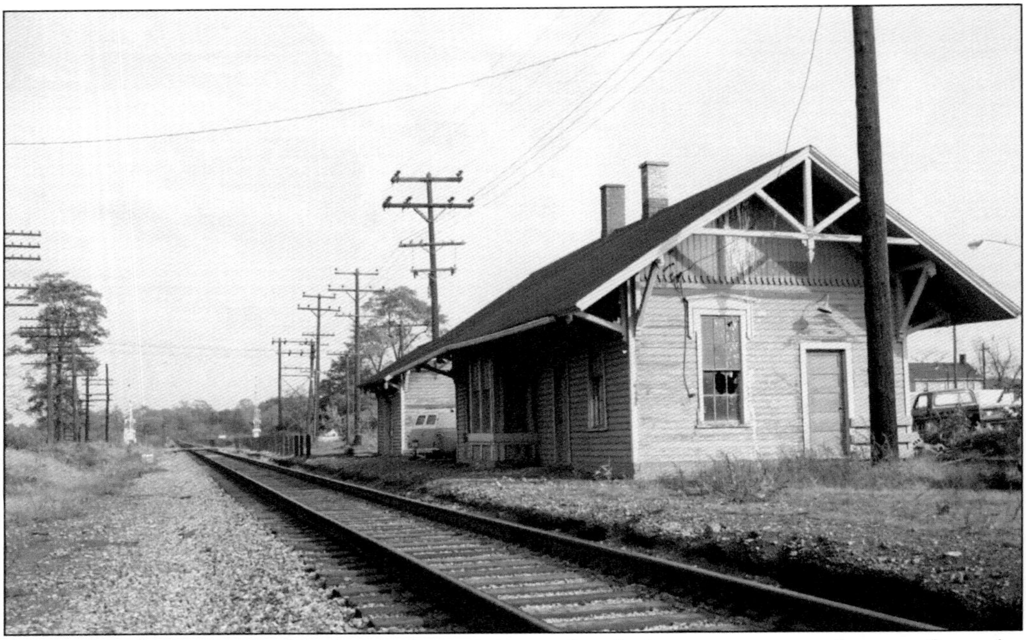

Willoughby had considerable freight business, so a freight house was erected across from the passenger depot. Painesville, being a larger city, had a larger passenger and freight depot. The Painesville freight house is out of view. The small building is a baggage shed. Note the difference that 20 years made. The Willoughby view was taken in 1966; the Painesville photograph was shot in 1947. By the 1960s, a number of portable frame buildings were placed adjacent to the depot for track maintenance use. At the crossing of the B&O was brick PE tower. Only a couple of small prefabricated railroad sheds remain in Willoughby and Painesville today. (Above, Charles Garvin photograph; below, Paul W. Prescott photograph.)

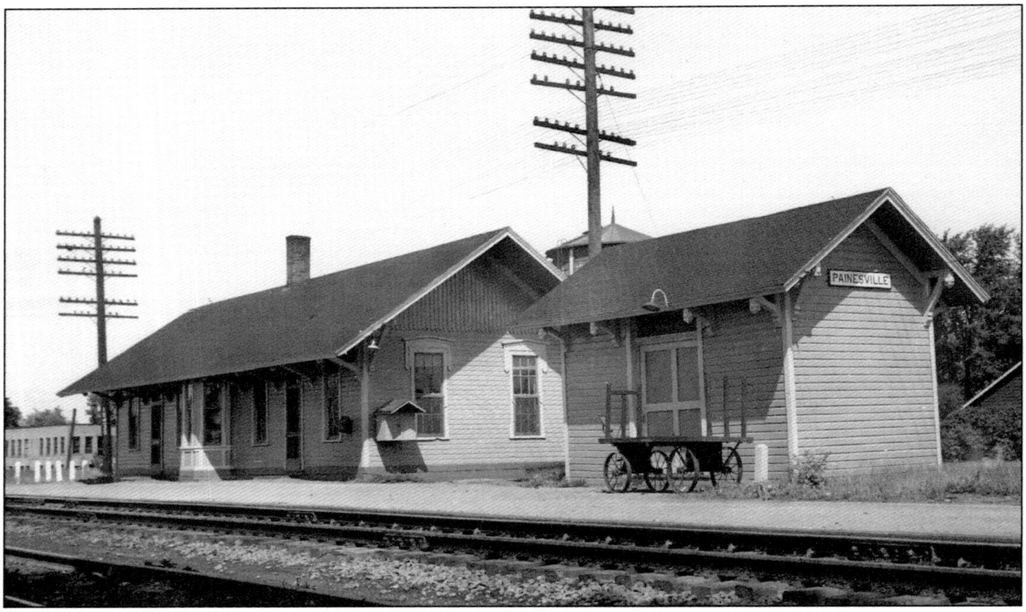

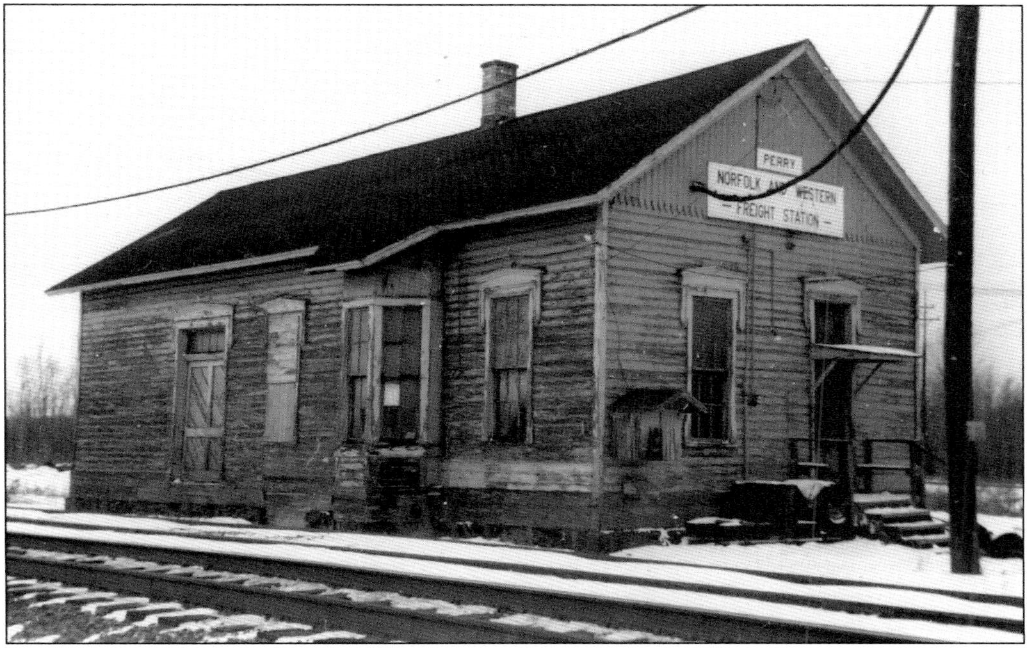

Perry's Nickel Plate combination depot suffered the indignity of having its roofline shortened to allow the passage of wider-clearance freight cars on the station siding. The depot is pictured in 1978; it would not last much longer. Below is an early-1900s view of the Nickel Plate depot and adjacent baggage shed at Madison. This vintage view shows the pride each agent took in his depot and the surrounding grounds. A freight house was also built across the tracks from the passenger depot. Sometime before the 1960s, the vestibule on the passenger depot was doubled in size and the roof overhangs at the ends of the depot were shortened. Today the freight house has been restored and the baggage shed moved to downtown; the passenger depot was torn down. (Mark J. Camp collection.)

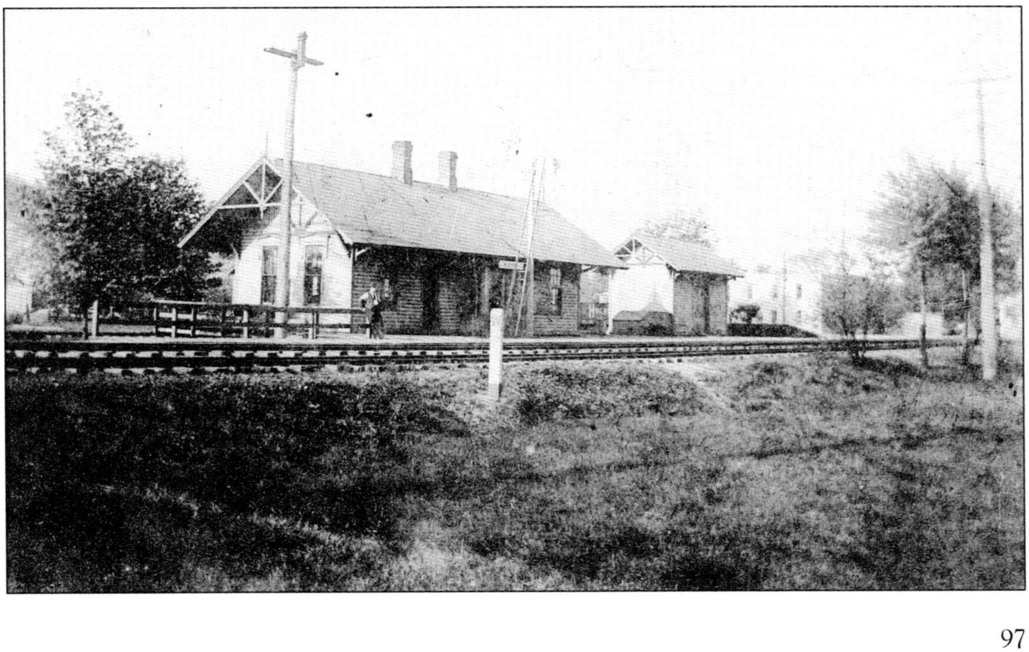

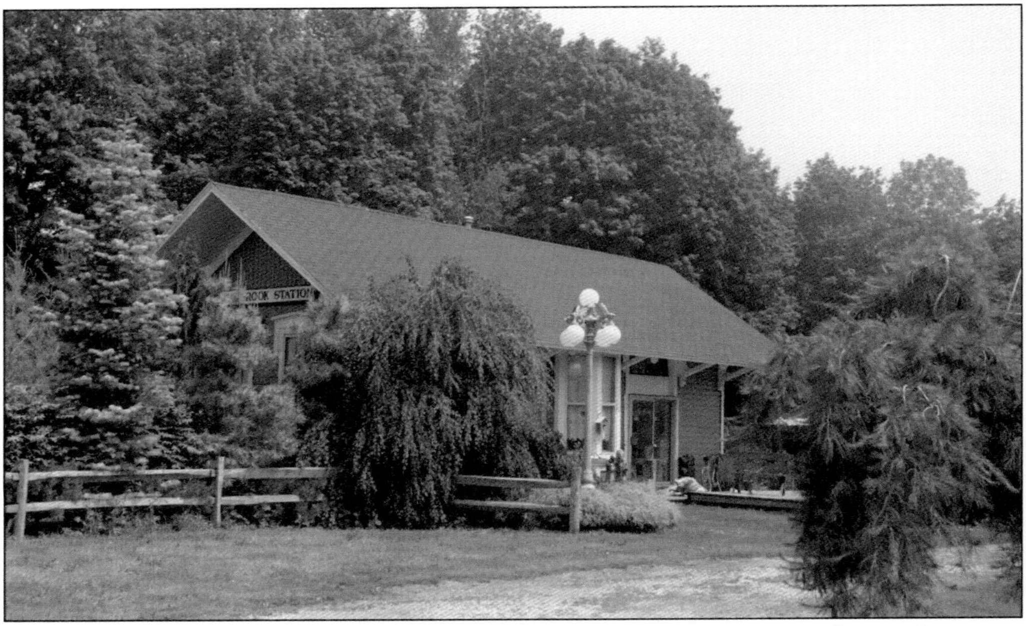

Saybrook's standard-design 1882 Nickel Plate depot was closed in 1950 and moved twice to its present location along Depot Road. Ashtabula was served by three main line railroads in later years: the NYC, Nickel Plate, and Pennsylvania Railroad. Although shops of the NYC and a terminal of the PRR were garnered by the city, the Nickel Plate chose to put its shops at Conneaut. Ashtabula had an 1881 standard-design passenger depot and freight house. At the crossing of the former LS&MS near Adams Avenue was NP tower. The concrete block tower dated from 1912 but has since been removed. The Nickel Plate passenger depot was demolished in February 1990.

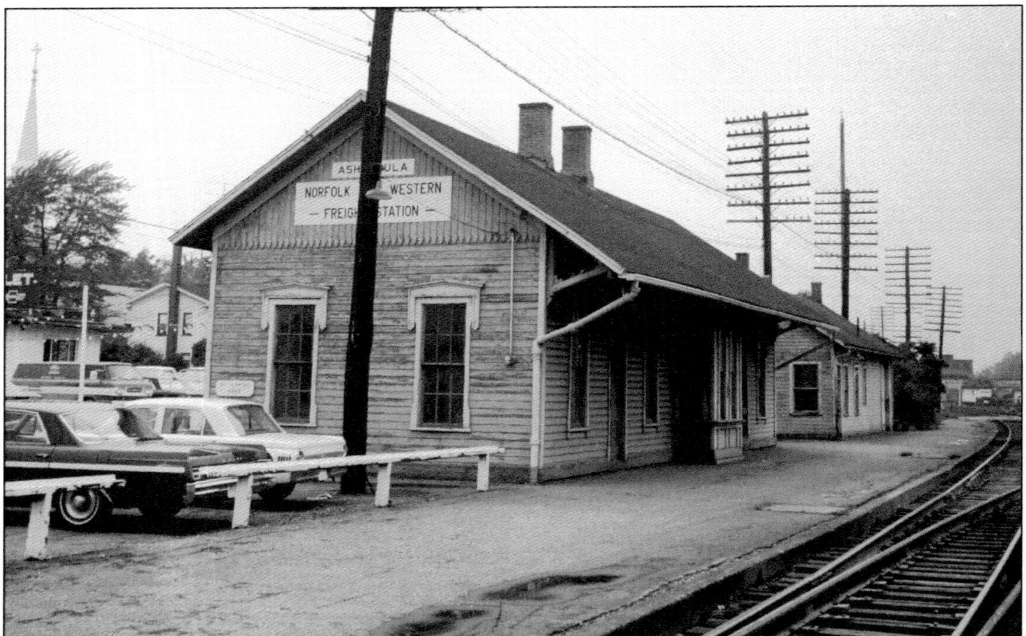

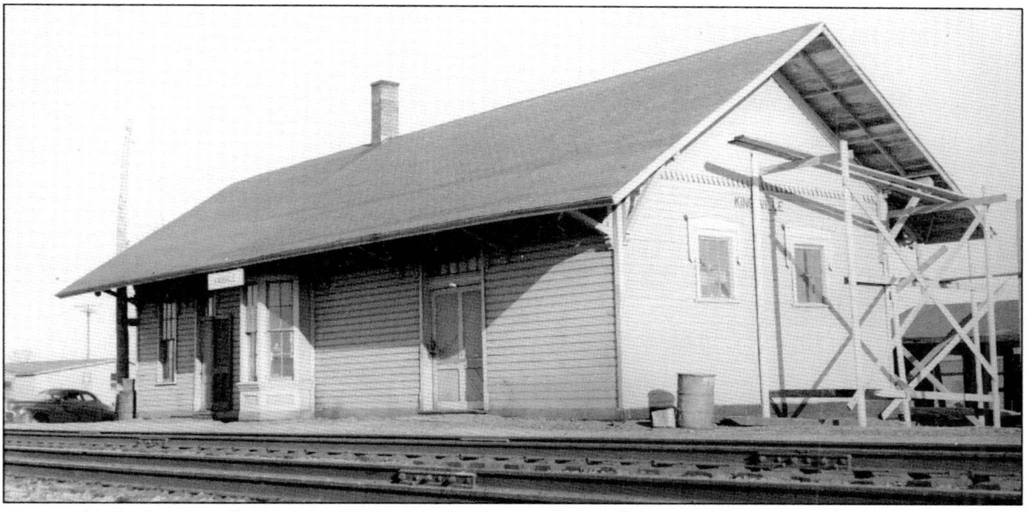

A standard-plan combination depot was built at Kingsville in 1881. In March 1947, the depot was receiving some roof repairs. Note that the town name was stenciled directly on the end wall, not on a town board. Kingsville remained boarded up along the track for a number of years before being moved. (Paul W. Prescott photograph.)

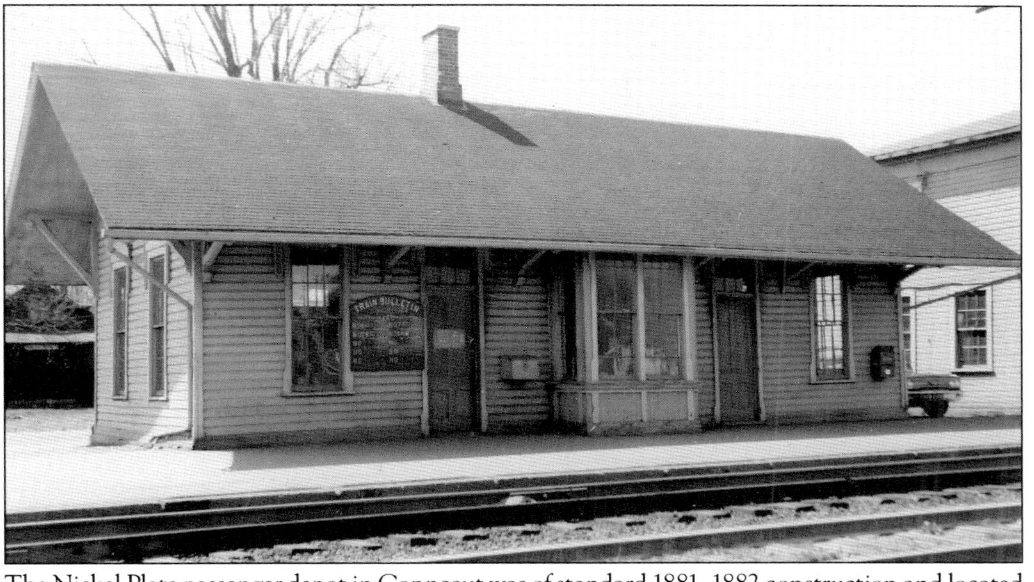

The Nickel Plate passenger depot in Conneaut was of standard 1881–1882 construction and located at the Mill Street crossing. Adjacent to the depot until 1966 was a baggage building. The depot was demolished on August 1, 1966. The adjacent engineers office, formerly a dining hall, was torn down in September 1967. The two-story division office building was the last significant Nickel Plate building to be torn down, lasting into the 1980s. (Paul W. Prescott photograph, 1963.)

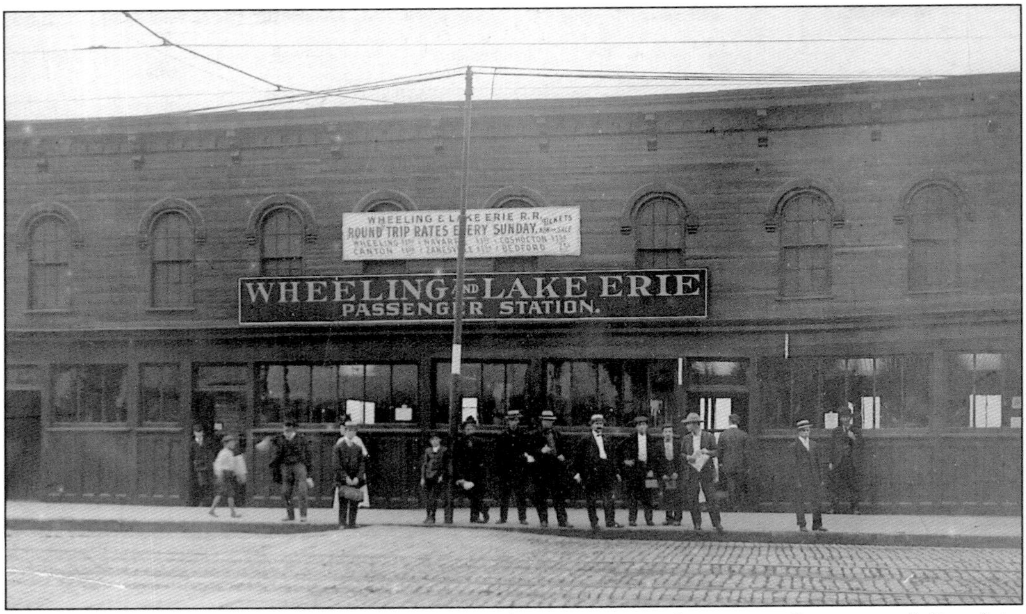

The narrow-gauge Connotton Valley opened a passenger depot on Commercial Road in downtown Cleveland in 1881. The above depot was opened on August 29, 1883, at the corner of Ontario Street and Huron Road on the edge of the Cuyahoga Valley, a part of downtown Cleveland known as Vinegar Hill. Financial problems hit hard in 1883, and the depot saw little use by its original builders. The W&LE took over this station in 1899 and replaced it with the depot below in 1909. The new depot was built adjacent to the old depot. The second Vinegar Hill depot was supposed to be a temporary depot, but it lasted until the area was needed for approach tracks to Cleveland Union Terminal in 1929. The older depot was located in the grassy area to the left. (Photograph collection of Cleveland Public Library.)

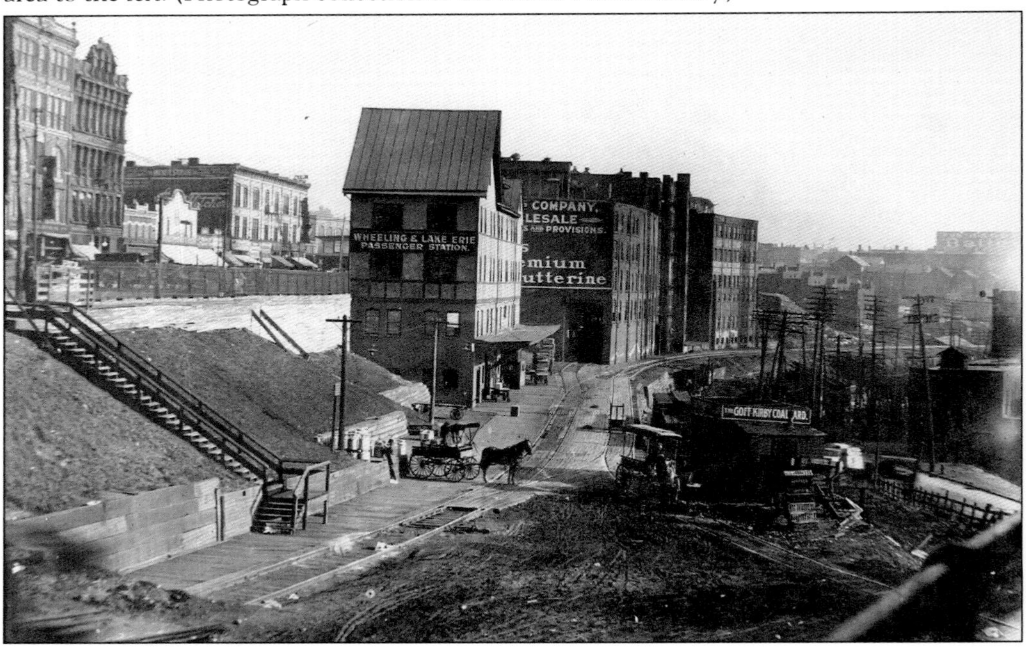

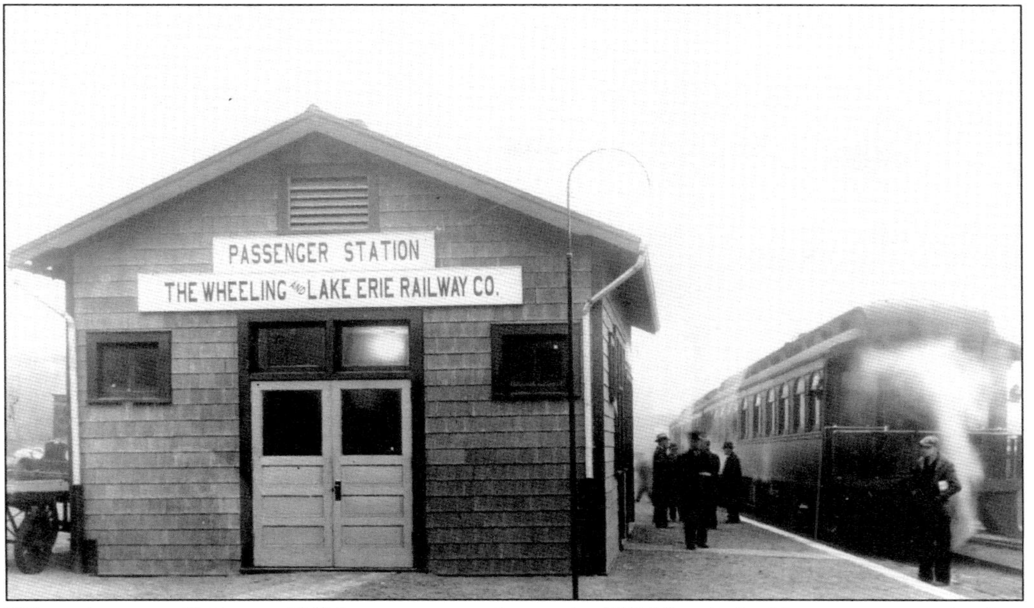

When the second Vinegar Hill depot was torn down, the W&LE switched its passenger trains first to the nearby Erie depot and then to this small frame depot on Commercial Road, shown brand-new in 1935. This was the last passenger depot to be built by the line in Cleveland. It served the city for less than three years before the W&LE terminated passenger service between Cleveland, Canton and Wheeling on July 17, 1938. (Photograph collection of Cleveland Public Library.)

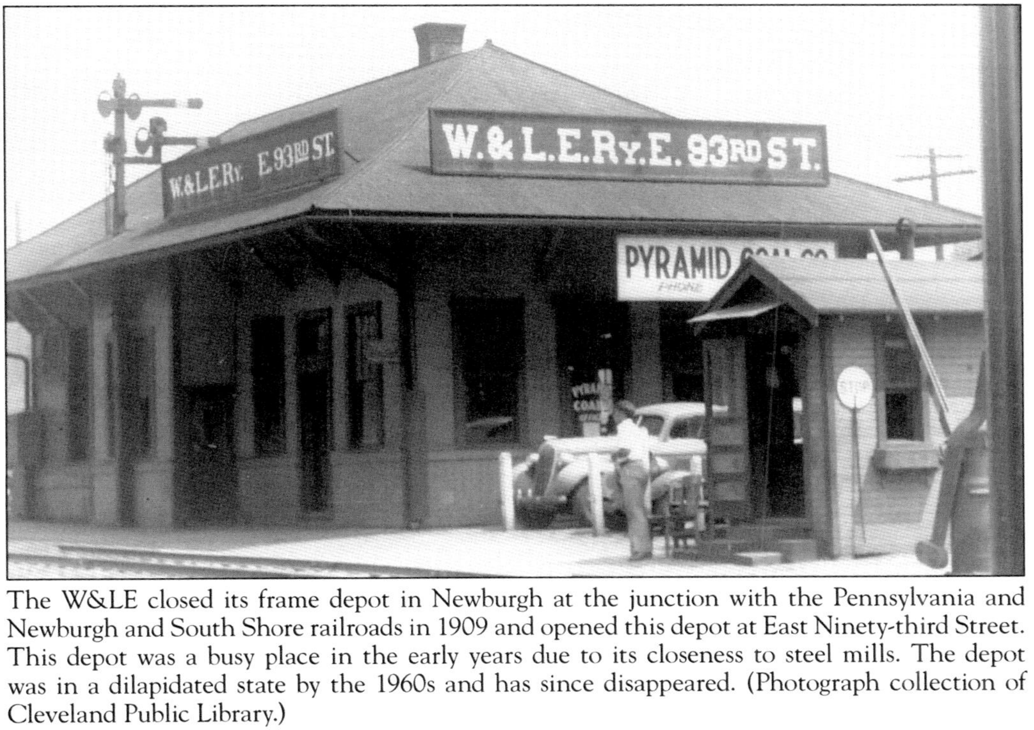

The W&LE closed its frame depot in Newburgh at the junction with the Pennsylvania and Newburgh and South Shore railroads in 1909 and opened this depot at East Ninety-third Street. This depot was a busy place in the early years due to its closeness to steel mills. The depot was in a dilapidated state by the 1960s and has since disappeared. (Photograph collection of Cleveland Public Library.)

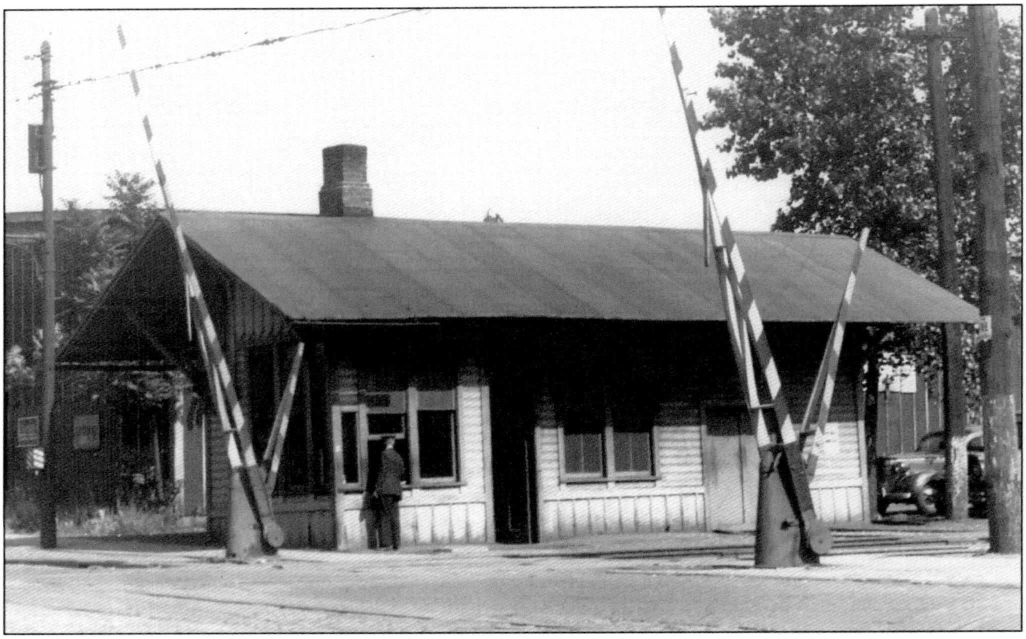

The W&LE depot at Miles Avenue in Cleveland was built to a standard plan. The agent talks to an assistant on a warm summer day in 1935. The pneumatic gates at Miles Avenue were controlled from an elevated watchman's tower. It was gone before the 1960s. (Photograph collection of Cleveland Public Library.)

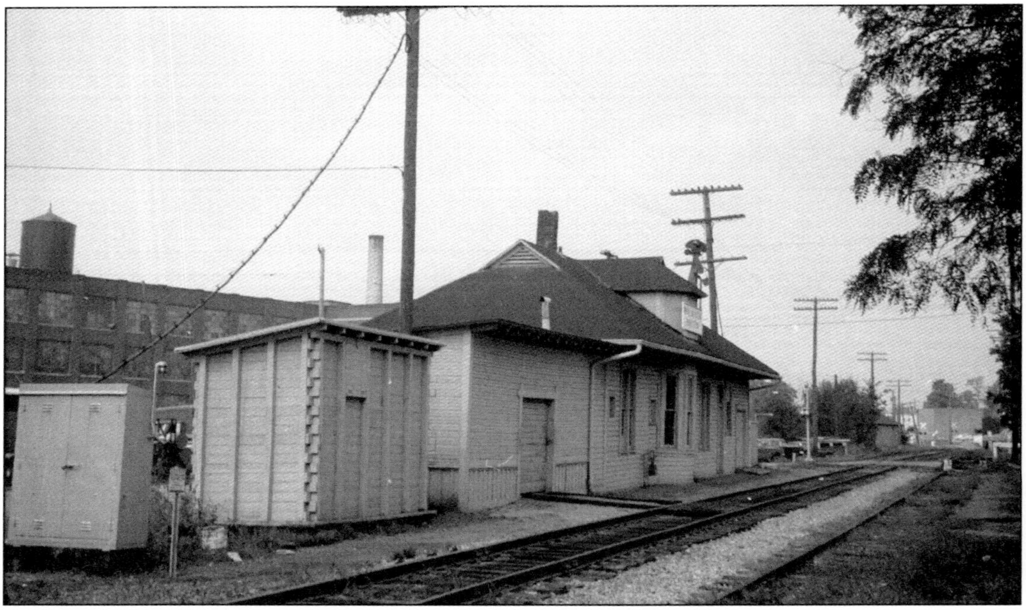

The W&LE depot at Bedford was built in 1881 by predecessor Connotton Valley. At that time the track ended here and passengers had to board trains of the Cleveland and Pittsburgh Railroad to travel into Cleveland. Around 1895, an open shelter was erected along West Glendale Street to serve passengers in that area. Bedford's depot has been restored and now serves as a railroad museum and chamber of commerce.

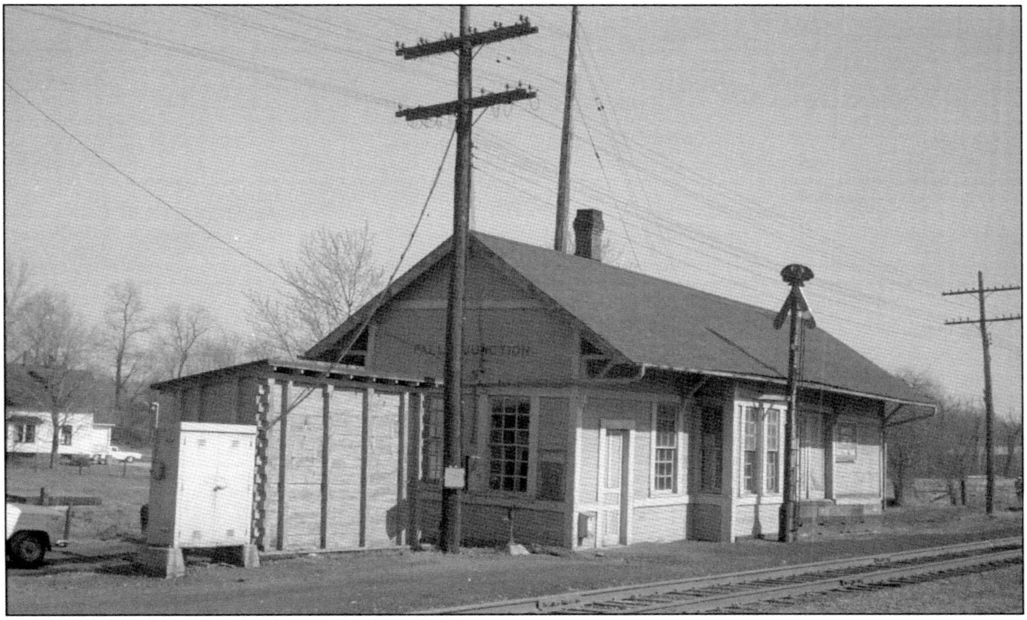

The CC&S erected the above depot at Falls Junction around 1890 where a line to Solon and Chagrin Falls joined. The depot was in active railroad use until 1974. In 1877, passenger and freight depots were opened on East Washington Street in Chagrin Falls by the narrow-gauge Painesville, Canton and Bridgeport Railroad, which ran from Chagrin Falls to the C&MV line in Solon. It was converted to standard gauge when the connector between Solon and Falls Junction was made in 1890. Passenger service to Chagrin Falls ended in 1932. The freight depot was then modified by the W&LE, as seen below in 1969. The Falls Junction depot remains on site, having been turned over to a railroad preservation group in 1993; the freight house from Chagrin Falls now resides in Claridon Township.

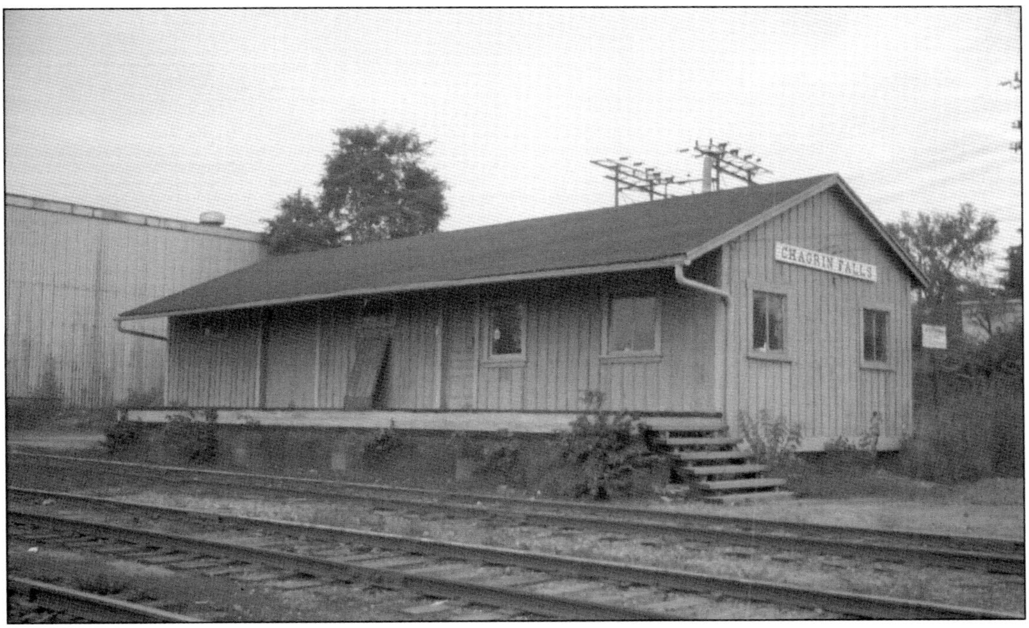

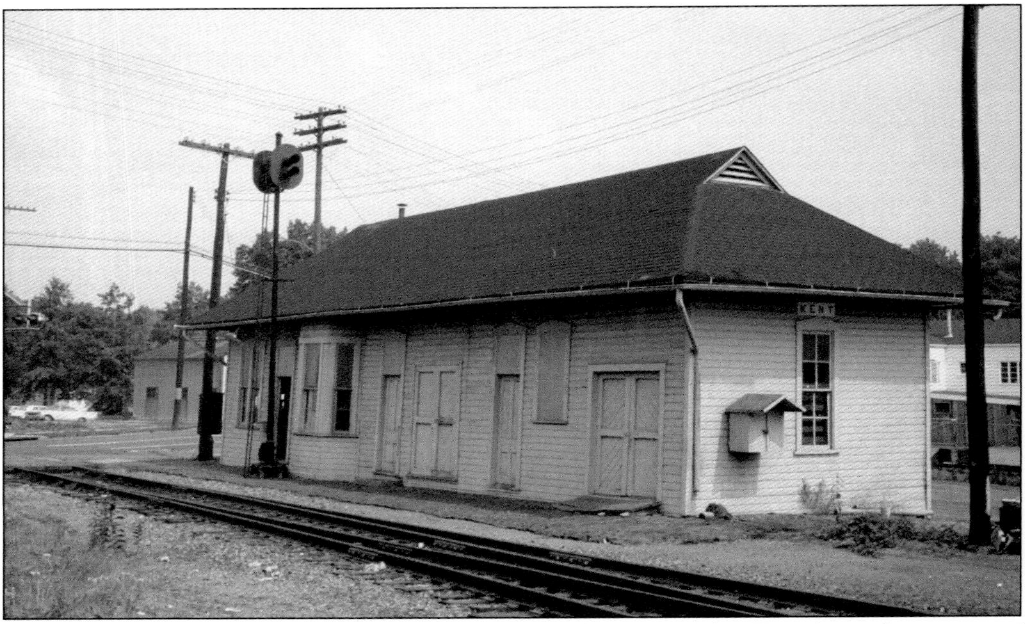

The W&LE also manned depots at Twinsburg and Moran. The Twinsburg depot was of Connotton Valley ancestry and dated from 1881. The rural Moran depot served mainly as a telegraph office and lasted from 1899 until 1948. Another depot of Connotton Valley vintage is the one at Kent. It dates from 1881 and is very similar to a towerless Bedford depot. It remains as a feed store.

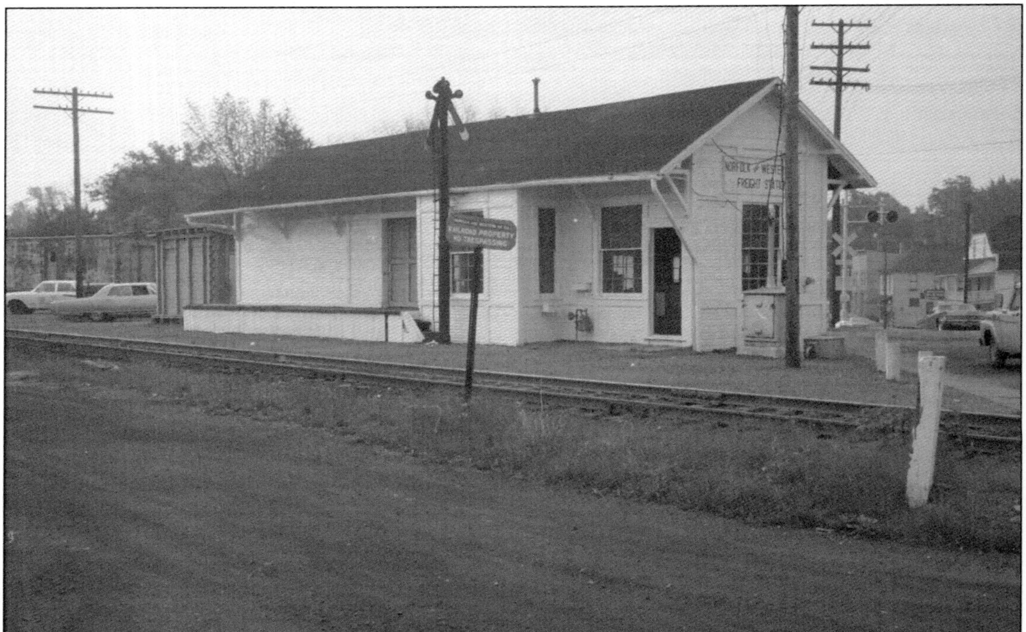

Mogadore's W&LE depot, shown here in 1967, is of standard design. It has been relocated in town and restored as a museum.

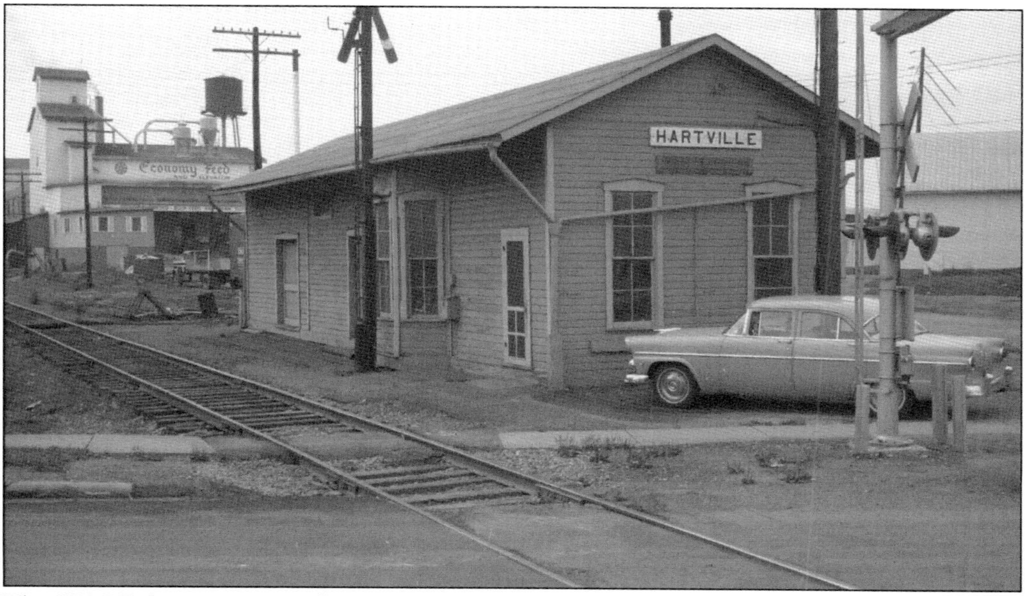

The W&LE depot in Hartville is still serving the Norfolk and Western Railway in this 1967 photograph. It has been restored by the local historical society.

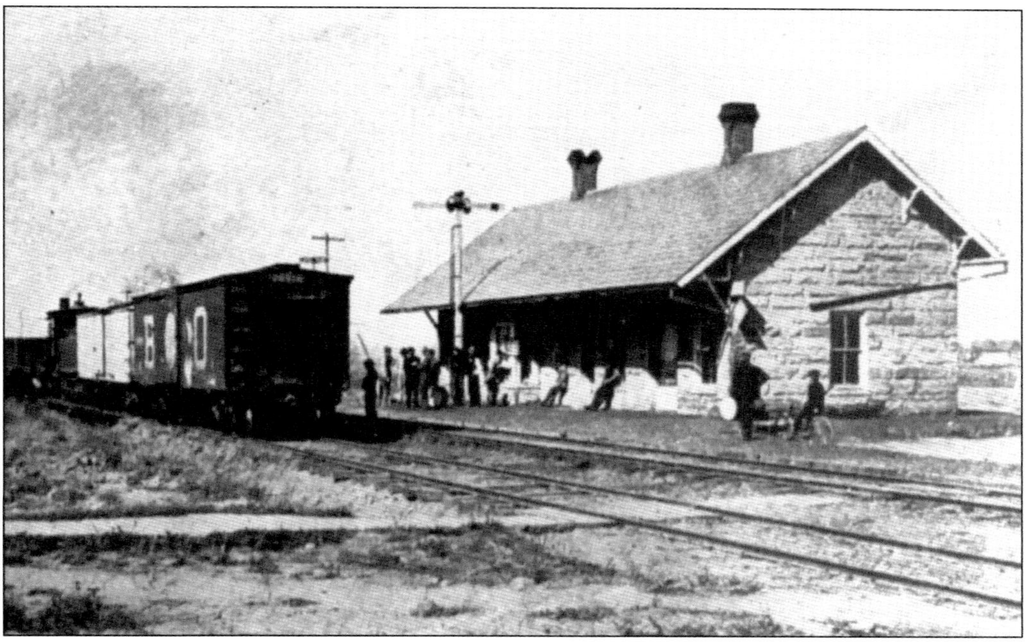
Back on the main line of the W&LE is a unique depot at Clarksfield. This combination depot was built of sandstone quarried from the dimension stone quarry in West Clarksfield. The depot probably dates from the 1890s. It was torn down many years ago. Just a few miles west at Hartland, the old W&LE depot was replaced by a metal prefabricated building by the 1960s. This structure has also been removed. (Mark J. Camp collection.)

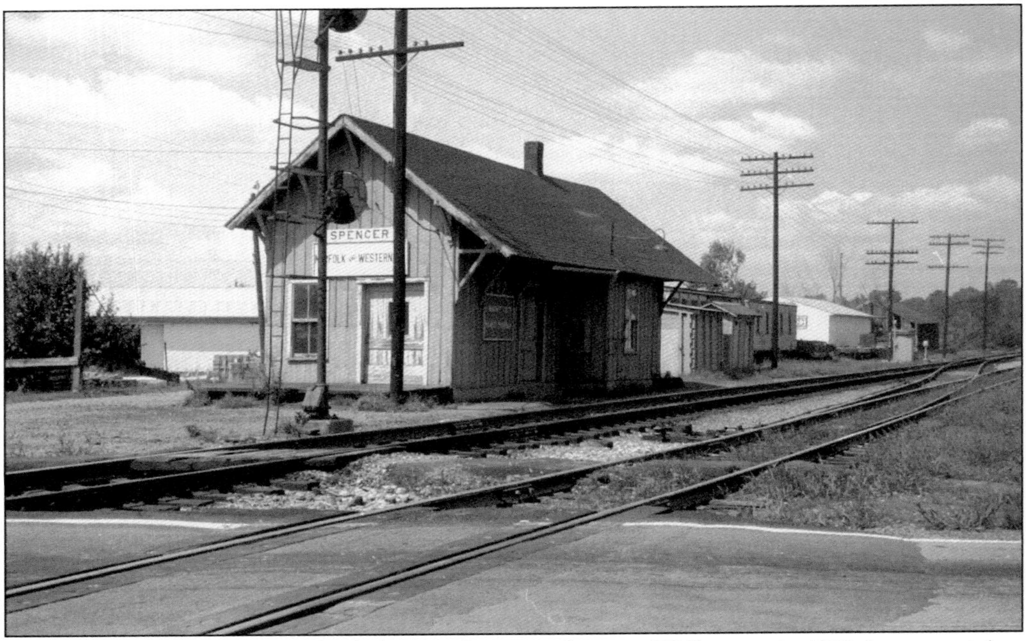

The W&LE built a large standard-plan combination depot at Wellington in 1881, however, it has been gone since the mid-1900s. Spencer was an important interchange with the Akron, Canton and Youngstown Railroad (AC&Y). The 1881 depot was a smaller version of the standard plan and is still in railroad use in this 1967 picture. Unfortunately, it too is just a memory.

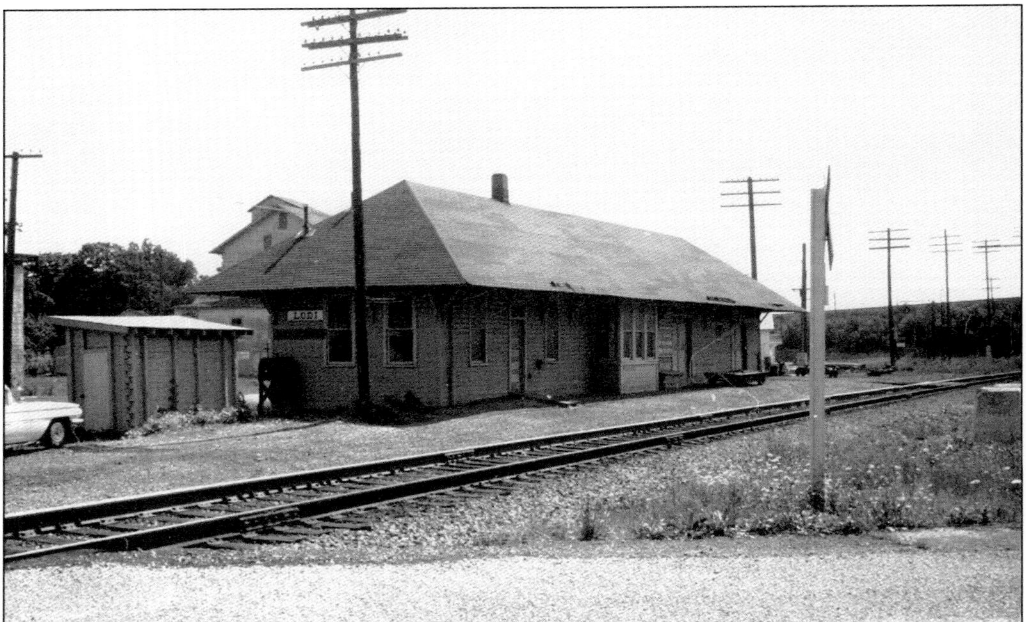

The W&LE combination depot at Lodi was busy with transfer business with the B&O that passed above town on its elevated right-of-way. It was built to a different plan than Spencer. In later years the depot served as storeroom for railroad maintenance crews. The depot remains in storage use.

Five

Pennsylvania Railroad Lines

Another early railroad in Northeast Ohio was the Cleveland, Warren and Pittsburgh Railroad, chartered in 1836. It was not until March 1847 and reorganization into the Cleveland and Pittsburgh Railroad (C&P) that track was completed between Cleveland and Ravenna. The C&P was completed to Wellsville and had constructed a branch to Akron and south to the main line of the Pennsylvania Railroad at Orrville by 1852. The C&P became part of the Pennsylvania Railroad in 1871. The Cleveland, Zanesville and Cincinnati Railroad (CZ&C) opened from Hudson on the C&P to Millersburg in 1852. The CZ&C became part of the Pittsburgh, Fort Wayne and Chicago Railroad in 1865. After a number of name changes the line was extended south of Millersburg to Columbus by 1873 and reorganized in 1885 as the Cleveland, Akron and Columbus Railroad (CA&C). In 1899, the CA&C fell under Pennsylvania Railroad control.

The Ashtabula and New Lisbon Railroad (A&NL) was chartered in February 1853 to build a line from Ashtabula Harbor to New Lisbon (now Lisbon). New Lisbon was a major coal mining region at that time. In 1870, A&NL's trackless grade between Ashtabula Harbor and Niles was purchased by the Ashtabula Youngstown and Pittsburgh (AY&P) Railway (the remaining grade to Lisbon eventually became part of the Erie Railroad). The AY&P, then under lease by the Pennsylvania Company, opened between Girard and Ashtabula Harbor in May 1873. Financial problems led to reorganization as the Ashtabula and Pittsburgh Railway and then as the Pittsburg, Youngstown and Ashtabula by 1887. It became part of the Pennsylvania Railroad in 1918. The line was removed in the late 1970s from Ashtabula Harbor to Warren. The Mahoning Valley Western opened between Ravenna and Niles in 1905. The Youngstown and Ravenna Railroad was incorporated in 1899 to build a line between the named cities.

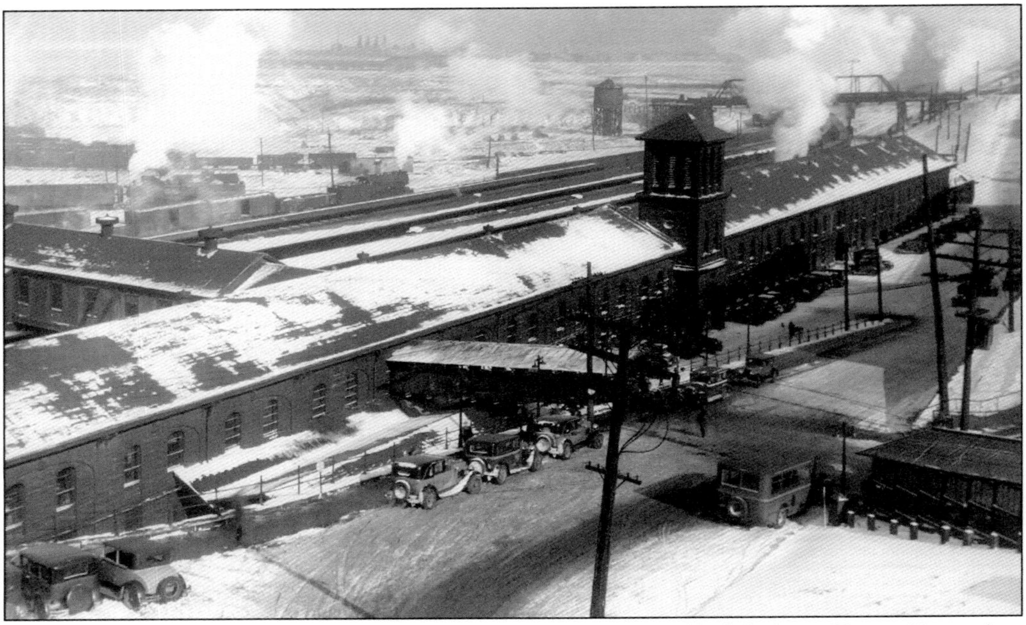

When Cleveland Union Terminal opened in 1928, the venerable lakefront Union Depot lost all its tenants except for the Pennsylvania Railroad (PRR). Renovation of Union Depot in the mid-1900s led to the removal of the arched train shed and its replacement with umbrella shelters between the tracks. This January 1930 photograph shows the depot a beehive of activity on this cold winter's day. The PRR used the depot until 1955 when the last passenger train left the by then rundown depot. The building was demolished in 1959. The PRR also had depots at Euclid Avenue, Woodland Avenue, and Harvard Avenue. Below is the Harvard Avenue depot in the 1960s. It dates from the early 1900s. The depot remains in business use below the elevated tracks. (Above, John A. Rehor collection.)

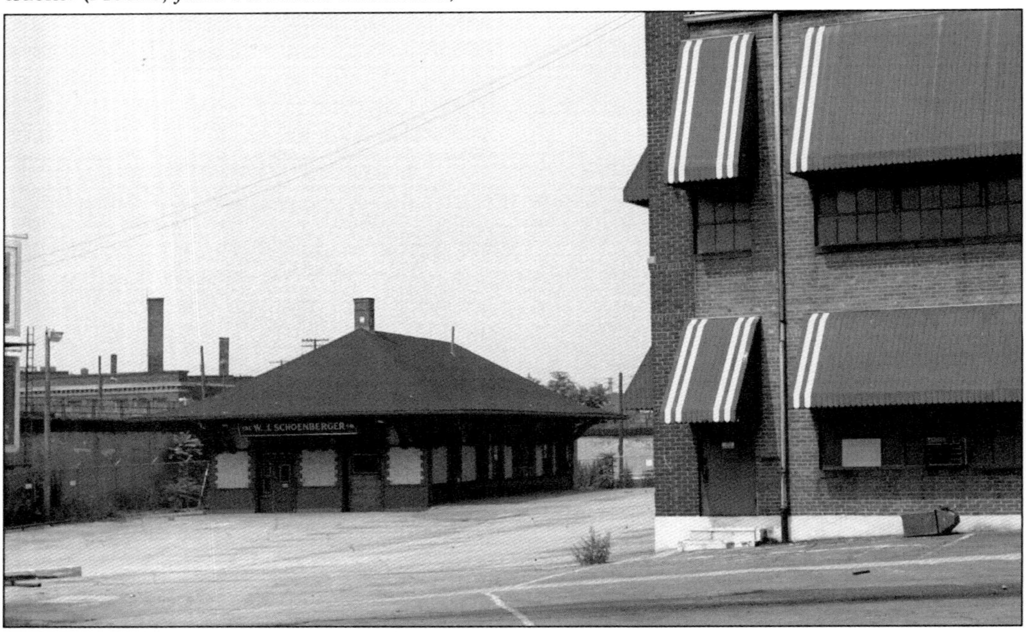

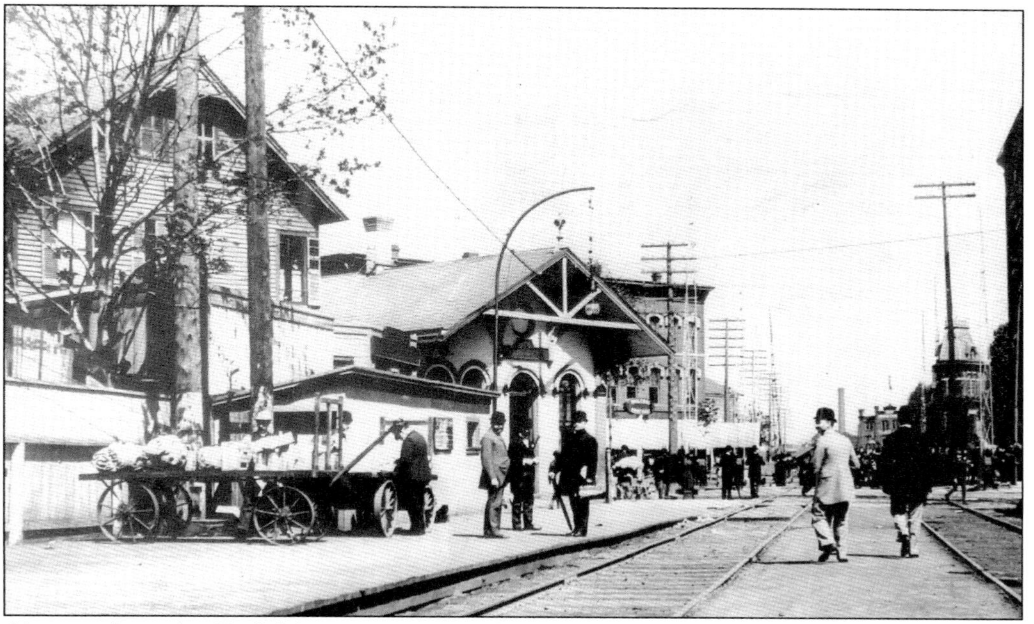

Above is the earlier Euclid Avenue passenger depot of the PRR. It was located at the corner with Wilson Avenue. It is close to train time in the Gay Nineties and the platform is vibrant with activity. The above depot was reportedly replaced in 1902 by the depot below. A track elevation-grade separation project in 1914 resulted in the construction of a new freight house across the tracks and required the passenger depot to be moved back about 40 feet to accommodate a covered concourse. During construction passengers used the old adjacent freight house. The Euclid Avenue depot became the downtown depot of the Pennsylvania Railroad after the closing of Union Depot in 1955. The last passenger train left the depot on January 29, 1965, for Youngstown. The once-busy depot is only a memory. (Photograph collection of Cleveland Public Library.)

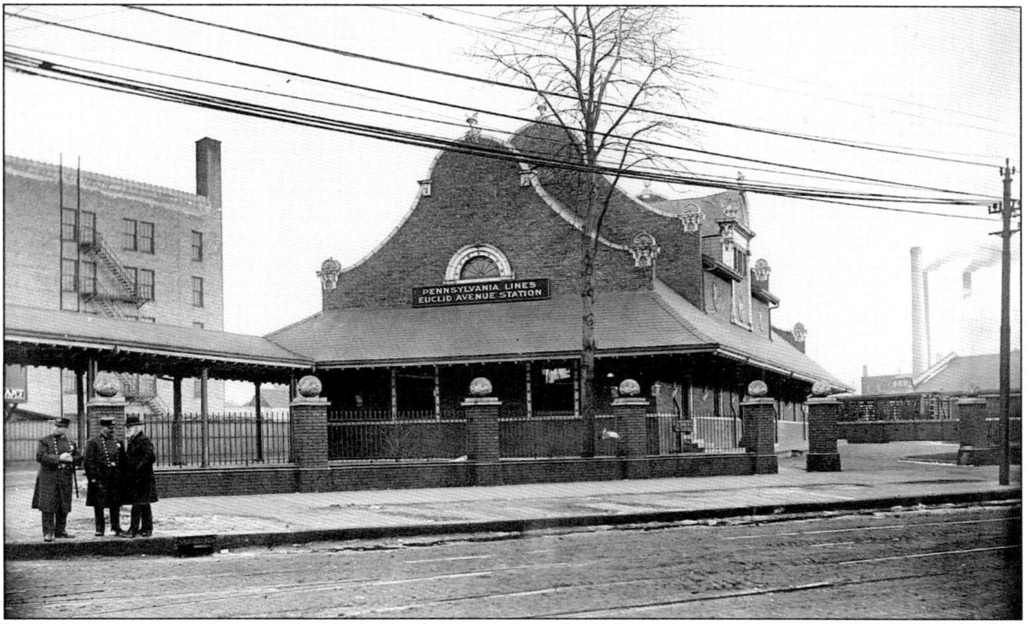

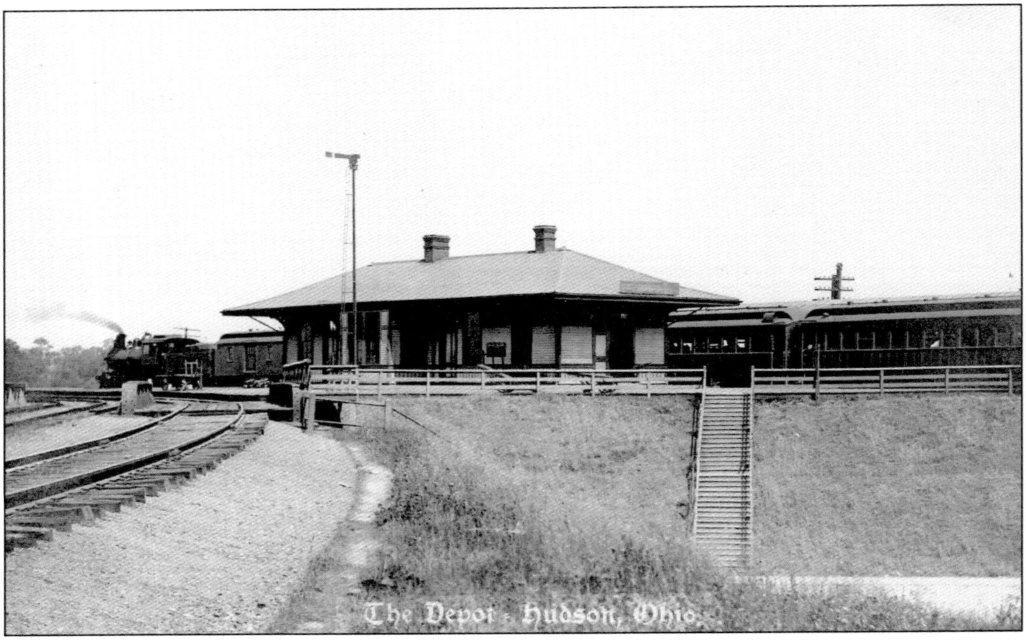

Hudson was an important junction on the former C&P and CZ&C railroads. The depots shown on this page were built around 1903 by the Pennsylvania Railroad at Hudson and Ravenna when the line was elevated, replacing earlier frame structures. This was one of the many standard depot plans to come out of the PRR's engineering department. Other than the obvious fact that Ravenna is of brick and Hudson is of frame construction, notice the variations in the vestibule. Ravenna's depot was located on an elevated right-of-way but also had covered platforms to serve the PRR low-grade line as well. In 1923, 24 passenger trains carrying Cleveland commuters passed each day. Ravenna is gone, but Hudson still remains on this site. (Mark J. Camp collection.)

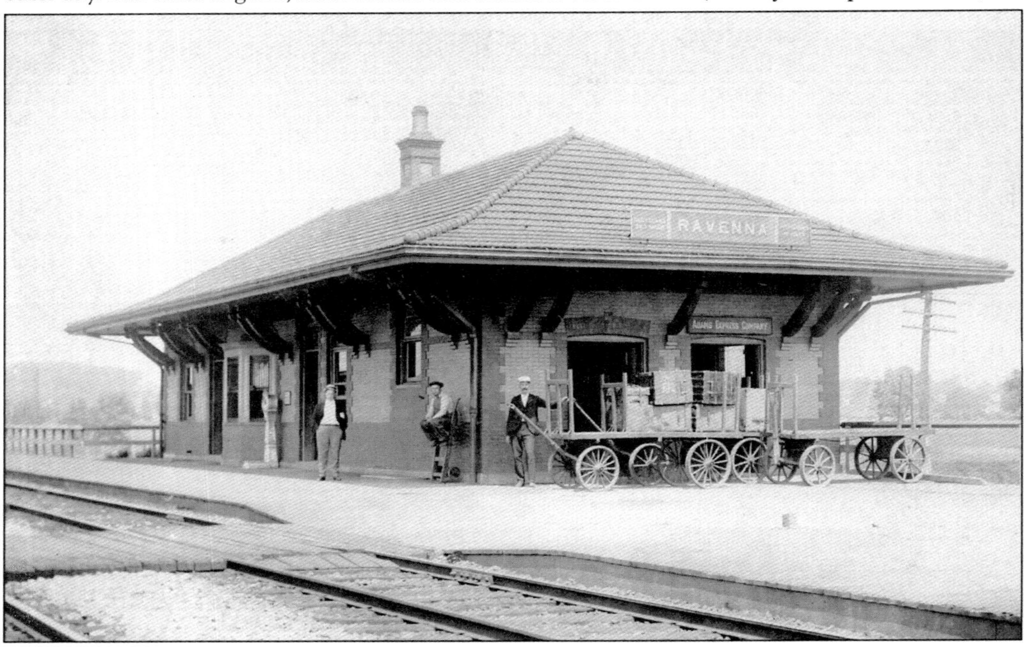

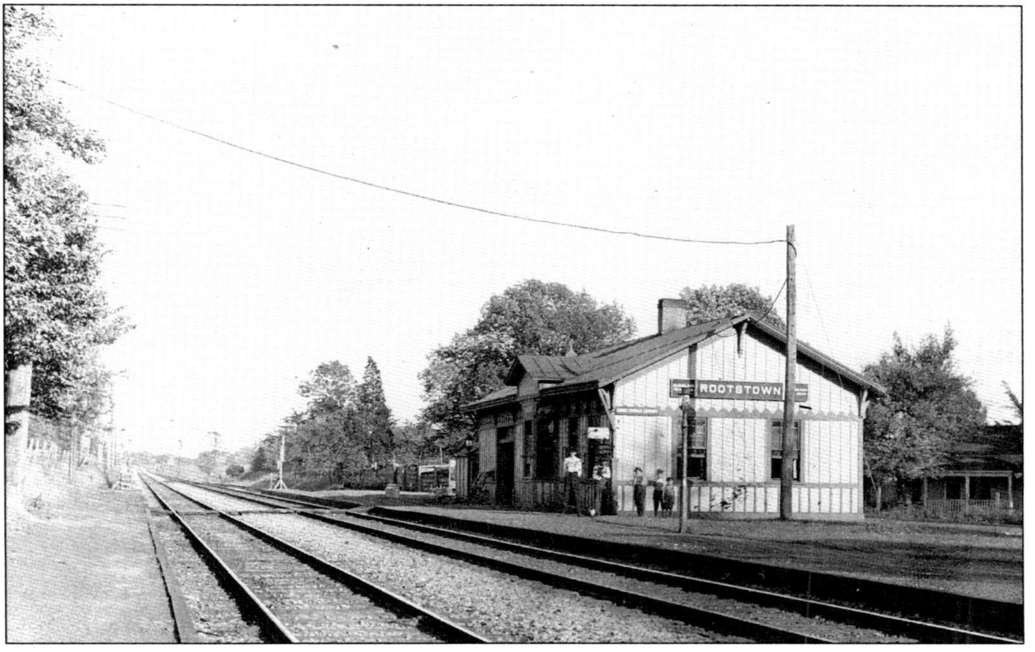

Another design used along the PRR is illustrated by the combination depots that once served Rootstown and Atwater. The PRR town boards offered the distance between the farthest stations on the line, in this case Cleveland and Pittsburg. (Mark J. Camp collection.)

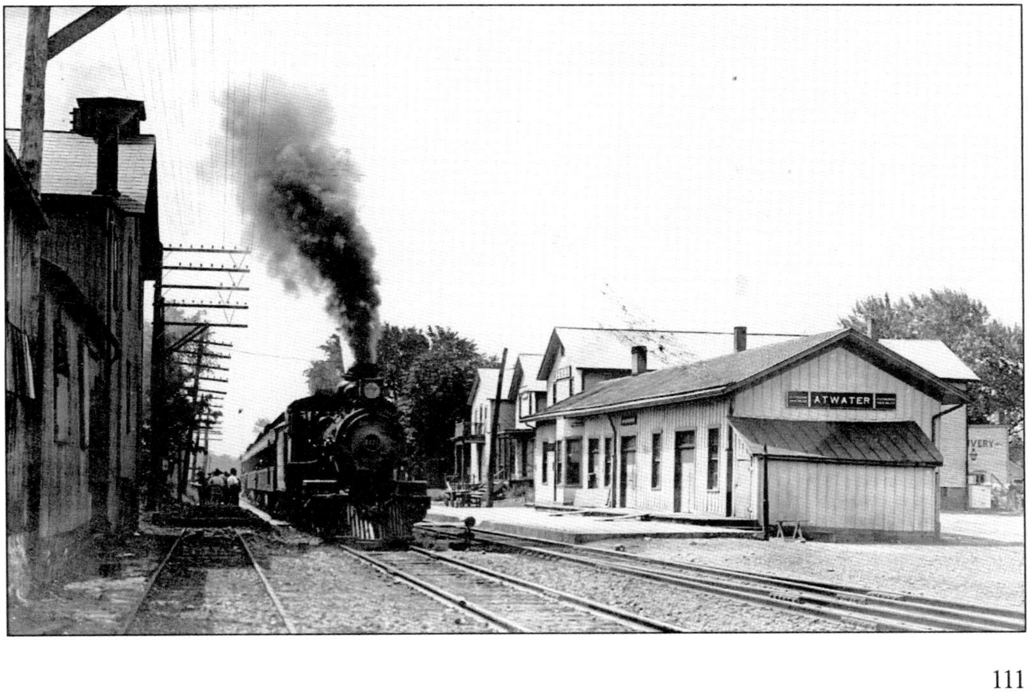

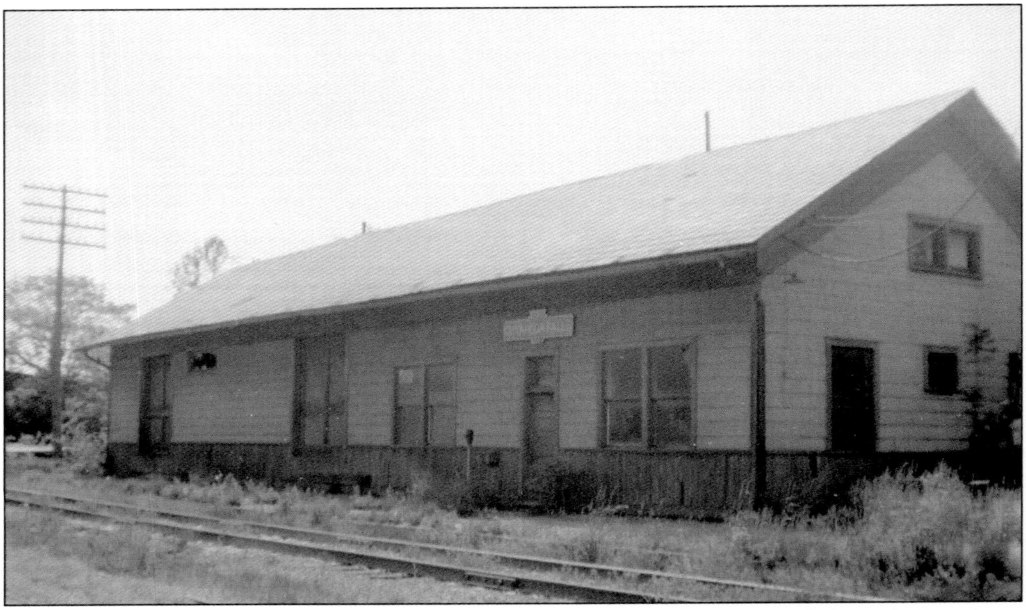

The CA&C stopped at this depot in Cuyahoga Falls. The first train passed through Cuyahoga Falls on July 4, 1852. By the 1950s, the frame combination building had been covered with shingle siding, and the last passenger train visited in 1955. The depot was still there in 1967 but has long since vanished.

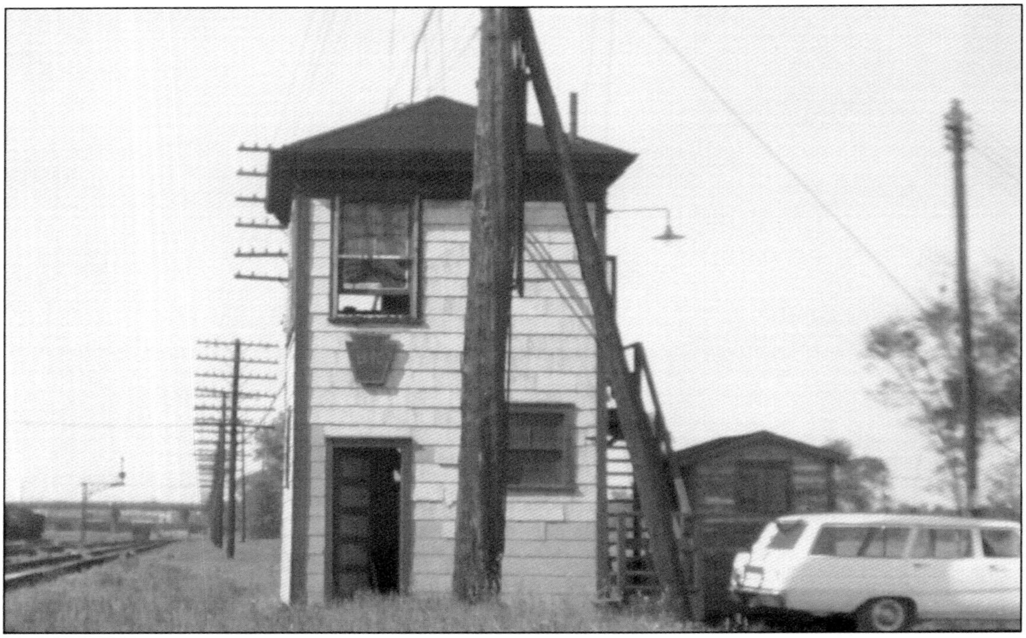

The C&P had a two-story frame depot near Mill and Summit Streets in Akron from 1852 to 1891. The C&P, by then PRR property, and the CA&C moved to Union Depot at East Market and College Streets when it opened in 1891. Union Depot was used by the Pennsylvania lines until the opening of new Union Depot in 1950. BN tower controlled the CA&C interlocking south of Akron in Barberton. The tower, photographed in 1967, was torn down long ago.

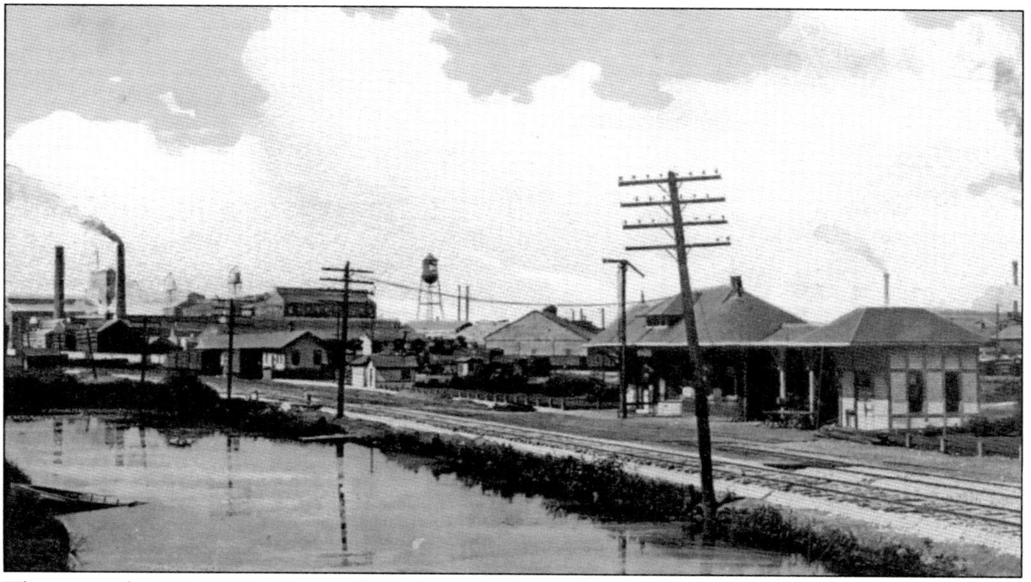

These are the CA&C facilities off Barberton's Tuscarawas Avenue around 1914. The passenger depot is in the foreground with an attached baggage building. In the distance is the 1885 freight house. In later years the brick passenger depot also served B&O passengers. In the late 1930s, the PRR and B&O transferred its passenger business to the nearby frame freight house and in 1940 demolished the vacant depot for a parking area. The freight house was deliberately burned down by the PRR in September 1965. (Mark J. Camp collection.)

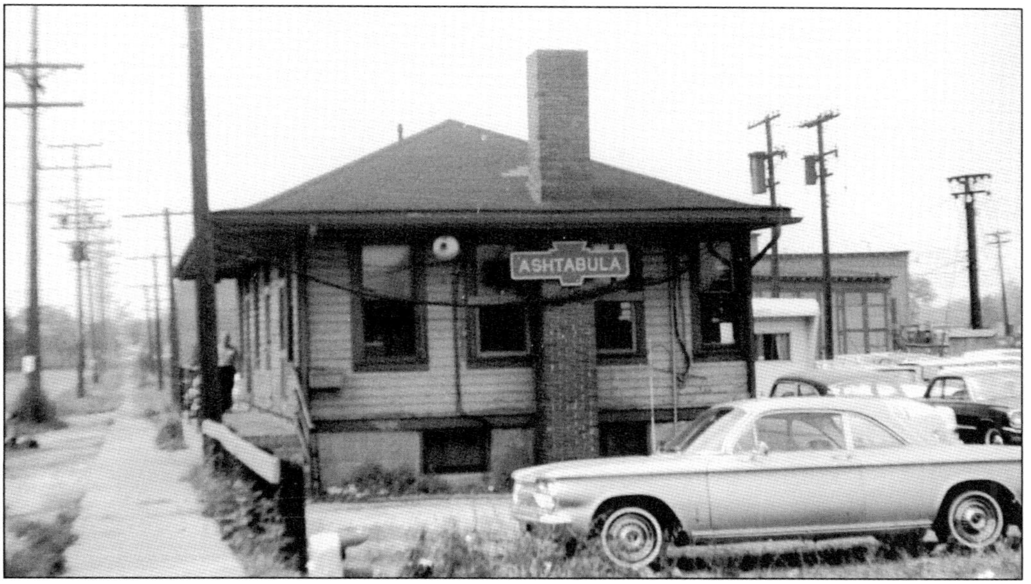

The Pittsburgh, Youngstown and Ashtabula (PY&A) line from Ashtabula Harbor south to Warren served this passenger depot in Ashtabula. The first regular passenger train to leave town departed for Pittsburgh on May 1, 1873. The original depot located on Center Street had a second floor for division offices. By the 1960s, it was a freight office. It has since been removed, only a roundhouse remains to remind one of the Pennsylvania Railroad's presence in the city. (Charles Garvin photograph.)

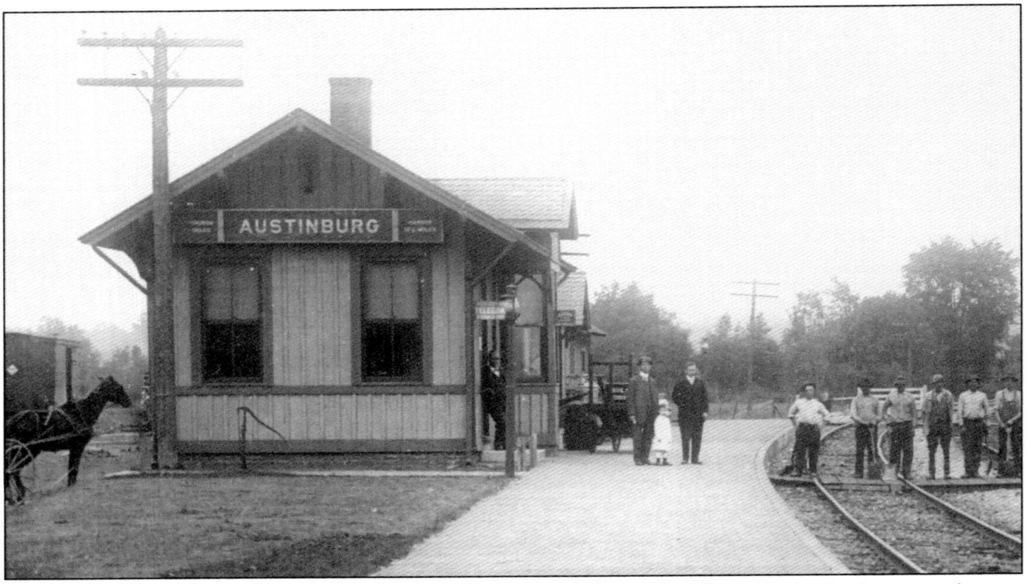

Gandy dancers, the agent, and others take time to pose for the postcard photographer at Austinburg's combination depot around 1908. A horse-drawn hack waits to the left for passengers wanting transportation to the downtown hotel. Four passenger trains stopped here daily in the early 1900s. Fresh bread was delivered every morning from Ashtabula bakeries. A local grocer was at the platform each morning and wheeled the baked goods to his downtown store in a wheelbarrow. (Mark J. Camp collection.)

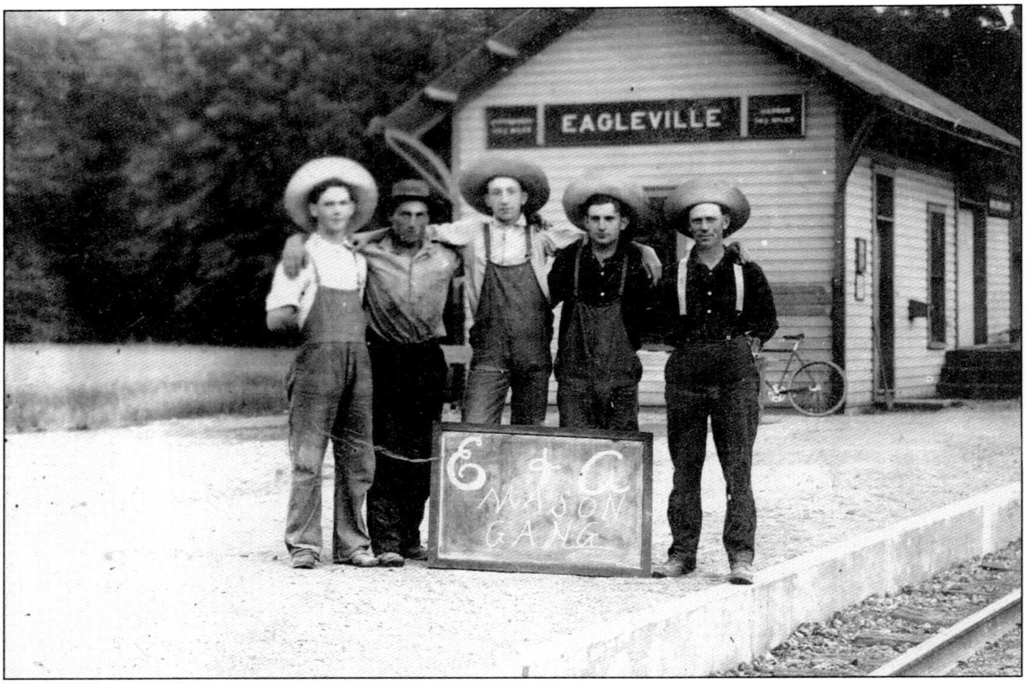

Some work is being done to the platform at Eagleville's PY&A depot around 1907. The masons proudly advertise their work. The depot was gone by the mid-1900s. (Mark J. Camp collection.)

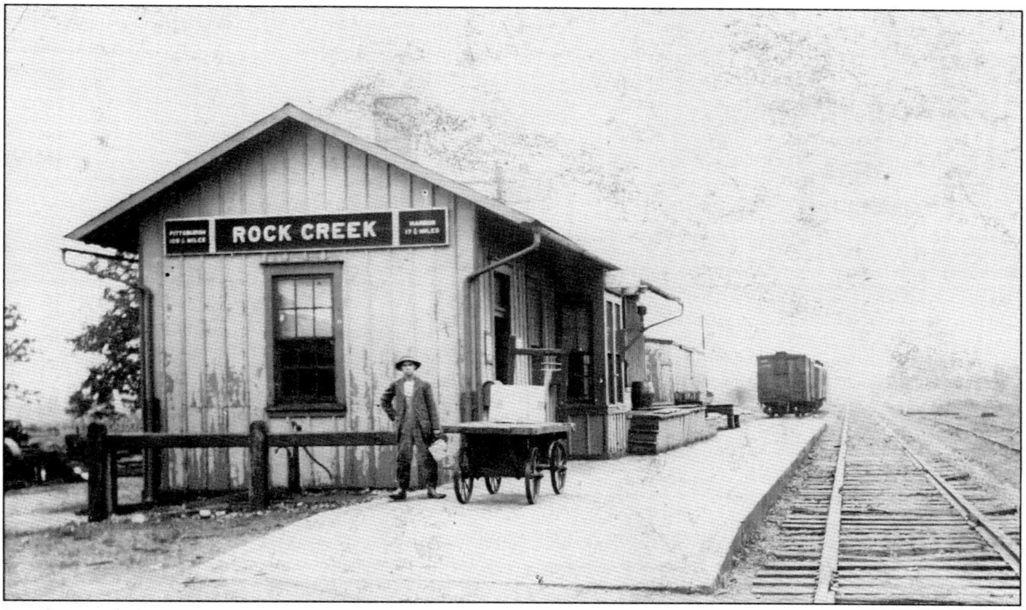

Rock Creek had another variation of the standard-plan combination depot probably dating from the 1870s. Behind the depot an old boxcar has been moved in to alleviate freight storage problems. Around 1900 the depot hosted five passenger and two mail trains each day. A local cheese factory was a major shipper. Rock Creek depot has been gone for many decades. (Mark J. Camp collection.)

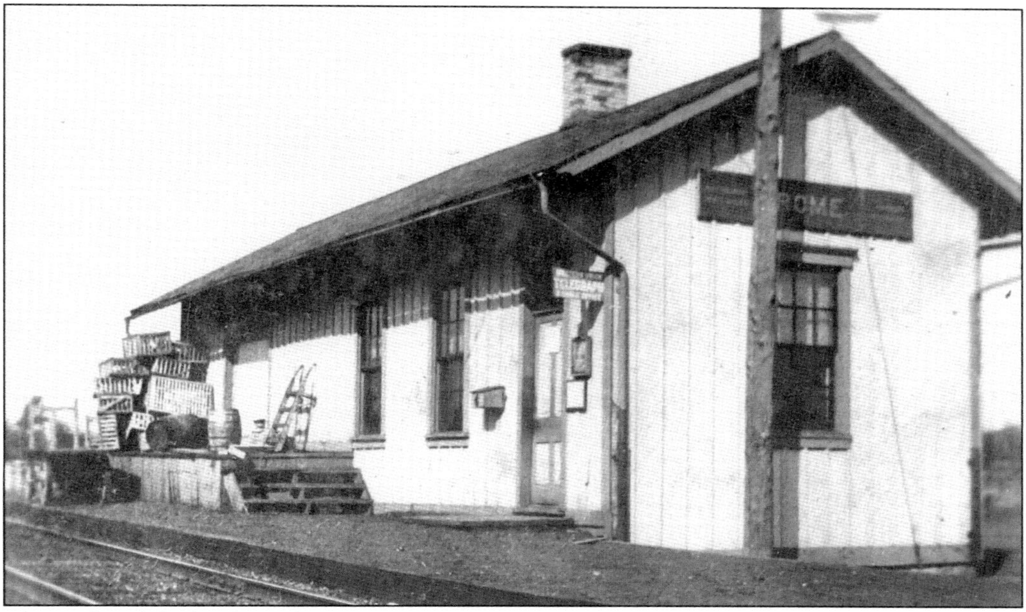

The railroad built through Rome Township in 1872–1873 passes east of the center. The community that built up around the depot became Rome Station. The depot is similar to Rock Creek, but it lacks a bay window. Empty poultry cages are piled high outside the freight room. The depot no longer exists. Another depot that no longer exists is the frame standard-design combination depot from New Lyme, just one mile south of Rome. (Mark J. Camp collection.)

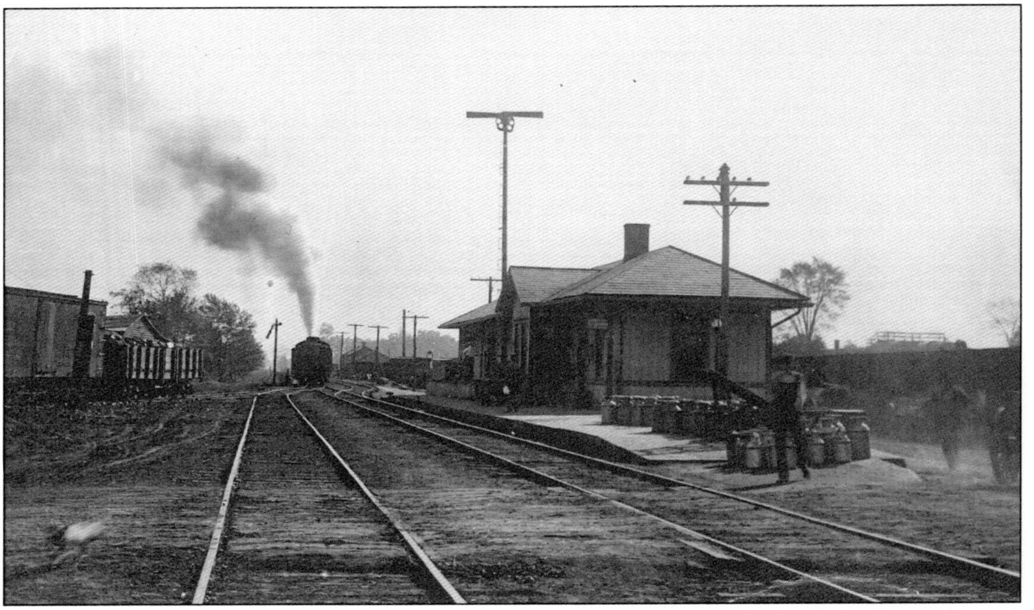

The 1874 PY&A depot in East Orwell was a major shipping point for local lumber mills and the surrounding farms in the late 1800s to early 1900s. A switcher works down the track. The order board and loaded baggage cart tells that a passenger train is due soon. The last passenger train stopped here in 1962. The building still exists although moved off the right-of-way. (Mark J. Camp collection.)

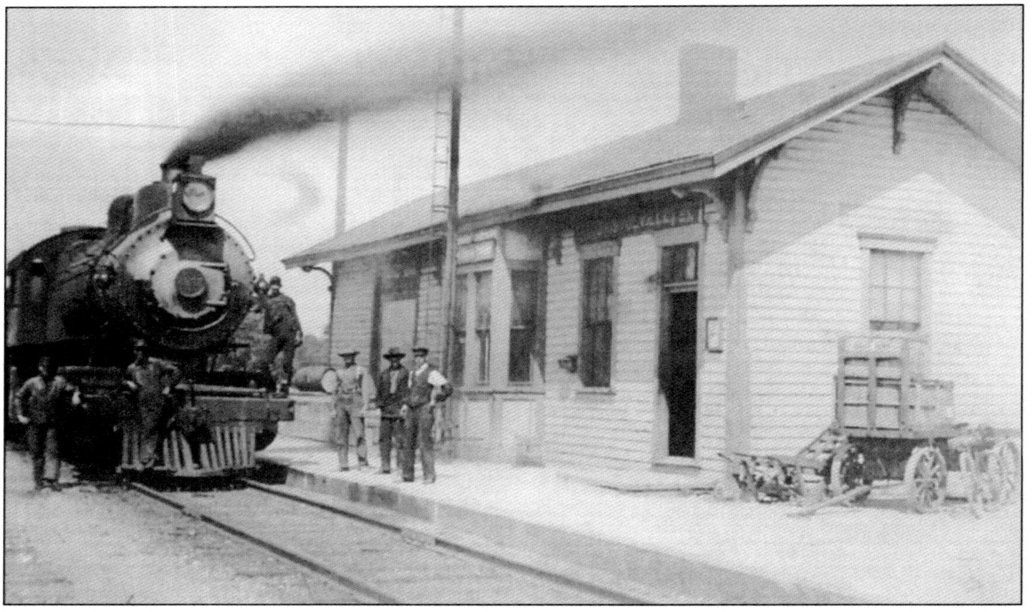

Bristolville's depot seems to be of standard PRR design and probably replaced an earlier PY&A design. It was actually located east of Bristolville at a location now called Spokane. The depot took the name of the community at the center of the township. The smaller community of North Bristol just north of Bristolville had a depot known as North Bristol Station (later named Oakfield) from 1873 until 1929. (Mark J. Camp collection.)

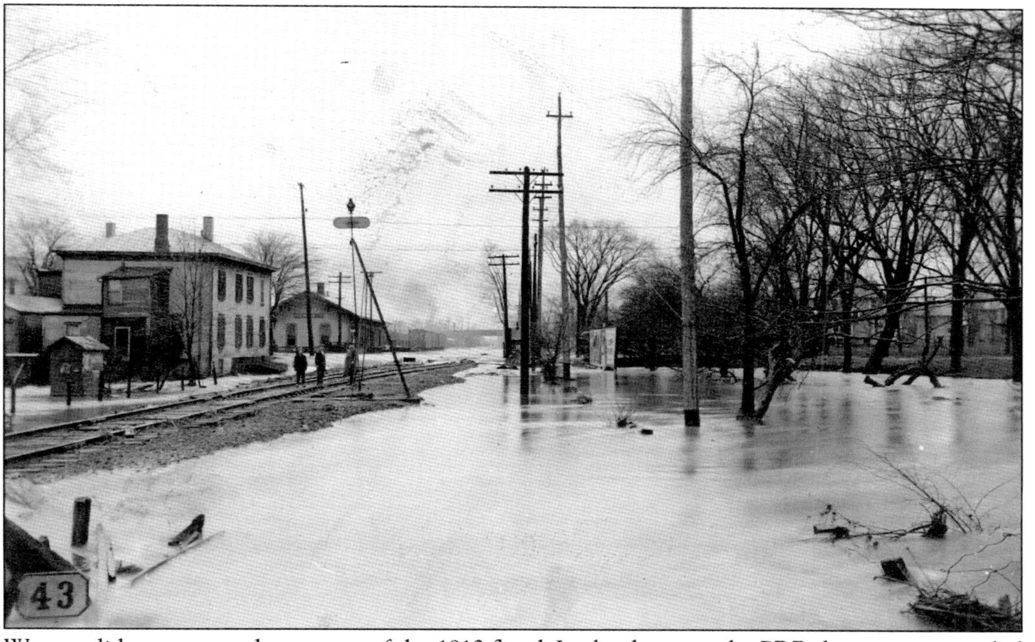

Warren did not escape the ravages of the 1913 flood. In the distance the PRR depot is surrounded by floodwaters from the Mahoning River. This side of the depot is a boardinghouse. In the 1950s, the frame depot was re-sided with shingles and converted to a freight house. It has since been torn down. (Mark J. Camp collection.)

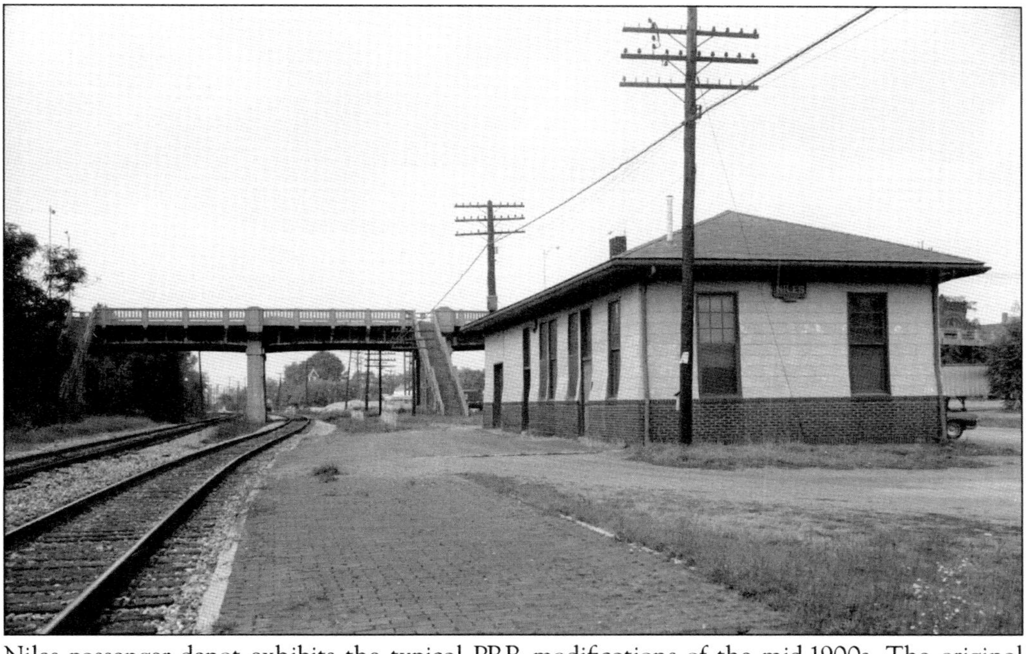

Niles passenger depot exhibits the typical PRR modifications of the mid-1900s. The original outside framed structure once had a peaked roof over the bay window. It sat along the Mahoning River with a freight house across the tracks. The depots have been gone for some time. (Charles Garvin photograph, 1969.)

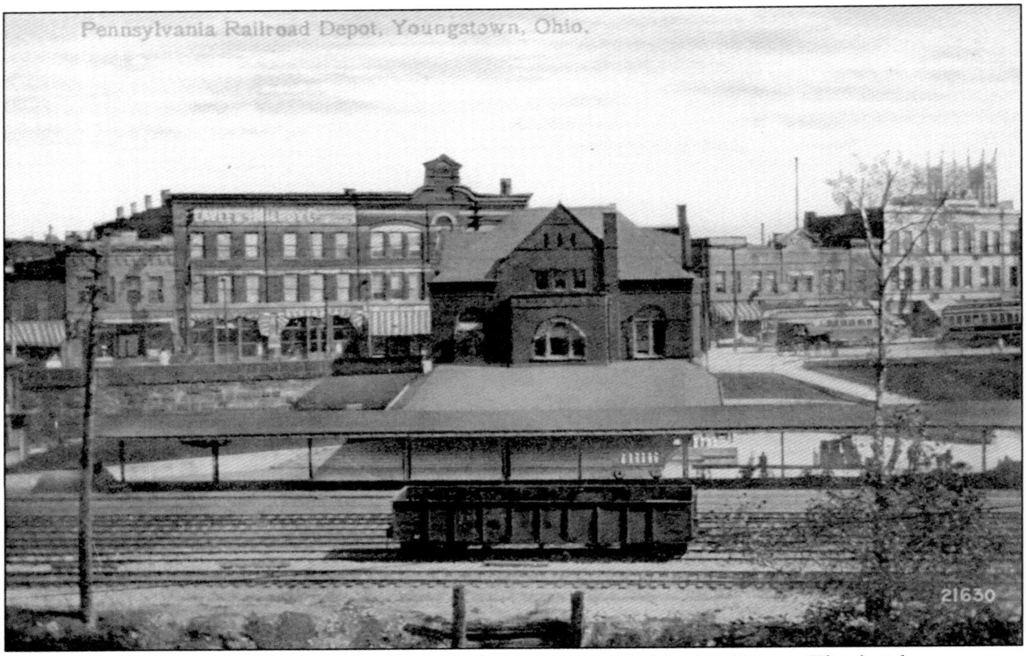

Youngstown's PRR station area was originally along the Mahoning River. The brick passenger depot is shown above around 1910. In 1948, it was replaced by the passenger depot shown below. In later years the depot also served as a bus terminal. The PRR depot is now part of a manufacturing firm on Martin Luther King Boulevard. Across from the PRR depot is a huge freight house once used by the Erie and P&LE railroads. Southeast of Youngstown a former PY&A depot houses a business in Lowellville. (Mark J. Camp collection.)

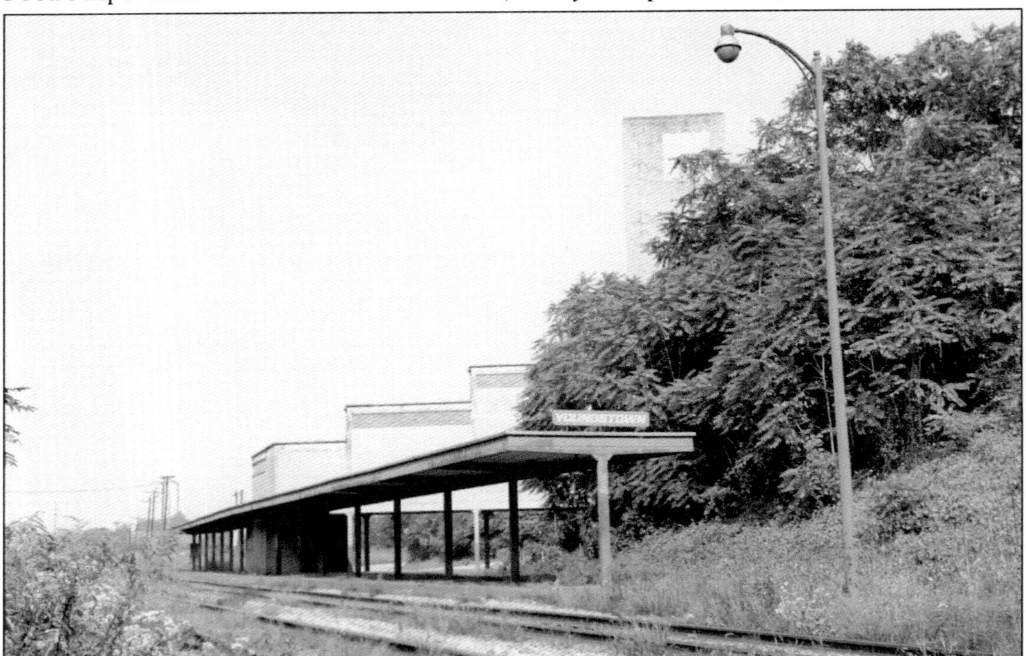

Six

Other Lines

A number of smaller lines were built across northeast Ohio. Some offering passenger service are briefly discussed; most were connecting lines around the larger cities and strictly industrial railroads.

In the early 1880s the Ohio Railway and Cleveland and Western Railroad were envisioned to be links in a narrow-gauge line across the continent. March 1890 marked the formation of the standard gauge Pittsburg, Akron and Western Railroad (PA&W) from these two lines. In August 1895, the PA&W became the Northern Ohio Railway, which the same year was leased by the Lake Erie and Western Railroad. East Akron was connected to Mogadore in 1912 by the Acron Canton and Youngstown Railroad (AC&Y), which stretched between the Northern Ohio line and the W&LE. The AC&Y leased the Northern Ohio Railroad in 1920, forming a line from Mogadore to Delphos. In 1944, the Northern Ohio and AC&Y Railway formally consolidated to become the AC&Y Railroad. The line never hauled many passengers; usually running mixed trains. Passenger service ended in July 1951.

The Ohio River and Lake Erie Railroad, chartered to build a line from Conneaut to Pittsburg, never laid any track, but was purchased by the Erie Shenango and Pittsburgh Railway in 1887. More mergers and name changes resulted in the Pittsburgh Shenango and Lake Erie Railroad by June 1888; the Pittsburgh, Bessemer, and Lake Erie Railroad by January 1897; and finally control by the Bessemer and Lake Erie Railroad (B&LE) in 1901. The B&LE was mainly a coal-hauling road, but passenger service to Conneaut lasted from August 1, 1892, until May 31, 1932. The B&LE had a frame depot just south of the old Main Street crossing; later at the foot of Liberty Street. The combination depot was demolished in March 1935.

The part of the Lorain Ashland and Southern Railroad in northeast Ohio was built as the Lorain and Ashland Railroad between Lorain and Wellington in 1906, but regular rail service did not start until after 1915 with the opening of a renovated line between Ashland and Lorain. The line operated for 10 years and abruptly terminated service in August 1925. The line never had a substantial passenger business; no depots remain. Although primarily a Pennsylvania line, the Pittsburgh and Lake Erie (P&LE) reached Youngstown in February 1879. The P&LE used a portion of the bed of the Ohio-Pennsylvania Canal as right-of-way. No depots remain standing in Ohio.

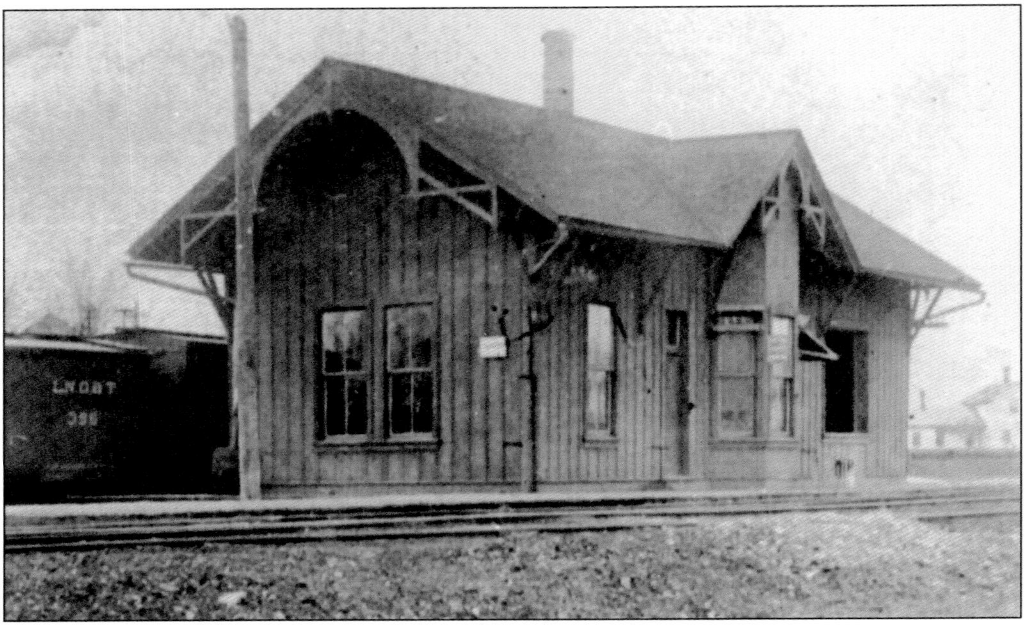

The depots at New London and Spencer are typical examples of the 1891 standard depot plan of the Pittsburgh, Akron and Western Railroad (PA&W). The view of New London shows the original appearance in the early 1900s, while the Spencer view shows the depots as modified in the mid-1900s by the AC&Y. In 1967, New London's depot was being used by the Railway Express Company and Spencer's sat unused. Both have since been removed. (Above, Charles Garvin collection.)

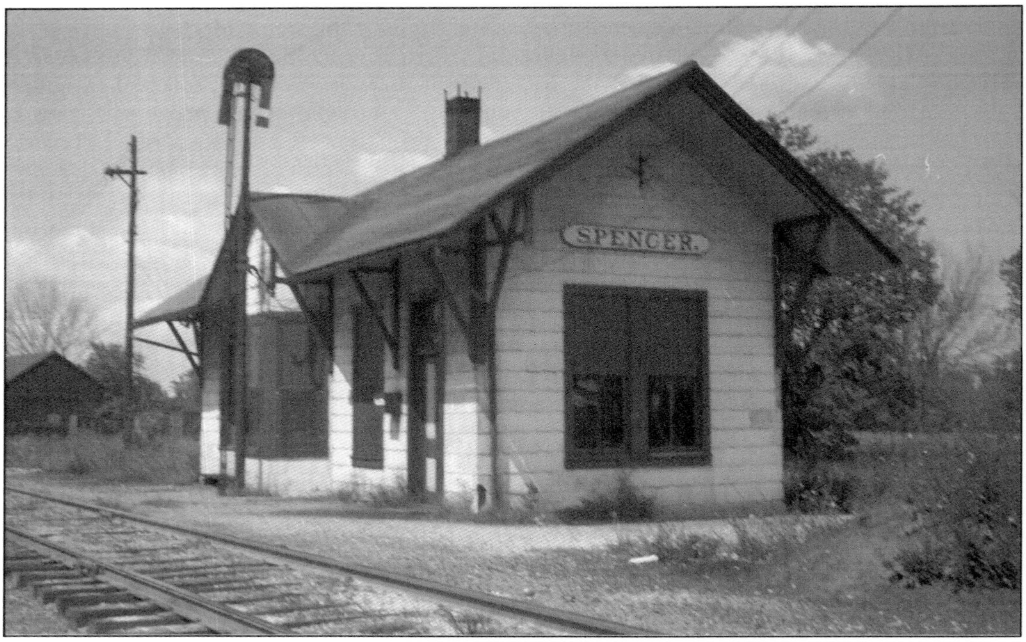

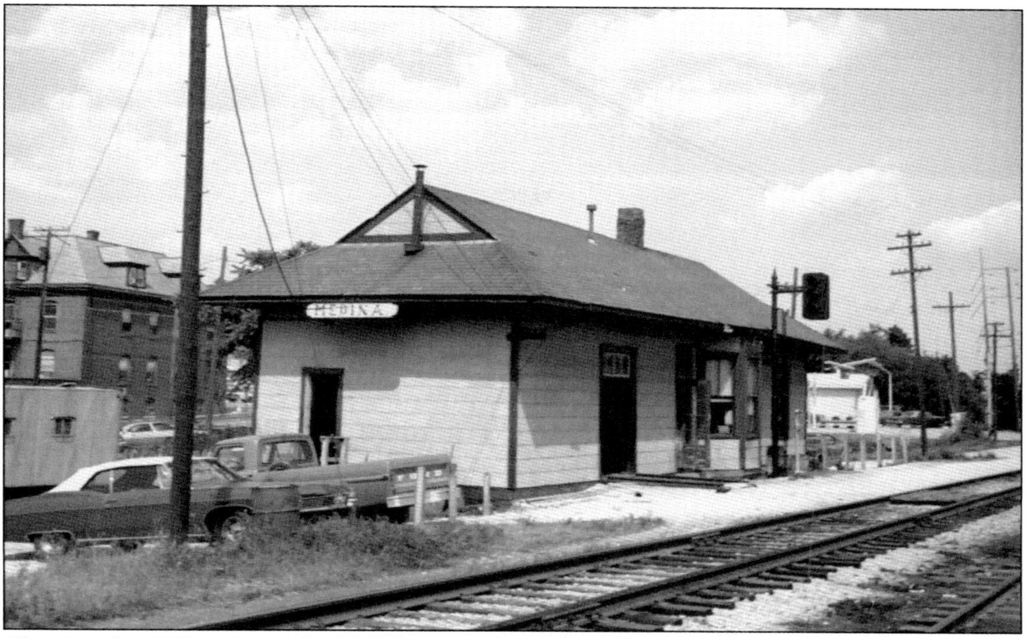

The first PA&W rails reached Medina in November 1890; service began in January 1891. Medina's AC&Y depot was built to a different pattern than other depots along the line. In later years it was re-sided and ornamental features were removed. It was demolished by the railroad around 1992. (Charles Garvin photograph, 1971.)

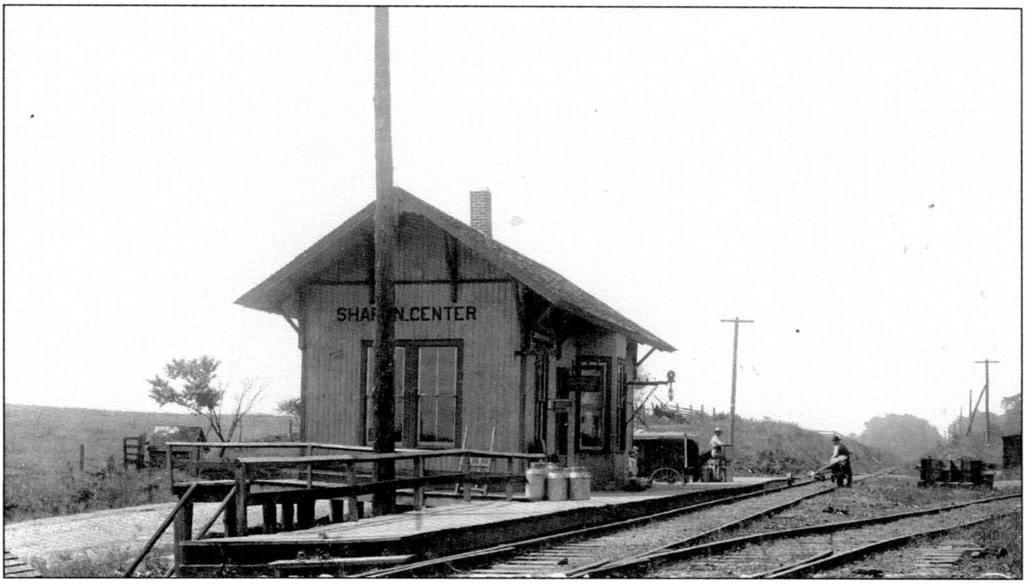
Another variation of the PA&W design was used at Sharon Center. Note the vestibule is not covered by a peaked roof and the gingerbread decoration differs. Dairy products are tended to, and a section worker is about to resume his check along the line while the next train is awaited. The last agent here, like many along the line, cared for more than one depot. The Sharon Center agent also handled business at Boneta, the next station to the west. The Sharon Center depot was relocated as a residence. (Mark J. Camp collection.)

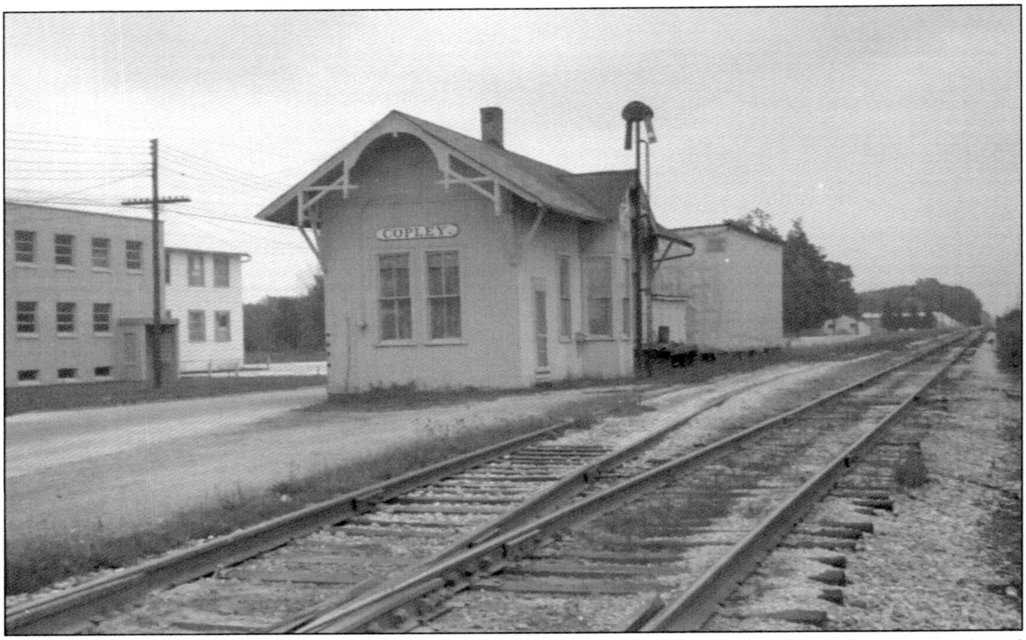

Copley's AC&Y depot dates from 1891 and was built to a standard plan. The depot was closed in the 1970s and if not for the action of the Copley Township Historical Society would probably have been torn down. The society moved it and restored the building over the 2000–2003 period; initially the society used it as a meeting room but then turned it into a depot museum.

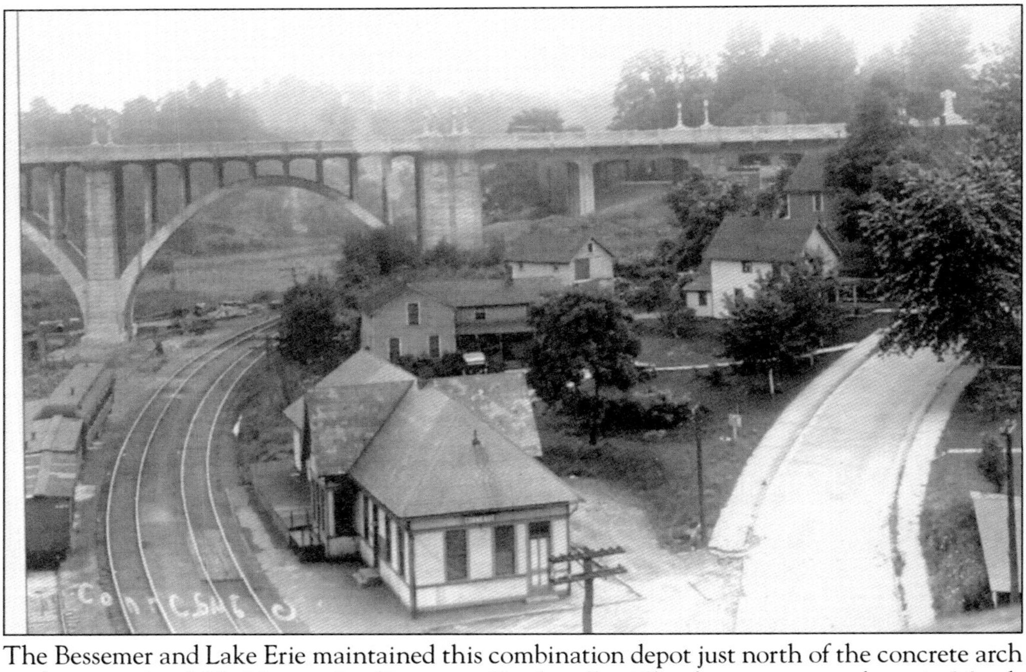

The Bessemer and Lake Erie maintained this combination depot just north of the concrete arch viaduct carrying U.S. 20 over the Conneaut Creek valley. The depot was torn down in March 1935. (Paul W. Prescott collection.)

Seven

Reuse of Depots

Some 73 passenger, freight, and combination depots remain standing in northeast Ohio, but few remain in railroad use. Obviously most have served their purpose and have either succumbed to wrecking companies, salvagers, fire, storm, train derailment, or neglect. In most cases as buildings became a tax burden on the railroads they were either demolished or offered for sale. Usually the requirement of a new owner was that the structure be removed from railroad property.

Northeast Ohio is lucky that so many have survived and that a number are well preserved and provide glimpses at the railroad age of the late 1800s and early 1900s. Railroad and historical museums are a common reuse of depots across the United States, and northeast Ohio is no exception. Some serve as headquarters of local or regional historical societies or model railroad clubs; others are simply external restorations of the buildings and may contain meeting rooms, city offices, or the local chamber of commerce. Museum and display depots like those at Bedford, Conneaut, Falls Junction, and Jaite remained trackside, but others like those from Copley, Mogadore, Rochester, and Vermilion were relocated. Sometimes depots were moved to historical villages like the Aultman depot at Burton's Century Village. Others like Berea's B&O depot were relocated to train and trolley museums. Boston Mill, Jefferson, and Oberlin's LS&MS freight house serve as a tourist line ticket office and museums. Both the passenger and freight depots from Andover have been preserved at antique engine show grounds near Wick. Amherst, Bay Village, Bedford, Middlefield, Valley City, and West Farmington depots serve as examples of restorations that serve as community centers. Depots from Farmdale, Geneva, Huron, Kingsville, Kipton, Leon, Lodi (W&LE), Lorain (B&O freight house), Saybrook, Wakeman, and Wellington's CCC&StL freight house are mainly in use as storage facilities. Vermilion's former LS&MS passenger depot has served as a school and church meeting hall. Depots that once served Lodi, North Kingsville, Sharon Center, and Sullivan have been converted to residences. Various businesses operate out of former depots from Akron, Aurora, Avon, Chagrin Falls, Collins, Garrettsville, Kent, Mantua, Medina, Mentor, Newton Falls, Perry, Simons, Solon, Vermilion, and Willoughby. Berea, Kent's Erie depot, and Mentor's LS&MS depot now exist as restaurants. Akron's Union Depot is now part of the University of Akron, and Cleveland Union Terminal anchors Tower City, a complex of shops and offices.

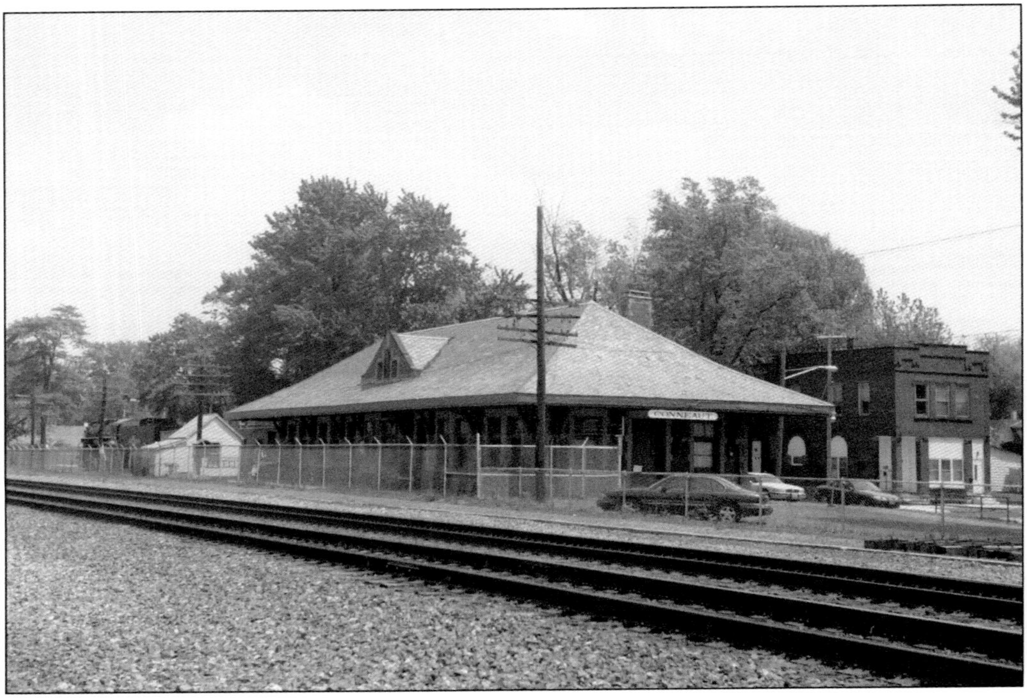

Historical and railroad museums are a common use of former railroad depots. Two examples in northeast Ohio are at Conneaut and Rochester. The Conneaut Historical Railroad Museum was dedicated in 1966, a pioneer among depot museums in Ohio. The depot was acquired in August 1963, shortly after being closed by the NYC. The Big Four depot in Rochester had to be moved off the right-of-way before any steps of restoration began.

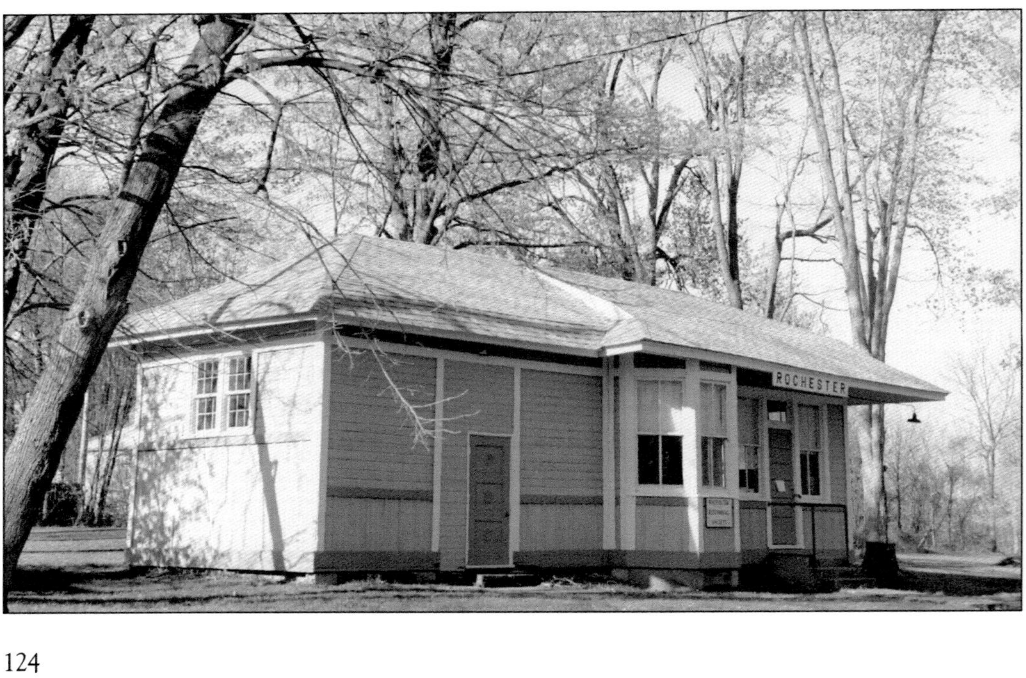

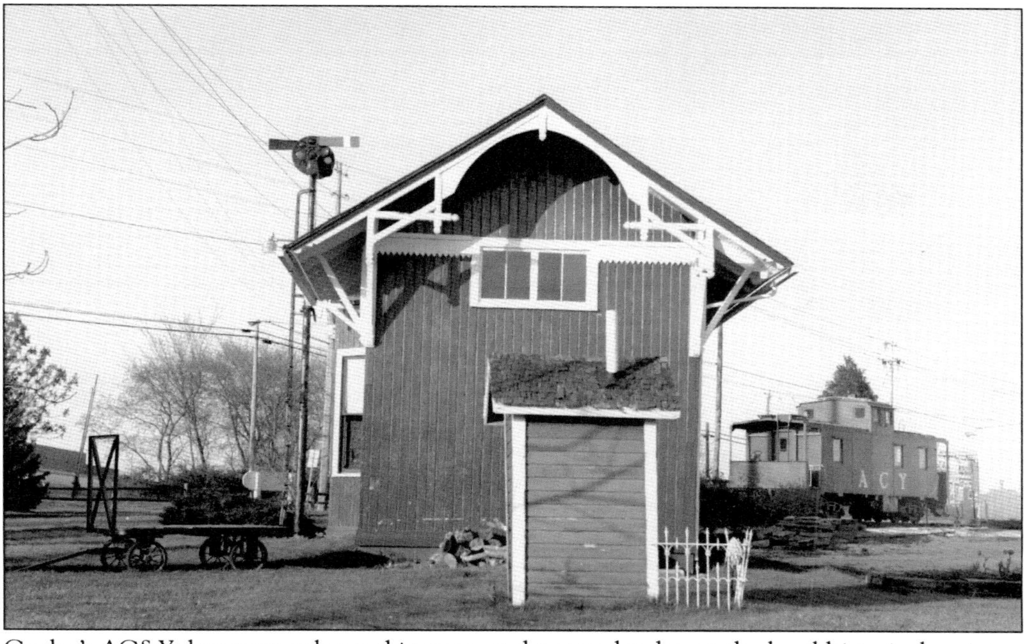

Copley's AC&Y depot was relocated in town and restored to house the local historical society.

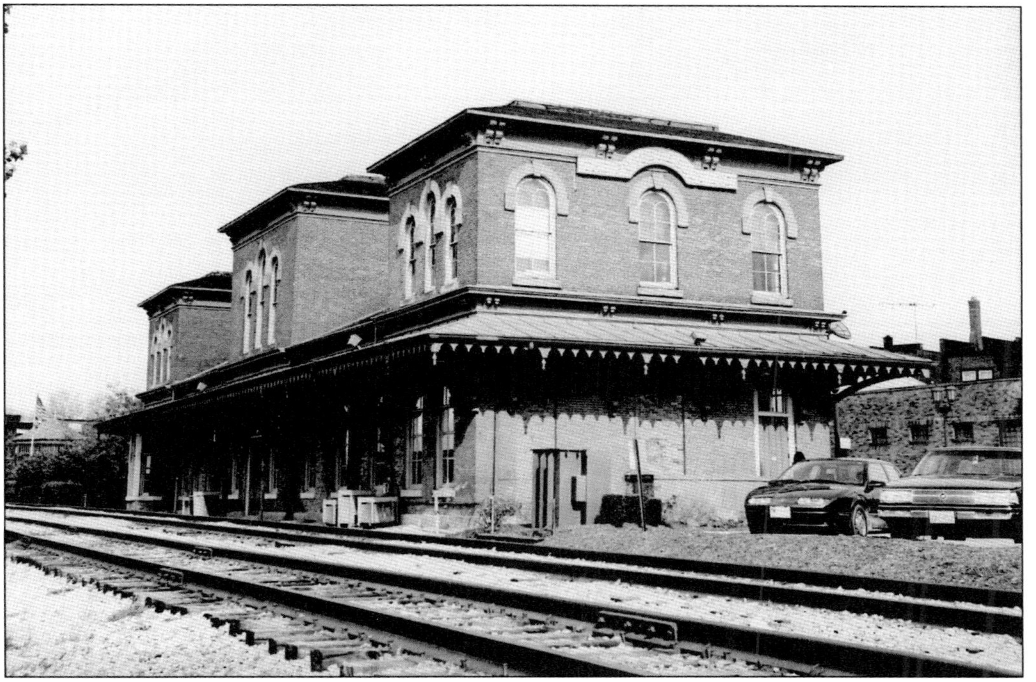

The Erie Railroad passenger depot in Kent reopened as a restaurant in the Pufferbelly chain in 1981. The railroad-themed eatery is a popular place and preserves much of the ambiance of the depot.

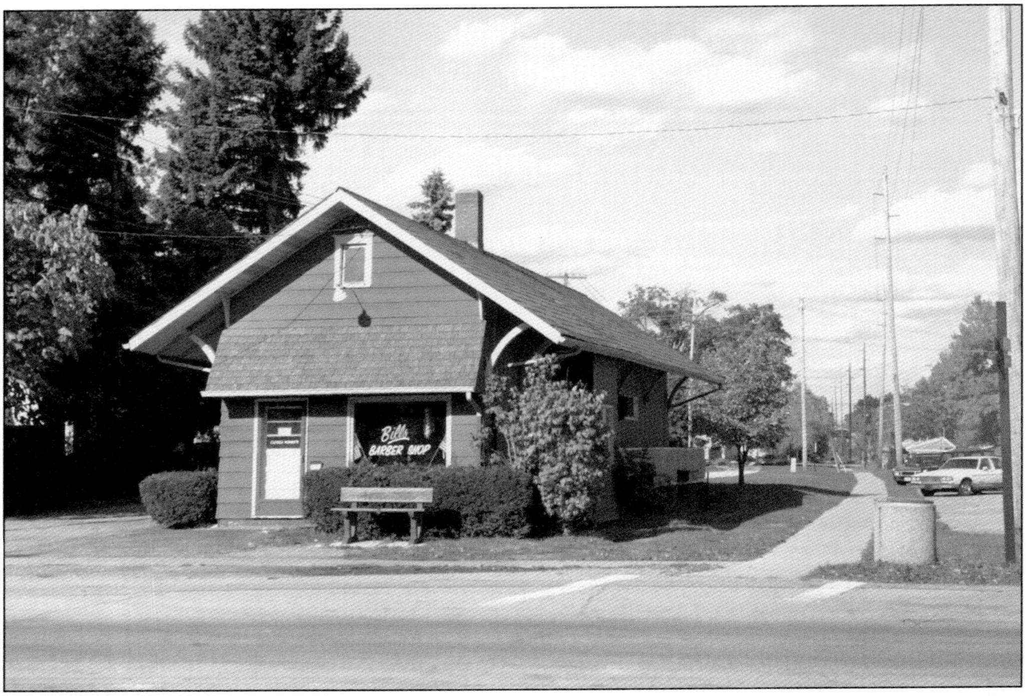

The former Lake Erie, Alliance and Wheeling Railroad combination depot in Newton Falls has been a barbershop for many years. Note the abandoned right-of-way.

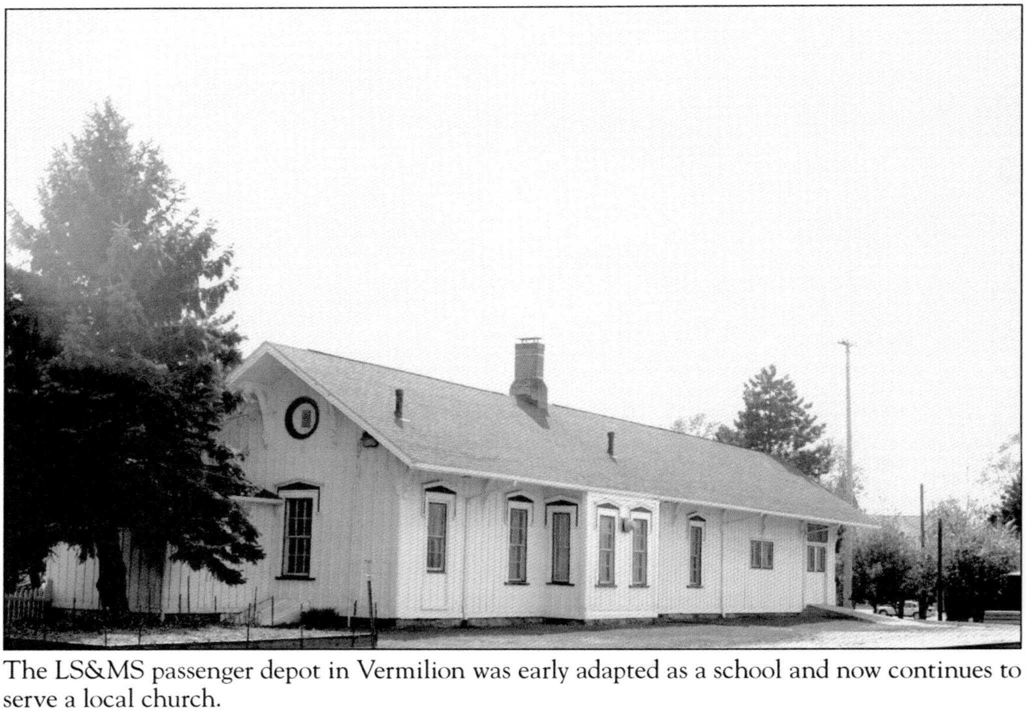

The LS&MS passenger depot in Vermilion was early adapted as a school and now continues to serve a local church.

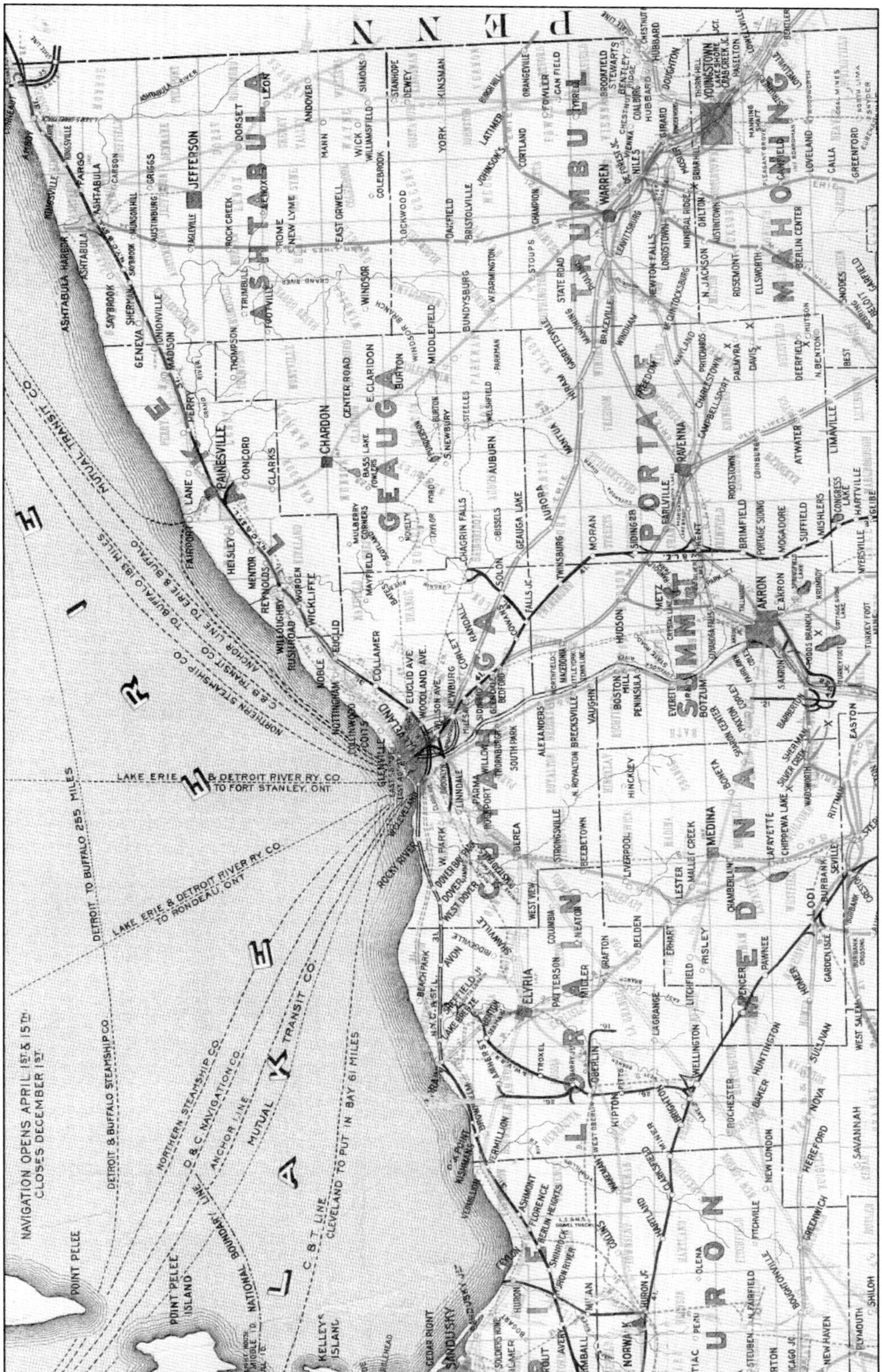

Railroads served many communities throughout the northeastern counties of Ohio in 1909. (Railroad Commission of Ohio state map.)